The Unity of Reason

THE UNITY OF REASON

Essays on Kant's Philosophy

Dieter Henrich

Edited and with an Introduction by
Richard L. Velkley

Translated by
Jeffrey Edwards
Louis Hunt
Manfred Kuehn
Guenter Zoeller

Harvard University Press
Cambridge, Massachusetts
London, England   1994

B
2798
.H357
1994
28928824

Copyright © 1994 by the President and Fellows of Harvard College
All rights reserved
Printed in the United States of America

This book is printed on acid-free paper, and its binding materials
have been chosen for strength and durability.

Library of Congress Cataloging-in-Publication Data

Henrich, Dieter, 1927–
   The unity of reason : essays on Kant's philosophy / Dieter Henrich;
   edited with an introduction by Richard L. Velkley ; translated by
   Jeffrey Edwards . . . [et al.].
      p.   cm.
   Includes bibliographical references and index.
   ISBN 0-674-92905-5 (alk. paper)
   1. Kant, Immanuel, 1724–1804.   I. Velkley, Richard L.   II. Title.
B2798.H357 1994
193—dc20
93-34705
   CIP

Contents

	Introduction: Unity of Reason as Aporetic Ideal *Richard L. Velkley*	1
1	On the Unity of Subjectivity *Translated by Guenter Zoeller*	17
2	The Concept of Moral Insight and Kant's Doctrine of the Fact of Reason *Translated by Manfred Kuehn*	55
3	Ethics of Autonomy *Translated by Louis Hunt*	89
4	Identity and Objectivity: An Inquiry into Kant's Transcendental Deduction *Translated by Jeffrey Edwards*	123
	Notes	211
	Sources	239
	Acknowledgments	243
	Index	245

Introduction: Unity of Reason as Aporetic Ideal

Richard L. Velkley

Dieter Henrich is widely known in the English-speaking world as a leading figure in German philosophy who, as teacher and scholar on both sides of the Atlantic, has sought over three decades to bring the German Idealist tradition into closer relation to the central questions and methodological approaches of Anglo-American philosophy. At the same time, his dense and subtly probing studies of major texts and problems in German Idealism have long been standard works for the interpretation and analysis of Kant, Fichte, Hölderlin, and Hegel. Yet until recently very few of Henrich's essays—even of the most frequently cited—have been translated into English. This collection will help to remedy that lack. It will also serve to disclose a principal aspect, indeed the very heart, of Henrich's philosophical endeavor, which has been little appreciated outside Germany. Since the appearance of his first publications in the early 1950s, Henrich has been engaged in a retrieval of the Idealist philosophies of self-consciousness, employing both close exegesis and systematic argumentation. The true goal of this retrieval has not been well understood: it is to lead twentieth-century philosophy beyond the Heideggerian critique of Western rationalism, by establishing the relevance of some crucial insights of post-Cartesian accounts of subjectivity for contemporary life.

Only fifteen years ago, such an enterprise would have been incomprehensible, or at best have seemed parochial, to most Anglo-American academic philosophers. Yet nothing could be more pertinent to the present philosophical situation, with its numerous controversies about the status of "subjectivity," "autonomy," "individuality," and other key modern concepts. In particular, contemporary Anglo-American thought is raising such questions as whether these concepts are compromised by their association with doubtful forms of "foundationalist" and "realist" epistemology and metaphysics; and whether the versions of these concepts in major thinkers such as Kant and Hegel may be construed as free of such presuppositions. The widespread interest in forms of political philosophy that develop Kantian and Hegelian themes—connected with the Rawlsian renewal of theoretical justifications of liberalism—has made such questions more pressing. This neo-Idealist trend confronts the deconstructions of the notion of the "subject" in various postmodernisms and, somewhat less drastically, in the hermeneutic-pragmatic standpoints of Gadamer, Habermas, and Apel. The emergence of these debates at the forefront of philosophy on these shores means, among other things, that Heidegger has become almost as central to American philosophy in the past decade as he was to German philosophy thirty years ago—although he is still for the most part an uninvited and unnamed presence.

Henrich entered into Anglo-American discussion and sought to influence it, well before it became engaged in an expansive dialogue with Continental thought. Thus he helped to establish in the 1960s (along with P. F. Strawson) that Kant's transcendental reflection on subjectivity discloses and amplifies the premises of the analytic discussions of self-identity and the knowledge of perceptual particulars. Henrich was one of the foremost scholars to show that a close reading of Kantian texts could contribute to the postpositivistic turn toward linguistically mediated transcendentality. As Richard Rorty, Donald Davidson, and others then made clear, that same turn makes possible the reception of Continental hermeneutics and poststructuralist thought, as well as the more radical critiques of realism they espouse. Of course this last development seems to render the status of the "subject" quite precarious, if not absolutely untenable. Henrich's writing on the Idealists raises the opposing possibility that some theory of the "subject"—perhaps based on the Kantian or Fichtean theories—may be indispensable to an adequate account of human knowledge and orientation within the world. In other words, Henrich compels us to consider whether the move from linguistic transcendentality to radical antirealism may not have too hastily jettisoned earlier modern ideas of the subject. And he requires us to wonder whether the postmodernist and Habermasian critiques of subjectivity are perhaps historically naive and poorly grounded. Essays that Henrich wrote thirty or almost forty years ago have surprising relevance for these problems. As the debates about realism, subjectivity, and rational autonomy become more sophisticated, the study of Henrich's writings becomes more essential.

In what follows I will offer some observations about Henrich's *oeuvre* as markers that should help to place his close historical studies of Kant within his larger project of providing the philosophical basis for a post-Heideggerian renewal of the Enlightenment: a retrieval of the modern philosophy of subjectivity that meets the challenges of the radical antifoundationalist critiques of modernity.

A Broken Wall and an Unbroken Tradition

In May 1989 thoughts turned to July 1789. One can assume that Dieter Henrich's audience at the Goethe Society in the city of Weimar of the former German Democratic Republic appreciated the coincidence of the French Revolution's bicentenary and the growing signs of the collapse of moribund Marxism—the Revolution's ideological stepchild, still commanding bodies but ever-fewer minds. Those present were no doubt predisposed to hear Henrich's message, which he could offer with authority as one of the twentieth century's leading interpreters of the tradition from Kant through Hegel. He told his audience that the potential of German classical philosophy had not been exhausted; it was an unbroken theoretical tradition in spite of many deformations and betrayals. Like that of the great political tradition of 1789, its task was not finished. Freedom, the central concept of both these movements, was far from being institutionally secured. The "unforgettable event" (as the Revolution was called by the founder of German Idealism) shared a common potential with its spiritual counterpart—ushering in a fundamental change in "man's self-description." In light of the signal "failures which German Idealism did not foresee," that potential would have to be realized today in a way not envisioned in 1790 or 1830. Yet society was still in need of direction from a comprehensive philosophy, and a philosophy that was both true and comprehensive—not just salutary myth—was still available. Clearly Henrich had in mind not Marxism, but rather the philosophy of freedom that Kant —following Rousseau, who gave him "all the essential motives of his thought"—saw as "a matter for all humanity," not only as academic doctrine. Its aim was "to liberate subjectivity" in the reflective process of a rational life in search of "self-unity."[1]

The roots of Henrich's conception of the classical German tradition and its contemporary relevance reach back to the founding years of the Federal Republic. As a student at the University of Marburg, Henrich lit upon the notion that Kant's thought as a whole might have a systematic form akin to that of his post-Kantian critics, thus uniting theoretical and practical reason in a distinctive, and hitherto unnoticed, fashion.[2] This recovery of a forgotten Kant might successfully meet the challenge of Heidegger's interpretation of German Idealism as only a late episode in the history of the decline *(Verfallsgeschichte)* of Western metaphysics. Heidegger's spellbinding and epic *Destruktion* of the "history of Being" was once again the main voice in German philosophy. Although immune to the allure of Heidegger's diagnosis of the malady of the West, Henrich, like many of his contemporaries (he became a student of Hans-Georg Gadamer in Frankfurt and then Heidelberg), acknowledged that the profundity of Heidegger's interpretations of central texts, and not least those of Kant, set a standard for future readings. Fundamental concepts of the great philosophers, not just problems of epistemology that presumed the validity of a tradition, had to be examined afresh.[3] Indeed, the validity of an entire tradition was at stake. If one was to go beyond Heidegger one had to read as well as he did. And in Henrich's view this also meant restoring for the present age the power of the classical German themes of self-determining reason, subjectivity, and self-consciousness, which had been reduced to derived and inauthentic moments within the happening of Being. He saw that these were the concepts of an indigenous intellectual tradition that could help legitimize a democratic modernity based on more than the right of self-preservation.[4]

So began Henrich's lifelong project of uncovering the basis of a "modern metaphysics" in the freshly and more originally analyzed ideas of German Idealist philosophy—through interpretations that would come closer to the spirit and intent of the classical authors. At the same time, he would present "argumentative reconstructions" that, among possible interpretations, proposed the best case for the validity of Idealist reasoning. Yet Henrich's first steps in the 1950s toward uncovering the unified structure of Kantian reason had already made clear that disunity and aporia were indeed intrinsic to Kant's system. Naturally he was drawn to investigate Heidegger's immensely influential effort to disclose systematic unity within Kant's transcendental analysis of the foundations of metaphysics—an analysis which in Heidegger's account was partially concealed from its own author. Heidegger sought to show that Kant pointed to the transcendental imagination (and its temporal schematism) as the "common root" of the faculties of sensibility and understanding, and thus as the source of human reason's unity. Henrich argued in an essay of 1955 that Kantian conceptuality could never in any constitutive sense permit an account of a common root or *Grundkraft* for the cognitive powers—and thus that Heidegger exegetically had no basis for his interpretation.[5] Kant at most could suggest, only regulatively, an "intrasubjective teleology" of the faculties, wherein they harmonize in the act of cognition.

Henrich's first reconstructive studies of Kant indicated his future direction: he would proceed to portray Kant as equally far from the Fichtean (counter-Heideggerian) ontological systematist whom he at first hoped to find and the neo-Kantian fragmented theorist of the sciences. Henrich gradually brought forth a renewed metaphysician of subjectivity and consciousness who, as a second "founder of modernity," revised the Cartesian heritage.[6] And he saw that Kant and his immediate successors provided the basis (but not the full elaboration) for a defense of that classical modernity against assaults from the major powers of post-Nietzschean thought: history (Heidegger) and language (Wittgenstein). One should look briefly at the *terminus ad quem* of this argument—Henrich's recent systematic discussions—to gain some sense of the philosophical context that is always being developed more or less explicitly (but not, of course, with prescience of all its later formulations) in the pre-1980 historical studies in this volume.

Modernity and Metaphysics

In both Germany and the United States historicist hermeneutics and analytical philosophy have been under siege by poststructuralist and postanalytic thinking. All routes taken by philosophers in the United States and Great Britain since the Second World War have been rendered problematic. In this situation Henrich's renewal of the philosophy of subjectivity is of much more than merely historical interest. Likewise in Germany the current postmodernist declarations of the end of the Enlightenment have brought to public notice the differences between the two leading German advocates of a "revised" Enlightenment: Henrich and Jürgen Habermas. In recent years they have engaged in a debate about what the project of modernity most essentially means.[7] Habermas delivered the first salvo when he said that Henrich's concern with a subject-centered metaphysics is incompatible with the antimetaphysical bent of modernity, and that it attempts to evade the paradigm-shift, since Nietzsche, from subject-centered discourse to linguistic discourse. Habermas charged Henrich with attempting to revive metaphysical infallibilism as well as ontological dualism and to restore the notion of metaphysics as a sovereign foundational science, ruling over the natural and social sciences. In all these respects, argued Habermas, Henrich fails to address the severest criteria of the philosophical probity of late modernity: "Henrich makes no attempt to defend the paradigm of the philosophy of consciousness brought to ascendancy by Kant, against the critique made against it repeatedly since Nietzsche."[8]

Henrich in reply has claimed that his proposed metaphysical approach meets most of Habermas's stringent requirements for modern, post-Kantian thinking. It is not a foundationalism working from absolute and self-transparent premises: Henrich abandons all "precritical" hopes of achieving a rational-deductive metaphysics (rational psychology, cosmology, and theology), and his fallibilism moves him yet further in a post-Kantian direction. Also, Henrich asserts, he has not meant to deny the significance of language (indeed, he has played a major role in promoting German interest in analytic philosophy), but he rejects any claim that linguistic interaction and intersubjectivity can supersede the subject; i.e, eliminate or trivialize the self-referential moment in discourse. The individual's concern with the truth of what is being said—a concern he has for *himself,* one not reducible to a search for agreement with, or argumentative victory over, another speaker—distinguishes genuine dialogue from mere linguistic game-playing.[9] Language has not been able wholly to dislodge the subject from philosophy, at least not *de jure.* Alleged paradigm-shifts may occur on the basis of insufficient reflection on whether earlier paradigms can and should be discarded.

Habermas's wholesale elimination of metaphysics thus strikes Henrich as a misreading of modernity and modern philosophy. If the "subject" is ineliminable from philosophic discourse, then philosophy is not just the clarification of an implicitly harmonious life-world, or the "illuminative furtherance of lifeworld processes of achieving self-understanding" (Habermas).[10] Subjectivity entails that disharmony and conflict are intrinsic to the human situation; conflict in turn makes necessary the human quest for resolution in unity. Hence the inevitability of "metaphysics," of the constant renewal of speculative questions that aim at the whole of human life and the world, or at final ends.[11] Since the life-world does not contain knowledge of such ends, albeit an interest in knowing them, philosophy must eventually leave behind the self-understanding of the life-world. In somewhat Platonic fashion, yet still with Kantian precedent, Henrich speaks of an "ascent" from perplexities inherent in the human situation that never permit doctrinal solutions or the closure of dialectic.[12] Although such metaphysical thinking is not explanatory—and thus ultimately eschews scientific forms of discourse, to which Habermas remains unswervingly devoted—it is necessarily integrative. Appropriately Henrich adopts the Kantian notion of nonconstitutive ideas of final ends or *Abschlussgedanken* (thoughts of closure) as providing the guidance of reason toward the unity it seeks.[13]

Although not discovering harmony in the life-world, metaphysical thinking is continuous with the strivings of ordinary life. Central to its integrative task is the unmasking of the falsifications and reductions of subjectivity committed by unnuanced and unlimited applications of scientific-naturalistic and linguistic-historicist thought. Metaphysics as critical is the enduring effort to counter the ever-actual threats to the freedom of the subject from manifold sources.[14] It especially needs to promote the awareness that the threats are not merely external but arise from inherent obscurities in the concept of freedom itself. That concept is essentially one that applies to a finite being, i.e., a being that cannot be construed as "sovereign subject" aiming at limitless mastery of Being. In Henrich's view it was never the intent of legitimate modernity, from Descartes through Hegel, to embark on the total conquest of necessity. On the contrary, the modern subject was always defined (in part) as self-preserving and thus bound to the body and to nature, in a manner that cannot be wholly clarified.[15] While the "subject" has some grasp of its own being apart from its involvement in the world, it is always confronted with the task of construing its relations, as "person," to the whole of the world. This experience of a fundamental dualism (not of substances but of individual and social modes of being) is inseparable from the primary reality of conflict. And that reality is merely flattened out and ignored, not explicated, by the communicative ideal of consensus.

It needs to be said that Henrich's renewal of a metaphysics of subjectivity goes beyond Kantian themes, and certainly beyond the Kantian formulations of those ideas. Thus his characterization of self-consciousness in terms of an irreducible, anonymous, and nonobjectifiable familiarity *(Vertrautheit)* is chiefly derived from Fichte.[16] Henrich readily concedes Habermas's charge that any account of this self cannot escape Fichte's paradoxes of self-objectification.[17] Those paradoxes (fully elaborated by Henrich himself)[18] point to only one of the regions of ineluctable obscurity *(Dunkelheit)* in human experience that provide the continuing impulse to metaphysical questioning.[19] Henrich does not commit the cardinal fallacy decried by postmodernism: treating the self as "self-presence."[20] At the same time, he acknowledges the force of the Hegelian disclosure of the importance of history; it is in Henrich's view one of the merits of German Idealist thought that it can do justice to history without subordinating reason to it—one can speak of the historical development of reason without falling into historicism.[21]

Furthermore, one will not miss a deep affinity between the hermeneutical approach to philosophy and Henrich's, insofar as the latter argues that the impossibility of arriving at a theoretical account of the "I think" brings about, already in the natural pretheoretical consciousness, the necessity for ongoing *self-interpretation,* taking the form of the various theoretical and practical self-descriptions of that being who is able to say "I." Henrich can thus claim that metaphysics is nothing other than the attempt to reach a definitive and comprehensive self-description, with the added proviso that the attempt is never successful.[22] It is in this connection that Henrich's writings on aesthetics and the philosophy of art—and the philosophic significance of modernity in the arts—also find their place. For it is precisely in its capacity to disclose the unforeseeability *(Unvordenklichkeit)* of the manifold forms of subjectivity, and the inscrutability of the grounds of consciousness, a capacity missing in discursive and theoretical reason, that art shows its metaphysical import, indeed, its indispensability. In this area of speculation (quite central to Henrich's entire philosophic project) his thought moves toward Hölderlin and the Romantic theorists.[23]

The Kantian Program

Most fundamentally Henrich's defense of modernity begins and ends with Kant and, in particular, with Kant's raising of the question "What is man?," to which all the primary questions of reason point.[24] Kant's thinking on this question (and the complex of questions relating to it) offers a sufficiently secure basis for a free and indefinitely revisable self-understanding of human life.[25] Although Kant's successors disclose unsolved problems in Kant's system, in various ways deepening the questioning that he began, they do not establish for Henrich the need for a wholly new basis for philosophy. Indeed, Henrich sees in Kant's successors the promise of a transformation of life through speculative reason that is no longer credible.[26]

In Henrich's account the elements of an enduringly legitimate modernity, first introduced by the Kantian philosophic program, are the following:[27] (1) a revolution in the relation of philosophy to ordinary consciousness, following Rousseau, in which philosophy is no longer pure theory but rather the extension of the primary natural questioning of the ordinary consciousness; (2) a theoretical inquiry pursuing such questions initially through clarification of the elementary procedures of the mind in its primary relation *(Grundverhältnis)* to an objective world; (3) the uncovering of dialectical and conflicting features within these procedures, in a surveying and analyzing of the internal complexity of reason that can be called a "second-level reflectiveness";[28] (4) a further development of such "reflection" into a novel form of deduction that is not a strict logical derivation from first principles, but rather a coordination of independent facts of reason into a coherent structure; (5) more specifically, the employment within such deductions (cognitive, moral, aesthetic) of given forms of ("quasi-Cartesian") spontaneous "self-relation" that involve a more complex sense of identity than can be found in earlier modern notions of "I think" or "I perceive"; (6) an ultimate orientation of all such coordinating deductions toward affirming and supporting freedom or autonomy as the fulfillment of human reason; (7) in particular, the elaboration of the primary questions of natural consciousness with the help of thoughts of closure or ideas of final ends that express the achievement, through the antecedent critical inquiry, of satisfactory notions of unity, i.e., notions that confirm and help realize the universal human interest in freedom.

This seven-phase structure can be reduced to essentially three elements: (1) the initial awareness of primary questions; (2–5) the foundational analysis in a critique of consciousness; and (6–7) the elaboration of a metaphysics of thoughts of closure. The second (2–5) and third (6–7) phases correspond roughly to Kant's division between the critiques of theoretical and practical reason, but it is more appropriate to think in terms of different kinds of philosophic reflection (for all phases are represented in each of the *Critiques*). The first phase is the preliminary *anticipation* of freedom as the goal of all inquiry, *justified* in the second phase and fully *elaborated* in the final phase.[29] Thus Kantian philosophy has a circular structure, involving "unity within difference." The practical end that is the theme of phase 6–7 is by no means deducible from phase 2–5; it is clearly presupposed in phase 1 and provides the impetus to all inquiry. Phase 2–5 in turn is not deduced from phase 1 in any traditional sense, but it has the deductive character of the search for the conditions of possibility of the ends anticipated in it. Those conditions involve "facts" of reason (the "I" of apperception, the forms of judgment, the fact of the moral law) that ultimately are not derivable from other sources, but can be coordinated to make a coherent structure that serves phase 1. The resulting edifice of reason is not, as is often said, simply the outcome of a construction of reason. Henrich prefers to speak of an "ascent" in which coherency evolves out of reflection on primary rational (not empirical) data.[30]

Henrich distinguishes this circular structure from other major forms of philosophizing: (1) the Aristotelian, which is characterized by a plurality of starting points and separate sciences based on them; (2) the various forms of naturalistic monistic philosophy in modernity (the latest being contemporary "naturalized epistemology," e.g., Quine), which tradition has proved to be the strongest rival for academic influence to the Kantian; (3) the post-Kantian systems of freedom, which are a variant of monism, radicalizing the circular structure of Kantian thought. In these, freedom is both the goal and the source of metaphysical argumentation. Thus in the Hegelian version all apparently factual aspects of reason are *aufgehoben*, i.e., integrated through a series of mediations that disclose these evidently given or immediate aspects of reason to be self-posited differences of reason. (Henrich has employed the term "autonomous negation" for this fundamental operation in Hegel's system.)[31] It is clear that Henrich has reservations about the possibility of overcoming such differences within Kant's structure. He also regards the "unity within difference" in the Kantian system as having a special kinship with Platonic dialectic.[32]

Internal Tensions in the Kantian System

Many of Henrich's studies of Kant locate within his principal arguments areas of tension, or "fractures," which are revelatory not of Kant's logical negligence but of his penetration into the fundamental and necessarily problematic sources of human questioning. For if a thinker's arguments were somehow "faultless" (the ideal of the philosophic journal article) this could only mean that analytic acumen is expressed at a superficial level of inquiry. The most central passages of a philosopher's thought, Henrich avers, are necessarily the most difficult and resistant to interpretation.[33] They are also the passages that are the most fertile soil for future philosophic developments. Henrich concentrates on three such problematic areas in Kant: the transcendental deduction of the pure concepts or categories of theoretical cognition; the attempts to deduce the moral law as the highest principle of practical reason; and the uncertainties and reticence in Kant's statements on his own methodology.

Henrich's famous discussions of the transcendental deduction have opened up new approaches to its tangled and perplexed reasoning, and have helped to establish that "deduction" in Kant is not a traditional logical-deductive procedure from a set of transparent and well-secured premises. Instead, a deduction (the evaluation of a claim to an acquired right, as in venerable judicial usage) is a reflective procedure according to a special eighteenth-century technical sense of "reflection": the pretheoretical examination of diverse and apparently conflicting cognitions, with coherence and unity in view, of which the theoretical sense of deduction is but an extension.[34] The claim to a right to universal and necessary employment on the part of the metaphysical categories is the subject of the reflection in the transcendental deduction, and the resulting judgment is of a limited right to such employment: to one solely *within* the limits of possible experience.

This argumentation is not, in Henrich's view, an attempt to justify the possibility of personal identity in terms of the objective account of temporally bound perceptual states as the condition for an enduring "I."[35] On the contrary, the argument makes use of a quasi-Cartesian concept of identity of the "I think" as a premise, albeit an insufficient one, which is reflectively coordinated with the concept of complex object implicit in the subject-predicate form of judgment. Identity as the "I"'s a priori knowledge of the possibility of employing rules of transition to connect all possible states (horizontally and transversally in time) of the "I think" is in need of *some* specific notions of regularity to fulfill the task of making the transitions. The human "I" *happens* to have available to it, for this task, the categories implicit in the forms of judgment that it employs in its discursive-logical thought.[36] Here there seems to be something especially problematic in Kant's argument: the step that attempts to bridge the two starting points, identity of the "I" (or "self-relation") and objectivity (or "world-relation"), and that can show only the fortunate concurrence of two ultimate facts of reason. From this concurrence, once acknowledged, certain universal and necessary presuppositions can be exposed, relevant to *those* original facts and only those, thus "legitimating" the categories. Kant, however, thought this exposure quite sufficient for his purpose: to settle the *quaestio juris* of the disputed claims of metaphysics to achieve knowledge of the whole, within and beyond experience. He made no attempt to overcome the duality of premises or to ground those premises in some deeper necessity.[37] The lack of such attempts in Kant was a primary source of the dissatisfaction of his critics with his system. But their dissatisfaction was necessarily with Kant's *aim,* since his manner of argumentation was perfectly in accord with his proposed goal.

The practical philosophy offers another case of irreducible duality within coordinated, not logically derived, unity. And in this case, namely, Kant's attempts to deduce the "respect for the law" or "autonomy" from rational spontaneity, Henrich discloses that Kant was himself initially not content with anything less than a strict unity of grounds (theoretical and practical). As early as 1765, under the powerful impress of Rousseau's notions of a self-legislative reason, Kant was confronted with the problem of how to relate the universality of an objective principle of the good (i.e., principle of judgment) to the universality of a subjective, yet not empirical, principle of motivation (i.e., principle of execution). In other words, how could one account for the remarkable feature of moral insight, wherein the apprehension of what should be done is immediately—not calculatively or prudentially in a means-end deliberation—accompanied by the consciousness of a commandment to act on the apprehension? How is it that the moral law by itself, without rewards or inducements, commands respect? Or again, how is it that human beings, having this responsiveness to the law, evince "autonomy"? None of Kant's efforts—from 1770 to the *Groundwork* of 1785—to derive this responsiveness (i.e, the effect of a purely rational principle on sensibility) from the theoretical spontaneity of reason was successful. Kant had to remain content with such responsiveness being an ultimate "fact" of reason, a view he first elaborates in the second of the *Critiques,* that of practical reason (1788). All the same, Henrich does not follow Hegel in regarding this admission as a mere "undigested log in the stomach," or anomalous irrationality within rationality; rather, he sees it as Kant's arriving at a deductive approach in the practical philosophy that is consistent in spirit and character with the reflection (in the coordination of facts) of the theoretical deduction.[38]

Kant's statements on philosophical reflection as the method of deduction thus entail a view of human reason as possessing certain regions of unavoidable obscurity, i.e., elements intrinsic to its structure that cannot be further grounded or analyzed, though they are not in themselves at all "clear and distinct." Transcendental elaboration of the coherence that such elements still afford replaces a foundational reconstruction or synthesis of knowledge on the basis of an analysis of cognition into primary intuitable elements, as is characteristic of earlier modern philosophy, empiricist and rationalist. Transcendental analysis presupposes such a "first-level" modern epistemic analysis (uncovering of the intuitive—empirical and spatiotemporal—and conceptual elements of knowledge), but as "second-level reflectiveness" it proceeds from an awareness of unclarified diversity and complexity in the first level, with its propensity for dialectic.[39] Henrich's reading of Kant provides, ultimately, a rejoinder to a Heideggerian charge that the modern philosophy of subjectivity, including Kant, achieves its clarity at the cost of an evasion of the inherent darkness and self-concealment of Being (as in Heidegger's claim of Kant's "drawing back from the abyss" of the transcendental imagination). On the contrary, Kant may more effectively show the inherence of *Dunkelheit* in the human situation by disclosing it in consciousness itself, rather than by ignoring the problems of consciousness and ascribing "question-worthiness" only to Being.

Henrich renders visible through Kant's case some interesting hermeneutical insights into an author's obscurity to himself. This obscurity is not adduced to "deconstruct" the interpreted author's alleged belief in his sovereign self-transparency.[40] Henrich is instead interested in inevitable areas of obscurity within reason that elucidate rather than undermine its powers.

Introduction

In addition to the areas already mentioned (the relation of identity to objectivity and the fact of moral insight), Henrich points to two other considerations, one more or less peculiar to Kant and the other intrinsic to philosophy. Kant repeatedly speaks of having a greater interest in setting forth his principles than in clarifying their foundations—a priority that Henrich relates to Kant's practical objective in initiating a revolution in philosophy which definitively justifies freedom.[41] This means that Kant, and perhaps every thinker who bows to the practical urgency of communication, accepts some *avoidable* unclarity. Further, all philosophizing takes the form of attempts to solve philosophical problems that are bequeathed to thinkers by their predecessors and contemporaries (no philosopher can be the *causa prima*, accordingly). But in the effort to gather the sense of what others are saying and to argue with it, a philosopher necessarily learns only late and imperfectly what the method of his own thinking has been. Some versions of phenomenology aside, "desedimentation" of a tradition does not ensure self-understanding, but instead points to its elusiveness. If Kant is especially enigmatic on his own method, it may be in part because, as Henrich suggests, his "second-level reflectiveness" involves a keen awareness of the dependence of philosophic inquiry on the clarification of philosophic tradition.[42]

Thoughts of Closure

Kant's critics and successors began their reflections with his principles of theoretical and practical self-relation, and further explored their implications. Variously they were dissatisfied with the elements of "facticity" in the Kantian system, finding them inconsistent with the primacy of a self-grounding autonomous reason.[43] In other words, they rejected the Kantian versions of philosophic "deduction" and "ascent." They instead opened up new lines of thinking in the areas of self-identity, autonomy, and ontology: to account for the possibility of the transcendental unity of the "I" of apperception, whose existence is merely presupposed by Kant (Reinhold, Fichte, Hölderlin); to give a more satisfactory grounding of the unity of the rational imperative and of sensibility, one which would offer more scope to the inclinations, emotions, and social existence than did Kant's moral principle (Fichte, Schiller, Hegel); and to overcome the merely presupposed ontology of the object of scientific knowledge in Kant, and in general to remove the disparity between the scientific and the prescientific worlds of experience (Jacobi, Schelling, Hegel).[44]

Although Henrich acknowledges the validity of many of their insights and improvements in these areas (especially Fichte's deepening of the account of the self and Hegel's revisions of Kantian ethics and ontology), he maintains the continuing importance of the unresolved *Dunkelheiten* in Kant, *as* unresolved. One might say that he is in fact more interested in these obscurities than was Kant himself. Henrich elaborates on the grounds for this interest in an apologia for a kind of metaphysics; thus it is of metaphysical significance that the human species is beset with irremovable ambivalence, that it can never be fully "at home" in the world. Most important, this species must acknowledge an intractable limit in its self-understanding, as it encounters the impossibility of producing objectifying theoretical knowledge of the ground of the existence of its own subjectivity. This stress in an aporetic reading of Kant is, by Henrich's own account, related to the increasing sense of the contingency of reason in the nineteenth century, and the even greater decline of confidence in reason in the catastrophic twentieth century; he avows his debts to the Heidelberg thinkers of problematic reason, Max Weber and Karl Jaspers.[45] Henrich argues that a flight from the problematic character of reason is the common feature of much philosophy in our time (pragmatist, semantic-reductionist, postmodernist), and this flight as a "refusal to think" is equivalent to the rejection of all metaphysical thought.[46]

Thus Henrich must apply Kant's questions to a situation in which Kant would find himself quite estranged: to an age of post-Enlightenment cataclysm, in which thought must expect satisfaction from something besides the hope of indefinite moral progress. One can say that Henrich indicates how his particular historical standpoint comes into conjunction with a metaphysics based on a Kantian view of the inscrutability of the grounds of subjectivity, to compel a revision of Kantian ethics, while not removing ethics from its position of primacy. This revision will further enrich and elaborate the notion of freedom. In recent essays Henrich has proposed a number of directions that such an enrichment might take, through analyses of the relation of ethical, epistemological, and metaphysical factors of conscious life.

One such direction is reflection on how speculative "gratitude" (as a modern version of classical *theoria*) is one of the most significant expressions of human freedom. Thinking as speculation about the whole is a fulfillment of freedom when it discloses the permanence of problems as a constituent feature of the unity of the whole.[47] Through this insight into the character of the whole, the thinker experiences a "gratitude for existence" unlike other forms of gratitude. This gratitude is distinguishable from communal thanks: the proportional reward for which human beings reasonably hope (from other humans or higher beings) in exchange for their practice of moral virtue. Such practice is indeed a starting point for thinking about ourselves and our freedom, and it is the core of much religious experience. Accordingly, Kant characterizes the free respect for the universal moral law, and the tribute it earns in a "moral world," as having incomparable authority for modern life. Yet what Kant describes cannot provide a satisfactory answer to his own question "What is man?" Beyond communal thanks for the blessings of morality, the thinker experiences contemplative thanks for the existence of the enduring questions of life, enabling thought to have its own freedom, beyond fear and hope. An essentially human possibility is to give thanks for beings, or Being, that cannot and need not acknowledge the thanks.[48]

With such thoughts Henrich develops reflections he began in earlier essays,[49] defining more precisely the trajectory of his central inquiry: experiences and actions that have the power to illuminate the totality of human life bear in themselves relations to unifying images of the world and therefore to essentially metaphysical conceptions. Whereas one can and must employ the traditional term "metaphysical" for the investigation of these relations, the term carries the meaning of Kantian "thoughts of closure" rather than that of scientific demonstration and theory. Taken as a whole, Henrich's interpretations of Kant, Fichte, Hölderlin, and Hegel seek to clarify these systematic connections and bring them back into the philosophy of our time.[50]

1
On the Unity of Subjectivity

Translated by Guenter Zoeller

It might seem superfluous to return extensively, once again, to Heidegger's Kant-interpretation.[1] After all, the agitated discussion that it provoked upon its first appearance in 1929 has faded in the consciousness of the scholarship.[2] And even Heidegger's own thinking grew beyond the horizon within which that interpretation had been accomplished.

However, the substantial reasons for a general reopening of that discussion weigh heavily enough. Only today is it possible to appreciate the extensive influence of Heidegger's book on Kant. For more than a quarter of a century, it determined the method as well as the interpretive goal of almost all publications in the field. Yet in most cases, that influence has not occurred in the light of conscious methodical discipline. And even the critical voices, above all those apparent in the essays of Cassirer and Levy,[3] are caught up in individual theses and textual interpretations and do not gain the distance from which Heidegger's attempt can be judged as a whole. Thus Cassirer and Levy ultimately rest on the very ground that Heidegger had intended to reveal in its utter lack of foundations. This is understandable and even necessary in the immediacy of a first encounter. But by now it should be permissible to place the criticism on a different ground. It would be easy to continue with what has been done, to a certain degree and in an excellent manner, by Cassirer and Levy, viz., to demonstrate Heidegger's distortions of Kant's doctrine and the ahistoric character of his interpretive method. Heidegger himself has made clear again and again—and among other places in the short preface to the second edition of his book on Kant—that he is not about to deny contradictions with the Kantian text. But he has also insisted that such contradictions can only make their appearance as distortions when one overlooks that a "thinking exegesis" necessarily has to go beyond what is said in order to enter into what is unsaid but truly proper to a thinking, something that cannot be accomplished or judged by means of historical philology. This claim has to be considered. To be sure, a "thoughtful dialogue between thinkers" will never want to transcend the level of philological textual exegesis in such a way that the explicit opinion of the text becomes something of no import compared with some dark genuine meaning. According to Heidegger, the exegesis has to be accomplished through an explicit understanding of what is said; that is, to be able to see the unsaid as such, one has to be certain about what is actually being said. Accordingly, the key references from Heidegger's Kant book will form the appropriate entry for this essay.

There is another reason for attempting to enter into the structure of the Kant book through an analysis of its basic approach. The Kant book has hardly found its place in the efforts to understand Heidegger's thinking and the course of its development, and yet it seems to me better suited to furthering such understanding than many of his other works. For nowhere else has Heidegger dealt so explicitly with a particular philosopher of the tradition, and nowhere else is he so open to something that is different in both language and terminology. It has never been overlooked that the interpretation is carried out by the "guiding preview" provided by fundamental ontology. What is called for is an adequate articulation of what is proper to Heidegger in his interpretation of the historical figure Kant. Yet it is a significant consequence of the systematic force of this interpretation that, from a perspective which is not entirely false but not sufficiently far-reaching, Heidegger appears fundamentally as a Kantian or as a follower of Hegel. This is all the more true since for Heidegger the self-differentiation from Hegel was always problematic. Heidegger's true identity will be revealed not least through the elucidation of his Kant-interpretation, which, though explicitly a reading of Kant, will also show itself to be secretly a counterproposal to Hegel's Kant-interpretation and that of speculative Idealism in general. It is the unavoidable difficulty of such an effort that one can neither simply adopt Heidegger's language nor simply polemicize from Kant's position. True understanding is indeed compromised if "followers . . . falsify what is problematic and so produce a clear-cut counterfeit answer."[4] However, even the hasty polemics of a self-assured Kantianism would at least have to recall Kant's words: "No matter how paradoxically and incorrectly a man of genius may write, one can always learn something from him. What is written with genius must be reflected upon."[5]

I. The Reduction of the Faculties to the Basic Power of the Soul

In the introduction to the *Critique of Pure Reason,* Kant speaks of the "common, but to us unknown root" (A 15/B 29), in which "perhaps" originate the two stems of our cognitive faculty, sensibility and understanding. Heidegger's Kant-interpretation attempts to comprehend the imagination introduced in the transcendental deduction as this unknown root. He wants to show that Kant himself saw imagination in this way, but that he could not explicitly elevate it to the rank of a principle, since this would have forced him to abandon the very ground from which the *Critique* is conceived. Heidegger insists that the true dynamic of the *Critique* has to be seen in the force of Kant's glance into that "unknown"—given that the unknown is not that of which we know nothing, but that which comes up to us as the disquieting in what is known (110). Thus anyone attempting to enter into a dialogue with Heidegger concerning his underlying assumption is referred to the interpretation of that passage in Kant. It comes as a surprise, then, that in the reviews of the Kant book, the reduction of the cognitive powers to the imagination is conceded without contest, and that the attention immediately focuses on the particular questions of that reduction. Here, in the face of Kant's text, emerges a helplessness that is not limited to the reviews but can be found in the literature quite generally, and this not accidentally.[6] For the exegesis of those Kantian sentences has a prehistory reaching from Reinhold to Cohen, with the result that Kant's own view and its historical presuppositions have become alien to us. To make them speak to us again in their immediate significance requires an explicit reenactment of that prehistory. The more extensive horizons of Heidegger's work will only become apparent once that movement from Kant through Hegel to Cohen has been understood.

Whether Kant thinks of the "to us unknown" common root of sensibility and understanding as something yet to be reached in our knowledge, or rather as something that is in principle inaccessible to us, cannot be decided as easily as Heidegger implies. Certainly, it could be the case that the sentence in question reveals the preliminary character of the system of the *Critique,* thus encouraging Kant's successors to penetrate its principles more deeply. This is how Reinhold, Fichte, Hegel, and Cohen have interpreted it, and Heidegger takes it in this way as well. But it could also be the case that the "unknown to us" is spoken from the certainty of the insight that the task of revealing the common root reaches beyond the limits of human knowledge, and that the "perhaps" merely concedes the possibility that there might be such a first principle, though there would be no reason to assume that it had to exist. It was thought that one could decide this matter without further examination in favor of the first interpretation, which is also seemingly supported on technical grounds. After all, it appeared difficult to explain why this sentence would be placed at the important point in the introduction that provides what needs to be said "by way of . . . anticipation" (A 15/B 29). Yet, the second interpretation is not so absurd that one should not try it by first looking for further information in Kant on the idea of the common root.

A first hint toward the concepts with which one would have to further determine the idea of the common root, a hint also about the difficulties of such a determination, as seen by Kant, can be gained from the final footnote of the essay "On the Use of Teleological Principles in Philosophy."[7] One might succumb to the illusion that the various phenomena (effects, faculties, powers) of knowledge could be reduced to a unitary ground (basic power) by subsuming them under a common title (general concept). This procedure would, however, be as insufficient as attempting to characterize the unitary principle of the powers of matter by defining these powers in terms of the common property of being a moving power, thus saying that the moving power is the basic power of matter. For the criterion of a basic power is that it renders intelligible the powers it grounds, such that the powers can be deduced from the basic power. Attraction and repulsion, however, cannot be gained from the mere concept of motion. No more are the activities of the cognitive faculty deduced by the fact that one calls them altogether representative powers. This methodological reflection must be kept in mind when one submits to the task of demonstrating such a basic power as the common root of the cognitive faculties, a task which, according to Kant, has to be faced unavoidably at the conclusion of empirical psychology, in which the analysis of the various faculties is accomplished.[8] Kant's skepticism regarding the possibility of solving this task is already here quite apparent.

In the two texts cited the idea of a common root receives its historical background. The remark on the "common title" is directed against the ontology of Christian Wolff. "Wolff assumes a basic power and says the soul is a basic power that represents the universe to itself." But "one attempts in vain to derive all powers of the soul from a single one; still less is it the case that the latter could be assumed to be the *vis praesentativa universi*."[9] For, as we already know, that would only be a common title for the powers. Wolff was led to this mistake by incorrect definitions of substance and power, and thus of the soul itself.

> Wolff wanted to derive everything from the faculty of knowledge, and he defined pleasure and displeasure as acts of the faculty of knowledge. He also called the faculty of desire "a play of representations," that is, modifications of the faculty of knowledge. Here, then, one believes to have unity of the principle ... But that is impossible here. Wolff came to this merely from the previously mentioned false definition of substances, that they were powers which thus had to be derived from a basic power. Now he assumed the *vis repraesentativa* to be a basic power, etc.—Yet power is nothing but the mere relation of accidents to the substance.[10]

Furthermore, the same illusion arises from "an incorrect definition of power. For power is not that which contains the ground of the actuality of the accidents (for that is the substance), but is merely the relation of the substance to the accidents."[11] Again, "it is already a mistake to say that the soul is a basic power, because the soul is defined incorrectly, as seen in the ontology. Power is not that which contains in itself the ground of the actual representation but the relation of the substance to the accident, insofar as the former contains the ground of the actual representations."[12] From these definitions the meaning of the "perhaps" in the passage from the *Critique of Pure Reason* becomes immediately clear. The passage on the common root does not point forward but refers back to the controversies of the eighteenth century concerning the system of psychology and its ontological presuppositions. Since, according to Kant, the concept of power regards only the relation of a substance to its accidents, "different powers can indeed be attributed to the substance (notwithstanding its unity)."[13] Thus they *can* be assumed; it is not necessary that a substance possessing different accidents stand to them in relation only through some basic power.[14] If, therefore, for reasons we have yet to investigate, knowledge of a common root cannot be achieved, then we can only say that sensibility and understanding *perhaps* originate in such a common root. The thought which today one is hardly willing to explicitly carry through, viz., that subjectivity is constituted of several mutually independent factors, contingent in their reciprocal relations, is here indeed assumed by Kant as a possibility that remains where all insight ends. Yet the question arises why we are dissatisfied with this determination of the principle of the unity of subjectivity when we are satisfied with a possible pluralism of powers concerning matter.

Christian Wolff's reduction of the powers of the faculty of knowledge to one basic power was not motivated by reasons that lie in the structure of the subject itself. Rather, those reasons stem from his attempt to turn the

Leibnizian concept of substance into the foundation of a systematic psychology. If it is granted that each created thing, including finite substances, is subject to changes, then the ground of these changes cannot be sought outside of this substance.[15] For that contradicts its concept of being the ultimate subject of all activity. The principle of change must therefore lie in the substance itself. Leibniz calls it "appetition," "entelechy," or "power."

It is through this power, not in need of solicitation, that the essence of substance can be further determined.[16] Since this power can only consist in the production of inner states of the substance, it must be capable of comprehending much in a unity, because changes are only possible gradually,[17] and it must satisfy the condition of pure interiority. Substance is thus in its essence representational power. Since, however, the world is a comprehensive relational system of substances, in which each substance stands in relation to every other substance, it must, according to its essence as representational power, carry the ground of all these relations within itself, thus being a "living mirror" of the universe.[18]

In his treatment of the soul Wolff adopts the Leibnizian line of thought unaltered. The argument for the content of the definition of power has changed, however, as a result of Wolff's abandoning the original meaning of Leibniz's preestablished harmony—a development that is especially clear in Wolff's student Baumgarten.[19] According to Wolff, the soul originally represents things to itself by reference to the affections of its body, that is, through sensations; according to Baumgarten, the soul is the ground of voluntary actions with reference to its body, thus it must also represent its body in the latter's individual position in the world. On Leibnizian premises, the soul is thus *vis repraesentativa universi pro situ corporis in eodem.*[20] That all phenomena of the soul must be derived from this, its essential power, already follows from the fact that only a single power can be thought in it. For the assumption of several powers that would determine the subject in different directions in their striving for actuality would immediately lead to different subjects, which would contradict the essence of the soul as substance.[21] The soul therefore perceives, imagines, remembers, notices, compares, forms concepts, judges, infers, aspires and detests, and freely determines itself to do or not do through one and the same power.[22] All these specific determinations or faculties of the soul are only modifications of its power. One must sharply distinguish those modifications (mere possible functions) from the power, the latter being that which contains in itself sufficient reason for the actuality of an action.[23] Kant rightfully objects to this procedure for providing the necessary derivation of faculties from the one power, arguing that it is nothing but the exhibition of a common factor. It simply consists in showing for a given faculty that the *vis repraesentativa universi* is indeed contained in it,[24] but it does not establish that the *vis repraesentativa universi* could not be thought at all without positing the respective faculty.

This criticism of Wolffian monism is by no means Kant's own accomplishment. In the first introduction to the *Critique of Judgment* he writes: "Yet it is quite easy to establish, and has in fact been realized for some time, that this attempt to bring unity into that diversity of faculties, though otherwise undertaken in the genuine philosophical spirit, is futile."[25] However, if we seek to determine who was the first to have that insight, then both Kant's text and Lehmann's commentary[26] remain silent. Yet it would have suggested itself to remember the "famous Crusius" (Kant)[27] who was certainly the most influential among the opponents of Wolff and whose theory of the basic power in psychology was highly influential.

In *Scheme of the Necessary Truths of Reason,* 1745, Crusius mounts some heavy artillery to combat Wolff. He argues that the concept of power as such simply means the possibility of an effect. Powers can therefore be easily abstracted from given properties.[28]

> Many, however, err in this regard in that, if they later easily subsume the effects to be explained under an arbitrarily abstracted general power, or might regard those effects as determinations of that which they assume to be contained in the general power, they immediately believe themselves to have explained the matter from its causes. This happens, e.g., if one fancies oneself to have found in the power that represents the world a power of the human soul from which everything that is contained in it can be understood. Yet it may very well be the case that what one has abstracted . . . is only an effect.[29]

Crusius goes on to provide rules for the determination of a basic power, so that in the explanation of things "we do not afterwards merely bring their properties and states under one and the same title; rather, we either discover the true basic powers or are able to approach the latter as close as possible."[30]

It was Crusius who instituted the term "basic power" in the general meaning it had in the psychology of the second half of the eighteenth century. By contrast to the merely abstracted general power, the basic power is that which constitutes something peculiar and different from other things "in a manner not due to our way of considering things." By the criteria provided, Crusius considers it impossible to base the human faculties on any single basic power. It is a mistake merely to suppose a basic power.

For "suppose there were things that had more than one basic power, which since it is possible, one cannot deny in advance, and indeed there are actual cases like that; then one would preclude without cause and in advance the way ever to come to know them. Thus let us assume that our soul had one single basic power, viz., the power that represents the world, in which, though so much perfection were contained that through it the soul could sense, meditate, infer, and so on, and could furthermore from its representations originate desire and disgust, pain and pleasure, and certain acts—those things, since they differ in more than grade and direction, would be impossible to conceive from a basic power[31] . . . The understanding of a rational but finite mind is not one single basic power but has to be imagined as a complex of certain basic powers and of other powers and faculties derived from them."[32]

Wolff, of course, had denied that a substance is determined in its actions by more than one basic power. And Crusius therefore turns even more generally against the very concept of power as determination of the soul's essence, and in this he goes much further than Andreas Rüdiger.[33] Wolff's principle furthers materialism, because power is not itself the subject of existence but must exist in a subject on which it depends, this being the only way to ascribe at all the predicate of existence to it, as is indeed required. Now if one determines the soul to be a power, then this suggests locating this subject in the body.[34] But it is not at all necessary to share Wolff's scruples regarding the unity of a subject that contains multiple basic powers. Crusius sees in the multitude of powers of the mind, which bring about different activities of the same subject, a specific perfection of the subject over and against matter.

That way, though, Leibniz's notion of power—to which the striving after changes in the manner of an entelechy was essential—is implicitly modified. In Wolff, too, that notion had provided the basis for the proof of a single basic power of the soul. But as early as 1755 Kant said that notion is "arbitrarily formed."[35]

Thus in Crusius's writing all those elements of the criticism of Wolff that we also found in Kant are advanced. To be sure, Crusius did not have to invent the pluralism of the cognitive powers of the soul. On that point he merely reestablishes an old tradition from which Leibniz had departed and which had found its foremost modern representative in Locke. The *Essay concerning Human Understanding* simply presupposes that a multitude of different powers and faculties inhere in the subject. The question how the unity of the subject is possible does not come up. That question arose only through Wolff and remained an issue thereafter, even though at first the criticism that was advanced from the standpoint of the pluralism of powers prevailed. Kant did not contest the merit that Wolff earned through his explicit realization of Leibnizian ideas. Wolff's thought even provides one of the unknown presuppositions for the Idealist speculation. As for Crusius, he has taken the question too lightly; he arrives at a multitude of irreducible powers, but lets them simply stand next to each other so that he can no longer determine the connecting unity which they obviously form in the subject.[36] Crusius's successors then had to reintroduce more of Wolff's ideas into the system of psychology.

The pluralism, though, remained. And this in spite of Bonnet,[37] who is opposed to Wolff in the details but agrees with his principal outlook. That situation is best demonstrated by Johann Nikolaus Tetens.[38] In his critique of Wolff, Tetens shares Crusius's arguments against a power the reality of which is exhausted in a general name for different phenomena.[39] And although he tends toward the view that in its ultimate constitution nature is simple,[40] Tetens sees no possibility of reaching that ultimate constitution through the only reliable method, viz., observation and analysis: "We do not know the basic power of the soul."[41] Tetens gives all his divisions a provisional character. And if he ultimately attempts to find a hint of the basic power in the capacity of feeling common to all powers, then he himself has already taken that back in the introduction to his work, where he apologizes for every instance in which he gave in to the "propensity to a uniform system." Considering the unsystematic, merely descriptive character of Tetens's book, it is unlikely that Kant profited from it.

There were more important motives driving Kant to confess to a pluralism. Among them are, above all, the distinction between the *objective* principles of sensibility and those of understanding, but also the foundations of moral philosophy. In the latter context Kant, under the influence of Hutcheson, took position for the first time against Wolff's system, which contains, at least in terms of its claims, a purely intellectual system of morals.

"Only in our times has it begun to be realized that the faculty of representing what is *true* is *knowledge;* whereas the faculty of perceiving what is *good,* is *feeling;* and that these two may not be confused with each other."[42] "For with concepts of such various natures, diverse basic concepts must, in all likelihood, form their foundation. The mistake, [which] some have committed, of treating all such cognitions (such as those involved in the feeling of the sublime and the beautiful; D. H.) as though they could be reduced to a few simple concepts, is similar to the mistake into which the early physicists fell—that all the matter of nature consists of the so-called four elements, a view discredited by better observation."[43] It follows from all this that opposition to the monism of powers does not presuppose a train of thought peculiar to transcendental philosophy. Moreover, it will become evident that even the impossibility of knowing the common root can be established from a point of view that need not be that of the critical philosophy.

The penchant for a uniform system, cited by Tetens as the reason for inquiring into the unity of the cognitive faculties, receives closer examination in Kant. Wolff's attempt to bring unity to the various powers of the soul is praised as "undertaken in the genuine philosophical spirit," for "it is always the maxim of reason"[44] to move the investigation in the direction of a basic power. However, Kant also states: "It is indeed the main rule of the philosopher to seek to reduce everything to one principle, to the extent that that is possible, in order not to multiply too much the principles of knowledge. But it does not follow from this that we also have cause to reduce the different powers in the human mind to a single one."[45] Thus there is no objective ground for the presupposition of a basic power in the manifold of phenomena but only a subjective, although necessary, principle. It is the maxim of reason to bring unity into the manifold of cognitions of the understanding. The idea of a basic power is thus a regulative one *(focus imaginarius)*.[46] As long as the motives for the presupposition of the idea are not understood by critical reflection, it will be impossible to resist the appearance, contained in the very idea of a basic power, that a being corresponding to the idea has to be presupposed. The search for the unity of the "faculties of the mind" thus becomes Kant's example in discussing the regulative use of ideas in the *Critique of Pure Reason* (A 631ff. /B 659ff.).

> The various appearances of one and the same substance show at first sight so great a diversity, that at the start we have to assume just as many different powers as there are different effects. For instance, in the human mind, we have sensation, consciousness . . . etc. Now there is a logical maxim which requires that we should reduce, so far as may be possible, this seeming diversity, by comparing these with one another and detecting their hidden identity . . . Though logic is not capable of deciding whether a *fundamental power* actually exists, the idea of such a power is the problem involved in a systematic representation of the multiplicity of powers . . . The relatively fundamental powers must in turn be compared

with one another, with a view to discovering their harmony, and so to bring them nearer to a single *radical,* that is, absolutely fundamental, power. But this unity of reason is purely hypothetical. (A 649/B 677; second emphasis is Henrich's)

In this passage Kant himself explains most clearly the idea of a common root *(radix),* and we understand why he cannot, as Tetens had done, assert that there is a basic power—although unknown to us—but can merely concede in the "perhaps" the possibility of its existence.[47]

II. The Unity of Apperception and Intrasubjective Teleology

In his rejection of the *vis repraesentativa universi* as the basic power of the soul Kant had accused Wolff of false definitions of substance, power, and soul. In the controversy with Eberhard this point receives further clarification.[48] One cannot simply identify substance and power, given that the latter belongs to a different category, viz., that of causality. The relation of inherence in a subject is entirely different from that of dependence on a cause. Although the substance must be thought of as endowed with power, through which it is the ground for the actuality of the accidents, it is not itself identical with that power. On that matter Kant agrees with Crusius.

Kant says here as well as in the essay on teleological principles and in the Pölitz metaphysics that power is the concept of the relation between substance and accidents *insofar* as the substance contains the ground of the accidents. That ground itself is contained in the substance as such. This subtle distinction receives significance in the rejection of materialism (see also Crusius) as well as Spinozism. "For the concept of substance ... is thereby (sc., by identifying substance and power) in reality completely lost ... just as Spinoza would have it, since he affirmed the universal dependence of all things in the world on an original being as their common cause, and by making the universal, effective power itself into a substance, he converted this dependence into inherence."[49] If one pursues these categorical distinctions further, then the semantic context of the passage on the common root becomes even clearer.

If substance is not itself power but merely the ultimate subject of the exercise of a power, then it follows, according to Kant, that in general it is impossible to know a substance as such through concepts. For a subject can only be determined through predicates. But predicates contain only the accidents of the subject in which they exist. Since being a predicate is the essence of a concept *qua* discursive knowledge, "we cannot have insight into the substantial being."⁵⁰ Here the problem emerges which Hegel will try to solve in his way through the doctrine of the speculative proposition.

It further follows that the concept of a substance, insofar as the substance is thought of strictly as ultimate subject and simultaneously as ground of the possibility of the accidents, includes the concept of freedom. "The concept of freedom is already by itself necessarily connected with the concept of a substance with respect to the intelligible (thus not in the case of *substantia phaenomenon* or matter; D. H.), because the substance must be the ultimate subject of its actions and cannot itself be the mode of action of another substance."⁵¹ But one cannot conceive of a subject that contains in itself the ground of the possibility of its actions except by positing the subject to be an intelligent being. Thus one will have to think the substance intelligent—a conclusion which Kant also draws, therein following Leibniz, from the impossibility of imagining inner states other than representations and activities dependent upon such representations.⁵² There is "freedom ... only where there is *causalitas intellectualis,* i.e., in intelligent beings who have causality through reason."⁵³ According to these categorial determinations, the concept of substance implies those of freedom and intelligence, and the concept of freedom implies those of substance and intelligence. But it is not possible to infer substance and freedom from intelligence.

Now one surely should not put too much weight on these cursory observations of Kant's. And yet through them, and immediately from the analysis of the concept of basic power, one gains access to central positions of the Kantian system. Kant has always emphasized that the consciousness of moral obligation is a peculiar "fact" that could not be derived and demonstrated from any other fact. From our earlier investigations it follows that the categorical imperative would have to be more than a mere fact of reason, if there were a cognition of human reason as a substance. For in that cognition would be included the cognition of freedom. If one could presuppose the freedom of the will, then the basic law of practical reason, which "forces itself upon us as a synthetic proposition a priori,"⁵⁴ would be an analytic proposition. The assertion that the imperative is a fact of reason thus presupposes that the concept of human reason as substance is indemonstrable.⁵⁵

Proof of this is provided in Kant's chapter on the paralogisms of rational psychology in the *Critique of Pure Reason.* Neither the thoroughgoing identity with itself nor the spontaneity of the intellect in determining objects permits the conclusion that self-consciousness is an intelligible substance or that such a substance must underlie it. The thoroughgoing identity could also be the identity of a state that is transferred between different existing subjects. (Locke had already shown that in the chapter "Of Identity and Diversity" in *Essay*.)[56] And the spontaneity of thinking must not be confused with intelligible freedom. For even if consciousness is aware of itself in all its thoughts as the ground of their being thought, it is still possible to imagine that the conditions that bind consciousness to the laws for the production of its own thoughts are not at all different from the conditions that underlie the material appearances in their transcendent substrate (A 358). Its capacity for thinking notwithstanding, the subject might be not a substance but, to put it in categorical terms, an accident or power that would receive the ground of its actuality from a substantial being not identical with the cognitive faculty, at least not with ours.

One can express the critique of the paralogisms in the terminology of the "basic powers" by showing why it is impossible to give any other concept of basic power "than the one that is taken from the effect and expresses only that relation . . . E.g., imagination in humans is an effect that we recognize as distinct from other effects of the mind. The power pertaining to it can thus be called nothing else but power of imagination (as basic power)."[57] The point holds with particular stringency for the case of self-consciousness. For only if one has shown that self-consciousness, which contains the condition of all thinking, cannot possibly be reduced to prior conditions does one have conclusive reasons to reject such a reduction for all other "faculties of the mind." The critique of the paralogisms thus first provides the possibility of understanding Kant's arguments for the unknowability of the common root of sensibility and understanding.

Self-consciousness is itself empty. There is nothing to be thought in it except the consciousness that all possible representations which it is supposed to be able to think as its own agree in the one predicate of being a representation of the "I" and harmonize with the conditions of such unity. For there to be anything to be thought by this self-consciousness, all predicates pertaining to what is being thought, besides the one of being thought, must refer to something given to self-consciousness for thinking. Self-consciousness is thus dependent upon a medium through which things to be thought can be pregiven to it, this medium being sensibility, which, according to the transcendental aesthetic, permits only knowledge of appearances. All reality that becomes accessible to self-consciousness has to be thought by means of the forms which guarantee its possible unity in all the different thoughts. It is inconceivable that self-consciousness could gain real cognition outside of that relation of itself—and the forms of possible unity—to pregiven thinkable data (appearances). But self-consciousness could only comprehend the conditions of its own possibility if the ground of its reality were thinkable independent of the conditions of its thinking, which is a contradiction unless one were to ascribe to that subject a higher faculty of thinking than the one based on the conditions of self-consciousness, i.e., an intellectual intuition. Thus it remains true: "But how this peculiar property of our sensibility itself is possible, or that of our understanding and of the apperception which is necessarily its basis and that of all thinking, cannot be further analyzed or answered, because it is of them that we are in need for all our answers and for all our thinking about objects."[58]

The "I," around which we "can only revolve in a perpetual circle" (A 346/B 404), cannot get outside itself and reach the ground of its own possibility. Kant does not, therefore, display unfounded skepticism when he believes he is able to say that the common root of sensibility and understanding, which might need to be assumed, is unknown to us. According to his principles that root is indeed unknowable and must remain so. One might further investigate and analyze thinking itself, but one cannot extend the knowledge of that "upon which this thought depends for its possibility" (A 398). And thus it is also not possible to inquire into the conditions of other, phenomenally distinct faculties in order to demonstrate their unity with self-consciousness. For in trying to get beyond their phenomenal diversity and reach the ground of their unity, one would have to look for such a unity in an area that pertains to the conditions of the possibility of self-consciousness. One would thus fall back into the first paradox of all self-knowledge.

There is yet another difficulty to face, though, in trying to realize the idea of the common root. Sensibility and understanding are different in their phenomenal presentation, and an identity of the two, no matter how hidden, cannot be assumed. "We cannot conceive how things so dissimilar could have sprung from one and the same source."[59] The reason thus lies in the discursive nature of the understanding that can determine homogeneity only through universal marks. That in which the homogeneous differs cannot be brought under one unitary concept. Thus an understanding that should have access to the problematic common root of sensibility and understanding would have to think nondiscursively, and the world in which this root could be thought would have to be the object of an intellectual intuition. This brings out completely the problematic meaning of the "perhaps."

Yet the faculties which together make up the human mind do not simply coexist such that one could imagine them arbitrarily modified and exchanged. Rather, they form jointly the unity of a structure through which knowledge is first possible. Thus the understanding cannot obtain knowledge without sensibility. And sensibility, in turn, must be so structured that the understanding is able to determine it according to the conditions of its unity, i.e., the categories. After all, appearances could be so constituted that the understanding found them not conforming to the conditions of its unity. Now the understanding in and of itself, viz., as self-consciousness, is defined through thinking alone. All representations of which it is conscious must already be determined according to the conditions of its unity. Since the representations do not stand under those conditions in and by themselves—considering that consciousness is an act of spontaneity—the understanding must be immediately related to a faculty other than itself, through which given representations are brought into consciousness. The imagination, then, is defined as a basic power. All three faculties—sensibility, imagination, and understanding—are necessary for there to be knowledge. But their existence cannot be deduced from each other. If one of the three conditions were not satisfied, all consciousness and knowledge would be impossible; the remaining actual faculties "would remain concealed within the mind as ... dead and to us unknown" (A 100). In its content the structure formed by the faculties of the mind is determined through the structure of finite self-consciousness, that is, through apperception and its categories. To that extent apperception and not imagination is, in Kant's words, the "radical faculty" *(radix!)* (A 114).

That holds even for practical reason. If Kant demands a demonstration of practical reason's unity in one principle with speculative reason,[60] that does not mean that moral obligation is supposed to be derived from self-consciousness. It cannot mean that, unless all reasons for the pluralism of faculties that we have attempted to explain are to be pushed aside. What needs to be demonstrated, though, is that practical reason is structurally identical with theoretical reason.

One can thus see why Kant can be *amazed* at the unity of the subject. For if apperception requires for its actualization other faculties which it cannot simply presuppose, then the fact that there is consciousness requires further investigation. One could term the thought developed by Kant on this matter that of an "intrasubjective teleology." It is a teleology in that the joining of the cognitive powers can only be explained from some purposive arrangement; and yet the teleology is intrasubjective in that the purposiveness in question does not refer to given objects.

"But we are absolutely unable to explain further how it is that a sensible intuition (such as space and time) is the form of our sensibility, or how such functions of the understanding as those which logic develops from the latter are possible; nor can we explain why it is that one form agrees with the other in a possible cognition . . . If we wanted to make judgments about . . . [the] origin [of the harmony of sensibility and understanding]—an investigation that of course lies wholly beyond the limits of human reason—we could name nothing beyond our divine creator."[61] Leibniz's preestablished harmony thus receives a surprising interpretation—one that for Leibniz, however, is completely inadequate, given that he considered the thought of a pluralism of faculties an absurdity.

Thus the circle of evidence begins to close. For in the intimation of an intrasubjective teleology the same thoughts recur that underlay the concept of a common root. "Despite their dissimilarity, understanding and sensibility by themselves form . . . a close union for bringing about our cognition, as though one were begotten by the other, or as though both had a common origin, which is impossible, or at least we cannot conceive [it]."[62]

The question of the basic power of sensibility and understanding concerns not the structure of subjectivity but the conditions of the possibility of such a structure. A need expresses itself in the question that stems, for one, from the demand of reason for unity of principles and that furthermore originates in the peculiar relation that the functions of the subject have to one another. The renunciation of an answer and the necessity of that renunciation did not come easy to Kant, just as he is asking a lot in calling upon us to follow him in that renunciation. At times Kant himself thought he knew more on several aspects of this question than he could later defend; such was the case above all with the substantiality of the subject and the deduction of the moral law. The standpoint of the mature critical philosophy thus emerges as the result of a development of its own. That standpoint includes the most consistent complex of thoughts that Kant ever reached in this question and which, as we may now say, he could possibly reach within his sphere of concepts.

The hint concerning the common root thus does not really point forward toward a context still obscure to Kant himself. Rather, it forcefully formulates an insight that has critical connotations without being critical in the transcendental sense. It throws light on several things that have remained puzzling in the structure of the *Critique*, e.g., the indifferent term *Gemüt* (mind), the synthetic structure and the apparently unsystematic disposition of the deduction, the separation of theoretical and practical philosophy, and much more. All attempts by Kant's successors to remove those scandalous "provisional" features would have seemed to him, had he wanted or been able to follow them, a return to positions he had overcome. The unity of subjectivity, in Kant's final construction of it, is conceived as teleological. Kant feels compelled to look beyond what is immediately given in consciousness, "to look beyond the sensible to the supersensible as the point where all our a priori powers are reconciled, since that is the only alternative left to us for bringing reason into harmony with itself."[63]

The speculative Idealists no longer saw the background of what to them seemed inadequate in Kant's work. The structural unity of the faculties that became visible in the transcendental logic so impressed Kant's followers that in their attempts to establish with ever-greater clarity the necessity of that unity they removed themselves, at first unknowingly, from the very framework in which Kant had developed it. The dispute over Wolff's psychology and the extensive work on the problems posed by it, which Kant had to accomplish in the period prior to the development of the *Critique*, were either forgotten or at least without any determining force. And thus the Idealists believed themselves capable of grasping the reality of being human immediately through consciousness. They no longer considered it meaningful to be amazed at the origin and unity of consciousness. The horizons still presupposed in Heidegger's method of interpretation thus began to delineate themselves.

It has been clearly established that Heidegger's way of interpreting the hint about the common root does not capture Kant's own view. Kant's foundational enterprise does not point "consciously toward the unknown" in a manner that would call for its elucidation (25). Rather, Kant stays on this side of the space occupied by what is in principle inaccessible. Moreover, the unknown is for Kant not, as Heidegger would have it, that which presses in on us as something disquieting in the known (110), but something entirely closed to us, which can disquiet us only as long as we are not certain of its unattainability. And even if one initially concedes that in the deduction Kant had a glimpse into something unknown that is still hidden in the essential structure of the imagination, it cannot have been the unknown to which he pointed with the idea of the common root.

We can no longer follow the thoughts that guide Heidegger's elucidation of the "essential unity of transcendence." To be sure, no one will want to assert that the duality of the sources of knowledge is a "mere juxtaposition" (24); rather, one will want to stress, with Kant, that the unification of the sources is predelineated in their structure—a structure through which alone knowledge can be what it is. The pull of the elements toward one another calls for a different interpretation than that of invoking coincidence, but it does not demand that "at first in the uniting, the elements as such spring forth." Yet Heidegger repeatedly puts forward that alleged conclusion (e.g., 39, 43, 53f., 95). That conclusion is indeed the presupposition of his interpretation. If one had to admit this presupposition then the thought that the transcendental imagination is the root of the two basic sources of knowledge does not seem remote, for it cannot be disputed that imagination is what provides unifying mediation. But there is no justification for the further claim that the mediation cannot be what it is unless that which is mediated originates in it. That claim stands as a sheer assertion against the subtle Kantian train of thought that leads to the plurality of faculties.

It will become evident that the assertion in question cannot be established in the horizon of Heidegger's book on Kant but that only *Being and Time* might provide means for supporting it. There is, however, one reference (93f.) in the Kant book that seems to presuppose an argument, though such an argument is nowhere provided. We are given the mere thesis that the formation of a unity is possible only if that which by its very essence does the unifying is also the origin of that which is to be unified (95).

Thus it may seem that Heidegger's attempt already fails in its methodological starting point, since it rests on a *petitio principii* and furthermore relies in its methodological conception on Kantian passages that, when correctly interpreted, mean the opposite of what they are taken to mean. However, we must now remember the difference between historical exegesis and the claim of a thinking interpretation—a distinction which Heidegger requires us to "contemplate" for the understanding of his Kant book. Perhaps we are now in a better position to draw that distinction and to explain it in more detail. Of course, such a consideration cannot obliterate the ambiguity that an interpretation acquires through the unjustified usage of the passage concerning the common root. But inversely, the historical interpretation in turn acquires an ambiguity of equal impact through the hints that are given regarding its presuppositions. For Heidegger explicitly distinguishes his attempt from the construction of a basic faculty that was at issue in the historical interpretation. The interpretation of imagination as the common root is not about the reduction of the given structure of cognition to some simple basic underlying powers but solely the development of that structure itself. The two approaches are not only different, but they are also opposed to each other. It will not be possible to think of the imagination as the soul's basic power. Nothing is further removed from Heidegger's "going-back into the essential origin of transcendence than the monistic-empirical explanation of the remaining faculties of the soul based on the power of imagination" (96). That enterprise is already ruled out by the fact that "in the end the essential unveiling of transcendence decides in the first place the sense in which one is permitted to speak of 'soul' and 'mind,' to the extent that these concepts are originally appropriate to the ontologico-metaphysical essence of human beings" (96). By attempting to render problematic the very concepts Kant employs, Heidegger's interpretation, already in its initial conception, goes beyond a historical exegesis that would let the author's own words speak.

Now one could immediately object that it is not an "empirical" explanation that is required in the idea of a basic power. Yet it cannot be denied that the idea of a basic power implies talk about the subject of substance and power. It remains to be asked how Kant justifies that usage. We must therefore now place Kant's theory, which thus far has been considered in the dimensions that it shares with traditional metaphysics, on its own ground.

III. The Problem of Justifying the Basic Concepts of Psychology

The concepts of faculty, power, spontaneity, and freedom are all predicables of relational categories. Their possible validity thus depends on the principle of apperception, in which they first originate as merely logical forms through which it is possible to think something. They can only bring about knowledge insofar as they are applicable to something pregiven. This critical restriction of their use also deprives them of their unquestioned role in traditional metaphysics, where they served without further justification for the determination of being in general—the role of a prior decision that also underlies the eighteenth-century discussion about the basic power. Thus Kant's discussion of the idea of a basic power does not have the unproblematic sense that it still possesses in Tetens. Since it had been shown that such a basic power lies beyond the sphere of the empirically demonstrable, and since the real use of the categories is limited to that sphere, it is even doubtful whether the problematic idea of a common origin of the faculties can at all be thought through the concepts of substance and power.

That point becomes even clearer when one remembers that the common root can only be assumed as the object of some intellectual intuition. For such an intuition, however, the separation of self-consciousness and pregiven being, which first defines the concept of the category, does not apply. It is therefore at least questionable whether the categories of a finite self-consciousness have any meaning at all with reference to an intellectual intuition. To be sure, finite self-consciousness is required to employ the categories when attempting to grasp the very concept of the unity of the cognitive faculties. But at the same time it knows that it employs the categories only analogically, and that therefore the idea of the common root merely indicates an "empty space." That idea does not contain the dogmatic thesis of an actually existing basic power; the concepts employed are no more than a necessary intellectual tool. All that is meant by such an idea is the inaccessible correlate of the (for us) contingent plurality of subjective attainments.

Something similar holds for the determination of the human faculties in the inner structure of knowledge. The critique of the paralogisms had shown that no being is known through self-consciousness. Instead only the condition of all thinking is thought. To know a being means to "determine" something pregiven through those necessary thoughts that are implied in all thinking. Given that knowledge is actual, it makes sense to specify and postulate the conditions under which that alone is possible—and those are conditions not exhausted by apperception. But then to know those conditions is no longer a transcendental task but a matter of psychology. To be known in their use and not just in their existence, they, too, must be pregiven to consciousness.

This is where Kant's doctrine of inner sense comes in and, accordingly, constitutes much of the transcendental deduction in the first edition of the *Critique of Pure Reason.* One can come to realize that knowledge would not be possible without the form of sensibility and the transcendental imagination. But those powers cannot be known as such, viz., in their transcendental meaning. What we know of them are always empirical derivations, such as attention or reproduction for imagination or the "affection of the empirical sense" through objects "as appearances" for sensibility. The transcendental cognitive functions are already presupposed in each cognition, including that of the empirical realization of knowledge.

Some functions can thus really only be thought of as faculties, which here means possibilities for attainments that have to be necessarily presupposed, but which cannot be established as real "powers," which cannot even be presupposed as such on the basis of some evidence. This fact must be seen as one of the motives for the reworking of the transcendental deduction, which, in the second edition of the *Critique,* is mainly limited to the logical analysis of knowledge and the systematic presuppositions of the attainments involved. The terms "imagination" and "sensibility" are now employed very carefully and are adopted by way of an analogy with empirically demonstrable functions. The sharp contours of Christian Wolff's rational psychology must fade.[64]

In this way the transcendental deduction assumes its methodologically peculiar position, which provokes revisionary attempts. For the logical analysis of knowledge leads to attainments that have to be presupposed but that remain essentially inaccessible in their own being. The analysis points back to the origin of knowledge without, however, being able to ascertain an original foundation for it. The provisional and fragmentary form of the subjective deduction is due not, as Heidegger thinks, to the fact that its development was not Kant's immediate intent, but rather to Kant's insight that it is impossible to carry it out in the manner endeavored by Heidegger. It is not the missed development but the analysis of the conditions under which such a development could possibly occur that keeps Kant in the conceptual framework of traditional psychology. For Kant believed that the concepts of traditional psychology could be derived from the concept of self-consciousness, that radical faculty of knowledge (A 114). Certainly, even this radical faculty, from which everything follows that has thus far been developed, can only be defined by the employment of the very categories gained from it, albeit in their merely logical use.

How else should one explain the determinations "act," "spontaneity," and "radical faculty," all of which are applied to apperception? The question arises which meaning those concepts have when applied to their own origin in an attempt to determine the "I." Usually the answer given is that all determinations of apperception are the result of a logical analysis of this possible thought in general. And indeed, apperception is the principle from which the necessity of the logical functions can be derived, and it therefore belongs to logic. But apperception belongs to logic only as its very condition, not because apperception is a logical phenomenon. One can examine concepts, judgments, and inferences again and again and analyze their relations indefinitely, yet never will one come across the concept of the "I," which must be presupposed for any theory of judgment and inference.

The "I" is thus an "original consciousness" which is not first derived from the analytic treatment of logical phenomena but which must be presupposed for it. And now Kant gets into the peculiar difficulty of not being able to determine in turn this supreme principle of all thought and knowledge. He calls it "an act of the understanding of the determining subject in general,"[65] a "thinking" (B 157), a "transcendental consciousness"[66]—all concepts that are designed to distinguish apperception from experience, intuition, and empirical action. What being the "I" has, insofar as it is such that it says "I" to itself, cannot even be expressed in its logical structure. Apperception cannot sufficiently define the movement in which, circling itself, it determines itself to be the condition of the possibility of all knowledge. That movement must be accepted as a fact whose far-reaching consequences can then be represented and analyzed. Fichte has founded his science of knowledge on the hint at this *aporia,* in such a way that he let it grow even more paradoxical in his theory of intellectual intuition. And Hegel's logic is based on the effort to make the "I" definable as a concept. If one wants to take up Heidegger's attempt in its systematic intention, he will have to place it in the line of those enterprises. (It will become clear only in what follows how Heidegger's differs in principle from those other attempts.)

One cannot just say that Kant avoided asking about the manner of being of the "I." This argument, which today is often mounted against Husserl, is ready at hand but conceals the fact that the meaning of such a question cannot be realized from Kant's standpoint. Conducting such arguments already requires a detailed concept of being, one that has been proved in a dialogue with Kant. The "overcoming of metaphysics" can never be accomplished with such formal reflections that block entry into its inner necessity, and Heidegger would be the first to share this opinion.

To treat the thought of the "I" not just as something evidently given but to ground it and to thus first make it definable is an attempt that is part and parcel of Heidegger's return to the "essential structure of transcendence." So far it has not become transparent, though, why for Heidegger such a question is necessarily congruent with the construction of that totality as totality.

Before turning to the prehistory of Heidegger's Kant-interpretation, and with it to the topic that is central to its intent, we must ask how the attempt to demonstrate the root of sensibility and understanding in, of all things, the imagination has to be judged through a historical interpretation of Kant.

Heidegger argues that there is a problem concerning imagination which is not considered in the first version of the *Critique* and which then threatens to explode that version. By way of evidence he points to the sharp contrast between those divisions in which Kant talks about the "two basic sources" of the mind and others in which he talks of "three original cognitive faculties." For Heidegger, this "homelessness" of transcendental imagination has only one possible explanation, viz., that the two basic sources refer back to imagination as the ground of their unity.

The difficulty in question can be solved with Kantian means if one distinguishes between understanding and sensibility as sources of objective contents of knowledge, and transcendental imagination, which has merely subjective significance. Understanding as the faculty of concepts and sensibility as the faculty of intuition contribute to every instance of knowledge of a specific content, whereas imagination has to be presupposed only for *the coming about* of knowledge. When analyzing any empirical proposition one will encounter only intuitions brought under concepts, never anything stemming from imagination, even though imagination alone renders intuitions ready for conceptualization. Exactly because it is the mediating act, imagination does not contribute to the material of knowledge.

To put the same point another way: when asking in what sense one could imagine the "cognitive faculty" in isolated acts, it becomes clear that even without the understanding sensibility would offer intuitions, albeit uncomprehended, blind ones. Moreover, without intuitions understanding would at least have the possibility of issuing concepts. But the imagination is essentially in need of given sensibility and pregiven concepts. It is absurd to think of imagination even as a merely possible activity without those two. Imagination is thus a faculty the actuality of which does not follow from the possibility of understanding. (Imagination does follow, though, from the actuality of understanding, since without perceptions given to the understanding, it would never be stimulated to thinking, which in turn presupposes the active imagination.) Imagination thus has to be assumed to be an independent cognitive power.

Yet since it is the task of the imagination to synthesize sensibility into perception in accordance with the possibilities of thinking provided by the understanding, it still makes good sense to say that imagination is a faculty of the understanding—the sense being that the understanding is immediately related to the imagination but that the latter is essentially in need of the unity thought in the former. Now, according to Kant, it is a futile enterprise to think about how that relation has to be represented in its details. It might be the case that the capacity designated "imagination" itself consists of many parts. We do not and cannot know how that capacity is able to apprehend the contingent form of time and whether it could only mediate that one form or other possible forms as well.[67] All such questions fail to understand the methodological skepticism toward the subjective deduction deemed necessary by Kant. After all, we do not know how and due to which conditions the unity of that which we know as thinking is possible. "Imagination" is merely the term for the unity of "activities" required, in addition to the objective principles of knowledge, to render intelligible the actuality of knowledge.

It thus becomes more and more clear how far Heidegger has moved away from the motives that gave rise to the form of Kant's system as we have seen it.[68] For virtually all crucial passages a historically more accurate interpretation discovers a meaning quite different from the one provided by Heidegger, thus establishing a totality of meaning which Heidegger simply left behind under the prior conception of his project. And yet this entire criticism is not yet sufficient, given that Heidegger precisely aims at rendering Kant's guiding concepts questionable. And had we ourselves not, in determining the "I," discovered a difficulty that emerged with regard to the very consistency of the critical philosophy? Let us only retain that the "glance into the unknown of transcendental imagination," which is said to have made Kant "shrink back" (110), cannot be taken in the literal sense of this somewhat dramatic phrase.[69] If indeed there were some merit to Heidegger's formulation, then that would be more visible to us than to Kant. For in Kant's thinking a "perspective which was broken open, so to speak, only for an instant" (116) had immediately again to conceal itself, and this on the grounds of some insight into what is true, not—as Heidegger would have it—out of fear of the consequences of degrading reason.

IV. The Construction of the Absolute "I"

It would be one of the most egregious mistakes in assessing Heidegger's Kant book to see its originality in the supposition of transcendental imagination as the root of sensibility and understanding and of all "faculties of the mind." Far from being new, this idea underlies the whole Kant-interpretation of speculative Idealism. And that not by accident but by necessity.

A simple line of thinking can already render clear this necessity. In all Kant's assertions regarding the basic power of the mind as a regulative idea, distinct from the structural unity of the cognitive faculties, the two-world theory is presupposed. The difference between the structure of knowledge and its intelligible condition—a difference also employed by the intrasubjective teleology—can only be thought with the help of the concept of the thing in itself. If one eliminates this concept, as speculative Idealism has done since Fichte for reasons that cannot be discussed here, but retains the postulate of the unity of the faculties, then the structural unity of the faculties becomes the only place for realizing that postulate. In such a case, though, it is necessary that the realization can be carried out. For the postulate and what it postulates are no longer distinct with respect to their manner of being. Now if one is predisposed to find Kant making good sense—and after all, speculative Idealism traced itself back to Kant—then transcendental imagination, which provided the structural unity of knowledge through the mediating link between the faculties, must become the ground for the realization of the postulate of unity. It will become evident

On the Unity of Subjectivity

that this line of thinking still holds for Heidegger, but with an important difference in the manner and the intent with which that interpretation of the imagination is carried out.

Heidegger himself says that his interpretation moves in a direction opposite to that of speculative Idealism (94, n. 196). For a better understanding of the contrary direction of Heidegger's movement we have to deal, with the requisite brevity, with the interpretation provided by speculative Idealism.

In his first system, Fichte assigns a role to the imagination which initially reminds one of Heidegger's Kant-interpretation. As is well known, the *Science of Knowledge* of 1794[70] takes its starting point from the analysis of self-consciousness. The "I," as the principle of the possibility of thinking, cannot be eliminated from any thought. Each reality that we might imagine is dependent in its being thought on the "I." Fichte infers from this fact (whether correctly or not is not at issue here) that the "I" as "I"—totally independent of all foreign reality—can be what it is solely through its own activity, that it must posit itself absolutely. The essence of self-consciousness is the absolute act.

If, however, the self is infinite activity, the question arises how the self can acquire consciousness in such activity. For consciousness, insofar as it is always the consciousness of something, means the reflection of the act and the positing against oneself of something nonactive, viz., that of which one is conscious in consciousness ("not-I"). This question thus presents the peculiar difficulty of explaining how it is at all possible that against pure activity there can be posited something nonactive, and this through pure activity itself. I say "through itself," because the "I" is the ground of all possible reality, and since it is absolute activity one cannot even conceive that something objective would offer resistance to that activity from outside. Fichte, not able to solve this contradiction, makes it the focal point of his system. It is inconceivable that the resistance come from outside; thus it must be possible to think it a check *(Anstoß)* occurring in the active "I" insofar as it is active. Because the check is essentially connected to the activity, one has necessarily to distinguish within the absolute "I" between "I" and "not-I." Yet this has to be done in such a manner that the active "I" is posited as absolutely active, thus as directed toward overcoming the resistance in its own activity. Yet it cannot overcome that resistance insofar as resistance is necessarily connected with its activity. Fichte's solution is that it *ought* to overcome the resistance. The check, previously inexplicable, turns out to be founded in the moral self-determination of the absolutely free act.

The crucial point is now how this "I" becomes conscious of itself in its inhibited activity. On Fichte's description, the infinite activity experiences an inhibition *(Hemmung)* and thus becomes finite, but because of its infinite nature it is again pushed beyond that inhibition, only to again experience it, etc. This brings about an oscillation *(Schweben)* of the "I" between finitude and infinity in the first step of the genesis of its consciousness.[71] This oscillation of the "I"—of the ground of all reality—is, according to Fichte, the imagination. "Our doctrine is therefore that all reality ... is brought forth solely by the imagination."[72] For this state of oscillation amounts to what we know as intuition. And the extensive nature of intuition, more specifically determined as space and time, is derived by Fichte from the productively self-inhibiting activity of the "I," which is now characterized as transcendental imagination. The understanding is evidently here so little identical with the "I" that it rather represents the opposite of rational self-consciousness and is reduced to "fixating" the structures already contained in intuition by conceptualizing them. Those structures themselves stem from the activity of the absolute "I" in the finite-infinite oscillation of the imagination.

Fichte early on realized that he was not simply rendering systematic Kantian thoughts but that he was attempting to introduce a completely different layer of reflection. Only later did he recognize that, in determining the "I" as absolute act, he also left behind the sphere of the Kantian theory of self-consciousness. To us, however, it is clear that his theory of the "I" that repels itself from itself, and thus produces reality, contains exactly that which is thought in the idea of a basic power. Indeed, Fichte always considered it a merit of his theory that his principle permits one for the first time to deduce the basic concepts of the *Critique*. Fichte's theory concerns itself overwhelmingly with the idea of the basic power so that in it the very "conditions of the possibility of thinking" are at issue. However, it becomes questionable whether the principle that is here called "I" still retains the subjective meaning of a "self," or whether one must instead think of it as a subjectivity that exists in itself and that ultimately returns us to the God of Leibniz and Spinoza. By the time Fichte realized this consequence Schelling had already, in the spirit of that consequence, reserved a fundamental place for transcendental imagination in his system.

To be sure, the term had to be dropped, but what it stood for, and that in which Fichte had already wanted to recognize the Kantian "faculty," remained. Whereas it still seemed in Fichte that transcendental imagination was a form of synthesis between "I" and "not-I," in Schelling it becomes clear that transcendental imagination is in reality self-consciousness itself.

This is expressed by the fact that the deduction no longer starts with the

"I" in its possible relation to something thinkable in general, but rather with the "I" in relation to itself as "I," which relation defines the "I." "I" means to relate oneself to oneself (Kant says: to be able to say "I" to oneself). In this act the "I" knows itself to be purely active (see Fichte). Yet we can make its activity intelligible to us only by distinguishing between two activities in it, one that is merely infinite production, and another that turns this production back unto itself—a reflection that is the essence of self-consciousness. The "I" now "oscillates"[73] between the two activities in an infinite contradiction, striving, as it were, to come to a consciousness of itself as the unity of the two activities.

Those determinations that in Fichte held only for the imagination, which produces intuitions, now simply define self-consciousness and have become the moments of the movement in which the "I" first realizes or objectifies itself through the different potencies of consciousness. Now it is openly stated that those two activities underlie the possibility of self-consciousness. They can thus not really be of the nature of an "I" in some subjective meaning, although they are necessarily presupposed by such an "I" and by it alone.

Schelling's further thinking was kept in motion by the closer determination of those activities. Yet he would hardly have let the opposition of activities underlie subjective self-consciousness so much more clearly than Fichte had he not been inclined, from the beginning, to take the "I" in an absolute sense.[74] In Schelling's account of the opposition within the "I," transcendental imagination is confirmed in its function of being the common root; in his doctrine of potencies, transcendental imagination provides the means for the construction of the identity of all activities of the subject. "Perfect science shuns all philosophical tricks through which the 'I' is, as it were, taken apart and divided into faculties that cannot be thought under a common principle of unity. Perfect science does not aim at dead faculties that have no reality and that only exist in artificial abstraction, rather it aims at the living unity of the 'I,' the latter remaining the same in all expressions of its activity."[75]

Hegel's approach is even more clearly reminiscent of Heidegger's than Schelling's is, and the question becomes more and more urgent how a principal distinction can be found in the face of their common polemic against the pluralism of faculties. Hegel's statements on Kant's philosophy in his essay "Faith and Knowledge" provide an appreciation of transcendental imagination that has been in many regards the immediate counterpart, and probably also the model, for Heidegger's treatise. The moments of Heidegger's interpretation that can be found in Hegel's essay include a hidden allusion to the passage on the common root;[76] the assertion that the unity of consciousness cannot be conceived as the product of opposite members,[77] but that transcendental imagination is the formative middle term of those members;[78] and the thesis that Kant was not able explicitly to retain that which he said because he had started from the already fixed opposition of the members. Yet Hegel does not permit the false idea to arise that Kant had shrunk back from something already seen because of a lack of intellectual courage. When Hegel claims that transcendental imagination is in reality the speculative idea, he does so in clear view of the fact that such an identification is thinkable only for us but not for Kant himself; that the truth has broken an initially invisible path behind the back of insufficient principles, and this solely through the force of the subject matter.

Like Fichte and Schelling, Hegel confers upon imagination priority over the understanding, criticizing the exclusive emphasis on the latter in Kant's presentation of self-consciousness. "The whole transcendental deduction . . . cannot be understood without distinguishing between the Ego which does the representing and is the subject—the Ego which, as Kant says, merely accompanies all representations—and what Kant calls the faculty of the original synthetic unity of apperception, the latter being the faculty of imagination, which is not to be understood as the middle term that gets inserted between an existing absolute subject and an absolute existing world, but as what is primary and original."[79] And thus we find in Hegel Heidegger's hint at the original unification on which the understanding is first grounded.

We cannot unfold here the complicated philosophical motives behind Hegel's interpretation—an interpretation that, like Heidegger's, aims not at being philological but at being systematic. Only this much can be indicated: What does it really mean to say that "activities" underlie the "I," that in it a "check" occurs, that an "opposition" of "finite and infinite activity" constitutes the essence of the "I"? This is merely using words. What is not being asked is whether something real is thought through those words and whether they are at all suited to determine what is meant by the absolute. At this point intellectual intuition must step in, meaning that the principle of construction implies the bankruptcy of thinking. And if a plurality of activities is to be posited, one has no idea how conceptually to distinguish this speculation from bad faculty psychology.

That is roughly Hegel's argument. And it is clear that in these thoughts, which form the basis of Hegel's logic, Idealism for the first time achieves a foothold that enables it to stand up against Kant, at least in principle. The logic, an enterprise Hegel first created in speculative Idealism, is designed to accomplish the tremendous feat of developing a system of concepts free of any presupposition and in which that which is thought, as well as the thinking through which what is thought is thought, coincide—an absolute method that evades the absolute skepticism with regard to the presuppositions of thinking. One can easily understand that this idea necessarily implies the elimination of the pluralism of faculties. There is no need to address more specifically how the pluralism is actually overcome and how entirely different motives pertaining to morality rule it out as well.

For if there is a self-grounding method, then through the very act of thinking something in general everything that can possibly be thought must be implicitly thought in this very thought as such, not just mediated by some presupposed universal interconnectedness of things. Now if this thought already contains the act of thinking and the "I" that thinks this thought—and this not as accompanying circumstances but in the very content of the thought—then the thinking and the subject that does the thinking can have only the structure of the thought in which they are already contained. They can thus not be externally constructed from pieces and faculties, rather, they must reflect in their possibility the essence of the unity of thought. Yet it must remain obscure here how it is supposed to be possible to gain the totality of knowledge from any thought whatsoever; this formal hint must suffice.

The development of Hegel's absolute reflection is furthermore the origin of contemporary philosophical consciousness. And this origin is so strong that its limits also appear to be the limits of Kant-interpretation. This explains the helplessness of Kant scholarship in the face of the passage about the common root, a passage that, when interpreted correctly, demands a look behind the premises and motives of speculative Idealism. Since Hegel, the essence of the subject has been determined in various ways. Almost never did one follow Hegel in determining it as something absolute. Today the tendency to think of the subject as dependent on a highest being has reestablished itself. Yet even when opposed, Hegel is so strong that on the question of the internal structure of subjectivity only answers that were unthinkable before him are possible. The unity of subjectivity is unquestionably certain, and this is especially the case where that unity is *de facto* not even thematized—a circumstance documented by the fact that its evident defect does not lead to its being considered problematic. The idea of an "intrasubjective teleology" in the critical sense is forgotten. We will soon have occasion to demonstrate this in Cohen's case.

Hegel had explained that it is contrary to the living feeling that the mind has of itself to think of itself as a "sack of faculties," and he emphasized that in that way the mind could never be grasped as a mind; that self-consciousness would then determine itself not as itself but only as one of its objects. All this had been said with such insistence that even where the means to leave behind the level of reflection critiqued by Hegel had been lost, Hegel's demands have found some measure of realization. Heidegger is the first to face Hegel at the level of genuine thinking. We will see that he does that also in the Kant book, which is exactly why the book is in an important sense a "thoughtful dialogue between thinkers." However, in spite of all neo-Kantianism, Kant scholarship was so determined by Hegel that it let pass as unproblematic the attempt to interpret the transcendental deduction in complete analogy to Hegel and did not object to the central supportive passages offered by Heidegger, which could have revealed the historical untenability of the enterprise from Kant's standpoint. Kant scholarship was especially induced into this attitude through the example of Hermann Cohen. For Cohen there were two reasons that made it impossible to look for the unity of subjectivity, thought under the term "common root," in a place other than the structure of subjectivity itself: the Idealist rejection of the "thing in itself" and the polemic of experimental psychology against the concept of faculties.

From the standpoint of empirical psychology, Herbart had quite correctly objected to eighteenth-century psychology's rigid treatment of mental processes, which had divided them up among isolated faculties and thus sheltered them from an observing and calculating empirical science. Herbart believed that he had to abolish altogether the concept of a faculty and to replace it with that of psychic laws and processes, which alone were considered experimentally observable. This polemic coincided with the rise of observation in psychology: in effect, Friedrich Albert Lange already believed that certain experimental results achieved the final detection of the common root.[80]

Cohen did not undertake to defend the Kantian concept of a faculty against this general tendency, even though this concept, as we have seen, covers not really existing entities but only the contingent fact of activities given within consciousness. Yet it lies outside the sphere of neo-Kantianism to reflect on such a contingency, the only possible exceptions to this being Paul Natorp and Richard Hönigswald. Instead Cohen tried to convince the psychological opponents of transcendental philosophy of the innocent nature of Kant's concept of a faculty.

The meaning of the passage on the root therefore has to be inferred from the nexus of the attainments of cognitive activity. And to that effect

Cohen treats the passage as the guiding thread of his commentary.[81] One must not think of sensibility and understanding as two independent capacities. Rather, the way in which what can be experienced is given is not different from the way in which it is thought; the forms of sensibility are themselves active attainments of the subject and have ultimately the same standing as the categories. Like Hegel and Heidegger, Cohen traces this reading to §26 of the second edition version of the deduction, in which Kant shows that an act of spontaneity is also required for consciousness of spatial and temporal representations.

However, for Kant this requirement holds only for the act of becoming conscious of spatial representations, not for their very givenness. After all, the spontaneity of the understanding determines the given "*in accordance* with the forms of sensibility," which therefore have to be presupposed as determinable. It is correct to say that as such, i.e., as mere receptivity, they cannot be made conscious. Nevertheless they must be presupposed, because only then is it possible to conceive the contingent nature of the spatial structure and the structure of intuitive discursivity (time) that we have. But this thought, too, is missing in Cohen, as it is in Fichte, Schelling, Hegel, and Heidegger.

According to Cohen, the hint at a common root contains an indication of the provisional status of the division of the *Critique* into an analysis of sensibility and an analysis of the understanding, a provisional status that is said to be overcome in the transcendental deduction. This explains, so Cohen maintains, the need for that preliminary reminder (cf. A 15/B 29). Yet it can be clearly seen that the preliminary remark refers only to the duality of the stems of cognition and that the hint at the common root outlines only briefly Kant's position in the dispute concerning Wolff, thereby dismissing the idea of a common root—though in a manner that was immediately intelligible only to Kant's contemporaries. For Cohen too, then, the "perhaps" has the meaning of an allusion to still hidden but answerable questions that form the proper center of the discussions that follow in the text; the "perhaps" is not seen as referring to a problematic idea. This renders yet more understandable how Heidegger's approach and his interpretation of the key passages remained uncontradicted.

We have thus reached the end of the prehistory of the interpretation of transcendental imagination. That prehistory allowed us once again to set off the concrete meaning of the idea of the common root in Kant from the intentions of his successors. It has became clear that the concepts of sensibility and understanding have always been taken in that close connection which they acquire the very moment the Kantian restrictions on the construction of a unitary subjectivity fall away. In that regard Heidegger is anything but original. He himself must have been clear about the continuity of the formulation of the problem that connected him with Hegel, as is evident in a number of hidden references. It is thus crucial to distinguish Heidegger in the proper manner from Hegel. And that should be possible on the basis of a discussion of methodology. For if there is sense to Heidegger's claim that his book renders problematic Kant's presupposition *in a countermovement to the interpretation given by speculative Idealism*, then his intent cannot be exhausted by a renewed realization of the methodological scaffolding set up by speculative Idealism. To explain the totality of subjectivity is the declared goal of both Hegel and Heidegger. Yet how can this totality be understood in a sense opposed to speculative Idealism?

V. The Totality of the Equiprimordial Moments of Existence

In answering our question we can no longer confine ourselves to the statements in the Kant book. After all, what had appeared shocking in the structure of its thoughts was that the interpretation of the passage on the common root presupposed the unity of the faculties as a demand that needed no explanation. We can only learn the reasons that justify this presupposition by placing it back into the systematic structure of *Being and Time*, considering that it was originally part of the latter's comprehensive design.

When abstracting from the richness of phenomenological analyses and focusing solely on the scaffolding of the progression of thought in *Being and Time*, one immediately recognizes that its driving force is the question concerning the unitary structure of the original totality of *Dasein*. In each methodological survey, the insight that a given fundamental structure of *Dasein* remains articulated yields the demand to move further ahead "until we can exhibit a *still more primordial* phenomenon which provides the ontological support for the unity and the totality of the structural manifoldness."[82] Yet how is this concept of the ontological structural unity of *Dasein* different from the speculative interpretations of subjectivity?

According to Heidegger, each of those speculative interpretations, from Wolff to Hegel, but also Kant's skepticism regarding the possibility of such an enterprise, presupposes that the unity in question, insofar as it is original and indestructible, must consist in a simple structural element. Heidegger considers this assumption unjustified and misleading, despite the fact that it appears totally evident. "The primordiality of an ontological constitution does not coincide with the simplicity and uniqueness of an ultimate structural element."[83] A fundamental structure affords us various ways of looking at the moments that are constitutive for that structure.[84] "The fact that something primordial is underivable does not rule out the possibility that a multiplicity of characteristics of Being may be constitutive for it."[85] Heidegger calls such moments constituting the unity of a structure "equiprimordial," thereby indicating that the structure cannot be derived from the moments as though they were something existing prior to it. "The phenomenon of the *equiprimordiality* of constitutive items has often been disregarded in ontology, because of a methodologically unrestrained tendency to derive everything and anything from some simple 'primal ground.'"[86]

Equiprimordial moments have no independent being, but they are also not reducible to one another. Rather, they constitute the unity of an ultimate, articulated totality of meaning.[87] Heidegger here employs the double meaning of the term "equiprimordial" *(gleichursprünglich)*, which points to an identical origin of the moments, but also indicates their equality in rank. This explains why the concept of the unity of faculties is replaced with that of the totality of subjectivity. For "unity" means identity of moments, which allows only gradual modifications, whereas "totality" signifies the being-together of different moments, with each essentially referring to the whole without any one of them being that whole. (According to that terminology, an organism is a totality, not a unity.) If, therefore, the question concerning the totality of *Dasein* in the structure of *Being and Time* is propelling the investigation, then this does not mean that the various characters are reduced to simple principles. The plurality of moments is preserved even in the ultimately reached unity, viz., that of temporality. And one can even go so far as to say that the underivability of the moments is irrevocably secured only by the fact that they are understood as members insolubly related to each other in the totality of meaning that is temporality. Once that is shown, it has become meaningless, according to Heidegger, to inquire behind the intelligible structure of subjectivity. For such a question leads out of the intelligible context of the meaning of *Dasein* and is likely to detract from the task of describing that context and thus stating what *Dasein* really is.

The concept of equiprimordial unity of meaning is thus formed in a conscious countermove against the categories of faculty psychology. Heidegger employs the concept in the Kant book in order to unlock the meaning of the passage on the common root—without, however, clearly stating the difference in method. Yet the historical intention of this passage points toward the basic power of the faculties, a power that would be a really existing structural element, to which, as to something primary and identically underlying, the multitude of the phenomena of subjectivity is to be reduced. We now understand how Heidegger can say that nothing is further from his attempt than to reduce the faculties to a basic power.

Since for Heidegger every regressively proceeding deduction conceals the structure of subjectivity, he must try to free Kant's transcendental analytic from the appearance of providing such a deduction. "The 'Deduction' is hence wholly different from a deductive, logical developing of the previously mentioned relations of the understanding to pure synthesis and to pure intuitions. Rather, from the outset the Deduction already has the whole of pure, finite knowledge in view. While holding fast to what is caught sight of in this way, the explicit taking-up of the structural references that join the whole together proceeds from one element to the other" (53). According to Heidegger, the sameness of the synthetic form is not the "identity of a tying-together which is formal and which works everywhere, but instead an original, rich wholeness composed of many members that bring about unity under the guise of both intuition and thinking" (43; translation modified). And the principle of apperception is "no principle that is arrived at in the drawing of a conclusion that we must put forth as valid if experience is to hold true. Rather, it is the expression of the most original phenomenological knowledge of the innermost, unified structure of transcendence" (81). Only with this presupposition is it possible to hold fast transcendental imagination as that which independently mediates the two stems. If, however, "the transcendental power of imagination is deleted as a particular grounding faculty . . . then the possibility of grasping pure sensibility and pure thinking with regard to their unity in a finite, human reason diminishes, as does even the possibility of making it into a problem . . . all re-interpretation of the pure power of imagination as a function of pure thinking—a re-interpretation which German Idealism even accentuated subsequent to the second edition of the *Critique of Pure Reason*—misunderstands its specific essence" (134f.). As soon as the imagination is assumed to be the essence of self-consciousness (Schelling) or of the absolute idea (Hegel), it loses its role as mediator and becomes the principle for the deduction of the faculties. Such a deduction then covers up the unity of the very structure that had been erected by the imagination in its function as medium between the equiprimordial stems, providing them with meaning.

Thus it is only from *Being and Time* that one learns the concepts which belong to the premises of Heidegger's Kant-interpretation—premises that cause him to ignore the historical meaning of his quotations. If, however, one asks for the justification of those concepts, then one faces considerable difficulties. The basic problem of the Kant book, which consisted in the efficacy of unarticulated presuppositions, can be found again on the level of *Being and Time*. Certainly, *Being and Time* accords high significance to the concept of equiprimordiality. Basically, though, that concept is presupposed from the very beginning. And the few things that Heidegger says about it stand in no proportion to the importance of the conclusions which are drawn from it in both *Being and Time* and the Kant book.[88] One thus has to try on one's own to approach that concept from other problems addressed by Heidegger which are less rich in presupposition. It is important to remember here that *Being and Time* was designed not with the intent of a theory of subjectivity but rather as the only possible guiding thread toward an explication and answering of the question concerning the meaning of Being.

This fundamental question of all ontology brings with it an *aporia* for thinking; in everything that might be thematized there is implicitly presupposed an answer to that question, for the simple reason that with reference to any subject matter whatsoever the predication, "is," must be meaningfully possible. Heidegger's phenomenology is methodologically attentive to this *aporia*. It explicitly performs the circular structure of understanding of Being and grasps the basic characters of a being or a sphere of being by means of a projection that provides justification in a retroactive motion. Now *Being and Time* employs such a projection in an attempt to uncover that being which is essentially understanding of Being, thereby making *Dasein* into the guiding thread for the explication of the question concerning Being in general. Because the idea of Being is the most fundamental idea that can be thought, one has to concede that if this idea is to be explained at all, it will have to be understood in a unitary sense. Thus *Dasein*, which in its nature is understanding of Being, will have to be projected toward the same unitary totality that is presupposed in the idea of Being itself. Assuming that to be true, one can also understand under which conditions that concept of unity has to be defined as the totality of equiprimordial moments. For if in the idea of Being as understood by *Dasein*, thus ultimately in the idea of Being itself, one had to distinguish several irreducible moments which constituted the unity of its meaning, then it would not be possible any more to reduce this most principal plurality to a really existing ultimate element, of which it could again be said that it *is*. "The ontologically elemental totality of the care-structure cannot be traced back to some ontical 'primal element', just as Being certainly cannot be 'explained' in terms of entities. In the end it will be shown that the idea of Being in general is just as far from being 'simple' as is the Being of Dasein."[89]

This formal elucidation may perhaps help clarify the concept of equiprimordiality, but it still appears quite extraneous to the proper content of *Being and Time*. The only reason the question concerning the meaning of Being does not get caught up in empty abstractions and does not revert to Aristotle's *pollachos legetai*[90] is that Heidegger all along anticipates the role of time and presumes that all modes of Being can be interpreted as temporalizations of time. The question as such could very well be asked from an Aristotelian point of view. It becomes significant only because Heidegger seeks an answer by means of the phenomena of subjectivity and temporality. Accordingly, the impulses that are active in Heidegger's Kant-interpretation point back to the phenomenological analyses of *Being and Time*. For time as the horizon of the meaning of Being is a totality of equiprimordial moments. It lies beyond our task, though, to examine those analyses and the arguments against Idealism that can be gained from them.

If, therefore, Heidegger declares in the preface to the second edition of his Kant book that the instances in which he went astray and the shortcomings of his endeavor became clear to him (xviii), that certainly does not mean that he had not noticed certain differences with Kant before then. Rather, one has to look for the point at which he went astray in the question concerning the meaning of Being itself. In the Kant book the world is still thought of as an encompassing horizon of beings constituted by *Dasein*, and this even where there is talk about *Dasein within* human beings, and where thus the transcendence of *Dasein* is more primordial than the human being as such. This constitutes the same deficiency that made it impossible properly to execute the "turning" in *Being and Time*.[91] The turning consists in the attempt to move from the determination of the horizon of all understanding of beings in time to a thinking of the Being of this time itself, as demanded by the universal meaning of "is." An interpretation of this attempt lies entirely beyond what can be accomplished in our reflections. But we already get an indication of the difficulties that are bound to come up when one tries to determine further the darkly paradoxical, multi-membered unity of time on the basis of subjectivity itself. In the subsequent turning to which Heidegger saw himself forced, that deficiency of the earlier attempt at a turning may have seemed so close to what he himself had interpreted as the essence of the transcendental deduction that in his later days Heidegger came to see the imagination in Kant as a station in the "history of the forgetfulness of Being," although he continued to see its structure in the same way.[92] An indication of this is provided by another passage: "Man as representing subject ... 'fantasizes,' i.e., he moves in *imaginatio*, in that his representing imagines, pictures forth, whatever is, as the objective, into the world as picture."[93] It is in this and only this sense that Heidegger now looks critically at his own Kant book. Its internal structure of meaning is not affected by that turning.

It seems significant to me that in the publications following the turning Heidegger ascribes the characteristics that determine *Dasein* in *Being and Time* to Being itself. This is so in the barely intelligible determinations of the "fourfold," in which the "four" are joined in "simple oneness" or something "humble" so that in each of them the other is already thought, without, however, permitting a reduction to one of them;[94] or in the thinking of the ontological difference and its relation to the "human being," in which relation neither the relata nor the relation itself has a being of its own.[95] Each time Heidegger distinguishes moments in some whole, in which the moments "jointly" constitute the whole, the structure of equiprimordiality is meant. (Heidegger at one point even says that the essence of the imagination's structure lies in its "conjointly" forming (89).)

Heidegger realizes quite clearly that the unity of subjectivity which he attempts to demonstrate by such means evades the concepts provided by the philosophical tradition. It seems as though the unity of a principle has to refer to the evidence of something altogether simple. How can an ultimate unity still contain a plurality of traits? Heidegger thought that this fact, which seemed paradoxical to speculative Idealism, points to the peculiar character of the "yet unasked question concerning Being." In the very idea of Being, with its basis in temporality, the finitude of Being emerges; finitude can only be understood in opposition to a knowledge grounded in some originary evidence.

"The ontological source of *Dasein's* Being is not inferior to what springs from it, but towers above it in power from the outset; in the field of ontology, any springing-from is degeneration. If we penetrate to the source ontologically, we do not come to things which are ontically obvious for the common understanding; but the questionable character of everything obvious opens for us."[96] For Heidegger, Kant's grounding is philosophical in that it consciously points to the unknown and not to the crystal clear, absolute evidence of a first proposition or principle (24f.). That is a direct reference to Fichte and thus to German Idealism, against which Heidegger formulates his own Kant-interpretation (94, n. 196).

Heidegger's interpretation of Kant, then, proceeds from all those presuppositions that emerge from the analysis of the structure of *Being and Time*. And one can say that this interpretation has little or nothing in common with the problems that determine the development of Kant's thinking. Surely Heidegger did not realize the extent to which his results diverge from the explicit position of the Kantian text. Those who do not know that position from their own studies will be led astray by Heidegger's interpretation, since the detailed textual references imply that it is a historical exegesis. But those who have mastered the basic outlines of Kant's system will understand Heidegger's Kant book properly when they see it as a reference to philosophical questions that make the Kant book part of the project of *Being and Time*. In the Kant book those questions are indicated in a hidden form; Heidegger immediately takes up the phenomena which, in his opinion, become visible in the *Critique of Pure Reason* in spite of the insufficiencies of its formal means.

Initially, though, this one-sided procedure, which does not let the interlocutor speak, will hardly appear to be a dialogue. And this holds especially for those parts in which Heidegger does not reveal any awareness of Kant's own opinion, as in the discussion of the common root of sensibility and understanding. Only after reflecting on the reasons for the misunderstanding and attempting to comprehend the origin of the revisionary interpretation will one be able to concede that even the misunderstanding stems from a genuine attempt at a dialogue.

2
The Concept of Moral Insight and Kant's Doctrine of the Fact of Reason

Translated by Manfred Kuehn

I. Ontology and Ethics

The question of the origin of metaphysics can at present be answered in two ways. One of these implies that basic metaphysical concepts have their source in the thought of the being of the entirety of particular beings. This idea was first formulated by the Presocratics and led, by a logical development, to the Platonic-Aristotelian doctrine of being as such. In the other approach Socrates also stands at the beginning of the ontological tradition of metaphysics. Plato's formulation of the question concerning the being of the good, influenced by the life and death of his teacher, brought metaphysics under way.

The second answer to the problem of the foundation of all philosophical reflection assigns a special significance to those phenomena that, since the division of philosophy into different disciplines, have received their subordinate place in "ethics." When Xenocrates divided philosophy into logic, physics, and ethics, the Platonic question concerning the measure of the good life had already become one of the special problems within a more comprehensive doctrine of *archai*. It continued to occupy this place in a tradition that lasted two millennia and in which it seemed Plato's question could be solved only if it was understood as the question concerning the ground and structure of a particular being that participated in the *logos*. This is the human being, understood as dependent on the more general structures of being itself and as constituting a special form in accordance with the principles of all existence. The moral good is an entelechy of the striving that finds its goal only in rational deliberation *(bouleusis)*. This view obliterated the Platonic fusion of ontology and ethics into one essential unity. Indeed, the title "ethics" itself suggests that the good by which the virtuous person is motivated does not originate from a reflection on being itself.

This kind of ethics formally remained—through various changes of content—just a part of an *ontologia specialis,* namely, psychology. Its basic foundation underwent a crisis only in the philosophy of the eighteenth century, a crisis that led to a renewal of the Platonic doctrine that made impossible a distinction between *prima philosophia* and ethics. In Kant's system and in the Idealistic philosophy that followed, the moral being of man became again a problem that was intimately connected with the problem of the being of all beings. In their works it became impossible to speak of an ontology that would lay the theoretical foundation of ethics, just as it became impossible to speak of an ethical theory that would leave ontology to a way of thinking uninformed by the essentially related question concerning the good. Since Kant, it has become possible once more to order problems according to the very laws that first governed Platonic thinking, and this even within *prima philosophia.*

The concept of knowledge itself was newly defined both at the beginning and at the end of the tradition of metaphysics. The Platonic question whether virtue *(arete)* forms a kind of knowledge *(episteme)* does not mean that the knowledge of the good should be subordinated to a concept of knowledge that would be fixed independent of virtue. It is, rather, an attempt to formulate adequately for the first time a concept of knowledge that can include insight into the good. The Idealistic conception of reason was meant to fulfill the same task. If we want to understand what it means to have insight into what is right, knowledge must amount to more than judgments about matters of fact. The unity of ethics and ontology is thus mediated by the problem of defining the essence of knowing. The concept of moral insight therefore transforms ethics into an element in the foundation of philosophy.

The concept of moral insight can, however, possess a meaning that transgresses the limits of a particular ethical theory only if we do not obscure the *special* structure of the knowledge of the good. We must make clear that moral insight is a phenomenon whose special character and possibility can only be understood if such insight becomes a motive in the revision of the theory of knowledge.

There exist three answers to the question of the nature of moral insight that keep one from seeing the problem in this fashion. (1) One may say that the good is present to us in the same way a stimulation is present to feeling, or that which we sense is present to one of our senses, or that which forms the goal of a drive satisfies that drive. If this were true, then insight would have no original meaning in moral life. To have insight into the good would mean only to notice with more or less vivacity what determines our life anyway. This determination could not then be differentiated from the observation of other facts. Knowledge of the good would thus also fail to modify our concept of knowledge. (2) It has been said that moral insight concerns the choice of the correct path toward the goal of our life. This formulation is also not designed to make knowledge as such the problem. For whether this choice is based upon clever calculation (as in the hedonistic calculus of the Platonic Protagoras) or whether it follows from experienced introspection, it must adjust the means to a given goal. We can easily explain such deliberate action by common rational procedures. (3) The phenomenon of moral insight might not show its significance for *prima philosophia* even if we avoid explaining morality either as feeling or as the choice of means. If moral insight itself does not become a central theme, we will fail. This happens whenever one assigns to morality a place in a teleology of rational beings that is based on the fixed concepts of a presupposed ontology. In this way, the scholastic tradition extinguished the autonomy of Aristotelian ethics by interpreting it as an applied case of metaphysics.

For this reason, ethics as a *philosophical* discipline must orient itself by the phenomenon of moral insight. We must locate it within the point of view of the subjectivity of a moral being, and we must attempt to obtain from it the concept of a special kind of knowledge. We must not restrict ourselves to developing the criteria of moral judgment. If we did so we would find moral doctrine and worldly wisdom, but not a discipline that has a place in the context of the foundation of ontology. Only by reflecting on the special character of moral insight can and must ethics transgress the limits that were imposed on it by the metaphysical tradition.

Moral insight is knowledge of the good. However, it is not the content but the reality of the good that is the problem of ethics within the context of first philosophy. Basic structures and rules of the good as well as the special kinds of moral goodness can also be uncovered within moral doctrine. Philosophical ethics asks only the question "What is the significance of the very existence of this good?" For what is unique in the epistemological character of moral insight, or the knowledge of the good, forms also the specific nature of the concept of the good itself. The essential characteristics that differentiate moral knowledge from scientific knowledge must also be elements within the formal structure of that which comes into the view of moral insight. If this insight is knowledge, then we will be able to find within it moments which belong to all that is known. However, if it is different from theoretical knowledge because it possesses characteristics that are specifically its own, then philosophy must ask what the basis and the possibility of this difference are. Since even what is known by moral knowledge possesses formal aspects that correspond to the special structure of this insight, the philosophical question concerning the good is identical with the question concerning the ground and the possibility of this special kind of knowing within us. The structure of the good becomes a problem only insofar as it is the consequence of the special way in which the good is present.

The question concerning the unity and difference of ontology and ethics can thus be reduced to the question concerning the origin of moral insight. For those who do not lose sight of the special character of this insight there are at first three possibilities, one of which provides the answer to the question of the origin of moral insight. (1) There exist several ways of knowing that are independent of one another. Moral insight is one of these; ontological knowledge is another. They have common characteristics that do not, by themselves, form a special kind of knowledge. (2) Moral knowledge is the origin and presupposition of all knowledge. We can derive all other forms of knowledge from moral insight. It provides the foundation for the belief in certainty that accompanies all kinds of knowledge. (3) Even though there exist two kinds of knowledge, the second can be shown to be a derivative of the first. Ontological knowledge, of which moral insight forms a part, is the presupposition of the mathematical and experiential forms of knowledge that themselves no longer exhibit specifically ontological and ethical characteristics. The formalization and application of ontological insight also lead to the loss of its original significance. The first answer concerning the relation of ontology and ethics was given by Aristotle; the second follows from Fichte's point of view; and Hegel's distinction between speculative and abstract knowledge is an example of the third.

A history of ethics that is written not only for the self-defense of moral consciousness but also for philosophical interests must find its orientation by means of this question. It must first investigate where the problem of moral insight was originally formulated in its independent meaning, and why this did not take place in other contexts. Such a history will therefore amount first and foremost to a history of ethics encompassing the period between Presocratic philosophy and Aristotle and the period lasting from

British empiricism to Hegel, namely, the two periods during which it was impossible to differentiate between ontology and ethics: they form the beginning and the end of the metaphysical tradition. This history will have to represent not the changes of moral doctrine but the foundation of the phenomenon of moral insight. It must investigate the place that moral insight occupies within the context of all knowledge as conceived in each system, and the theory of the relationships between ontology and ethics that assigned this place to it. Such a history must also investigate whether this theory of the relationships between ontology and ethics agrees with the structure and spontaneous development of moral consciousness. It could become clear at the end of this history of ethics that the disjunction of the three answers concerning the question of the origin of ethics—and thus also the relation of ontology and ethics—is not exhaustive.

These three answers have a common presupposition: they assume that moral and ontological knowledge stand either beside each other without any connection or in a relationship of one-sided dependence. For Aristotle, the duality of the forms of knowledge is the last word. Fichte derives theoretical knowledge from moral knowledge, and Hegel derives moral knowledge from speculative knowledge. However, if it is not admissible to separate moral insight entirely from ontological insight, and if it is not possible to reduce the one to the other, then philosophy must seek a way to mediate between the two. This has not been attempted thus far. We can see how in this situation the method with which Plato and Kant have approached the problem of moral insight and the relation between ontology and ethics must have great weight. Plato held to the unity of ethics and ontology from his "middle period" onward. Yet he did not conceive of such a unity by deriving the one from the other.

Kant's rational foundation of morality is also based upon the principle of the unity of theoretical and practical reason. Although it is one and the same reason that expresses itself in both dimensions, we can derive neither theoretical knowledge from practical knowledge nor the practical from the theoretical. There is also no previously determined sense of reason that would allow us to understand both its forms. The critics of Plato's and Kant's philosophy have always considered this a shortcoming. For them, Plato and Kant seem to have failed because they did not reflect sufficiently on the connection of the different parts of their theory. Although it has been recognized that Plato in ancient and Kant in modern philosophy were the first convincingly to bring out the character of moral certainty as insight, still it is felt that neither found the principle of the unity they themselves established. Aristotle gave this reproach as the reason for his rejection of Plato's ethics; and it became, in the wake of Reinhold and Fichte, the justification for the Idealists' attempting "to go beyond" Kant.

Aristotle and the Idealists offered this reproach for different reasons. Aristotle wanted to give up the unity of ethics and ontology that Plato had maintained but not proved, and he wanted to preserve only the epistemological character of moral insight *(phronesis)*. Speculative Idealism first and foremost intended to construe this unity that in Kant had remained a presupposition. Thus, though Aristotle and speculative Idealism are opposed in their solution to the problem, they are close in their alternative formulation of what makes a solution possible: ethics and ontology either stand beside each other without any connection or they follow from each other in a one-sided dependency. Therefore they are also in agreement that the Kantian and Platonic point of view is either unsatisfactory or of only protreptic significance.

Kantian philosophy, like the Platonic, developed in a direction opposed to the point of view of its most important critics. When Aristotle criticized the Platonic theory of the unity of ethics and ontology he had in mind especially Plato's late thought, whose theory was formulated in the context of the doctrine of the *idea tou agathou* as the ground of *mixis* and *eide*. Plato progressed from a formulation of a questioning that was orientated by the life of Socrates and the corrupted community of the *polis* to an ontology whose highest concept was that of the good. The Kantian development followed the opposite course. When Kant (under Platonic influence) discovered the rational character of the certainty of the good, he first believed that he could understand the possibility of moral insight from theoretical reason. His theory of the incomprehensible facticity of the rational law of morals is the late result of such efforts at a deduction. He finally became convinced of the fruitlessness of such attempts. The critique of the Idealists is thus directed strictly against the mature and not the preliminary form of his doctrine.

Once we learned to read the Platonic dialogues as evidence of Plato's philosophical development, the route which his thinking took on the question of the unity of ethics and ontology became clear. Kant's road toward the theory of the fact of reason was traversed during eleven years of silence between the publication of the "Inaugural Dissertation" and the *Critique of Pure Reason*. It must therefore be reconstructed from the documents of the literary remains. I shall attempt this reconstruction in the following essay. However, this attempt makes sense only if it contributes to the substantive question concerning the relation of ontology and ethics. Even though this question had already been formulated in Greek philosophy, and even though it contributed significantly to the foundation of the metaphysical tradition, it has still not been answered.

II. The Structure of Moral Insight

Any investigation into the connection of ontology and ethics must orient itself by the characteristic features of moral insight that differentiate it from other forms of knowledge. For only through its characteristic aspects can moral insight lead to the question concerning the original sense of the concept of knowledge and thus allow the relation of ontology and ethics to become a problem for first philosophy. These characteristics have emerged from the history of ethics as a secure possession.[1] Although they are usually not sufficiently considered, we may count on agreement when we appeal to them. I shall mention only four of the most important aspects.

(1) Moral insight does not view the good as an arbitrary matter of fact. It does not simply recognize what is "good." There cannot be any knowledge of the good without an act of approval. Someone who says "This is good" means always that what has revealed itself to him as good is also accepted by him in its being. What is correct makes sense, what is good is originally affirmed. Without this response of the one who knows the good, moral insight would be impossible.[2]

We can approve only what fulfills the conditions of possible acceptance, all the same. Even though the good comes into view only in approval, it is not good *by virtue of* this approval. Affirmation must be preceded by a demand of the good that calls for acceptance. The legitimacy of this demand is immediately comprehensible. It is the basis for affirmation *(complacentia)* without which we have no insight into the good. This demand is thus a basic phenomenon of the content of moral insight. This is also the case where it is not explicitly fulfilled, as in the situations of immediate morality which Hegel called the "substantial" morality, such as that within the community of a family. Even here we originally accept the good, and that means that we affirm it as a legitimate existence.

The good is not affirmed because of something else. We do not accept it as a means to an end that we have already chosen. Comparing it to calculations that assure success would cover up the special character of moral insight. However, it would also be wrong to say that we consider it good because we can derive its goodness and the sense of "good" by means of unambiguous logical operations from given principles. What is accepted as good is "evidentially" good for moral insight. It does not need justification. Someone who wants to answer the question concerning the ground of the good before he approves of it has already lost sight of it. This does not mean that the content and form of moral insight cannot be made comprehensible by reasons that are prior to it. However, the question which leads us on this way is not itself required by moral consciousness as a condition for our approval.[3]

Because the moments of demand and approval constitute the sense of the good, the relation of consciousness to its act in moral insight is different from that in theoretical knowledge. The consciousness of moral insight has been fixed, as it were, by the originally legitimated demand and by the approval that has always taken place already. It is "bound to" the good in its insight.

This becomes clearest when we compare it with reflection, one of the most important topics of the more recent Idealism. We can go beyond any truth by asking a question that reflects on the conditions of its possibility. We can obtain "unconditional" certainty only in a highest principle that is either a clear presupposition of reflection itself (Fichte) or a principle that has been obtained as the result of the process of reflection as a whole (Hegel). The approval of the good in moral insight is independent of this process of reflection. Although it can become part of it, the certainty of the legitimacy of the good does not have its foundation in this process. The legitimacy of the good cannot be overcome or questioned in moral insight.

The structure of moral insight suggests, therefore, that it is the highest form of all knowledge. It held this position in Plato, in Fichte, and in a certain sense also in Kant. However, its dissimilarity from theoretical knowledge, even from one that is ultimately founded, raises again a methodological problem for attempts at such a close connection between the idea of the good and the principles of knowledge.

(2) In the history of ethics the relation which holds in moral insight between demand and approval has often led to a denial of the character of moral consciousness as insight. Since we cannot achieve the theoretical distance of proof and deduction in the case of the good, the good seems not to be present to us as knowledge. The demand appeared to coincide with the imposingness of a perception, and approval could be conceived as a felt response. This coincides with the circumstance that the concept of the good cannot be defined without inclusion of an element of meaning that indicates the passivity of moral consciousness in understanding the good. This is clearly different from our affirmation of what is true. Aristotle covers this up in an incidental remark that comes out of the tradition of the *polis,* namely, that the good person acts *hos dei* (as he must).[4] The same

feature returns in the Stoic discourse on law *(lex)* and obligation *(obligatio)*. It comes most incisively to the fore in the Kantian formulation of the categorical imperative.

We cannot doubt, however, that moral consciousness can only be described as insight. The demand is not a case of factual being-affected. Its legitimacy is something that is understood. We can achieve the assent to the good that we affirm and approve only if we understand it. Affirmation does not depend on the intensity of an emotion. Motives which might keep me from doing what I have approved may be much stronger than my approval itself. Approval can take place without an emotional reaction of noticeable intensity. Its significance is entirely unaffected by the intensity with which it takes place. If it were merely a feeling, the opposite would be the case.

We understand the meaning of the good to which we give insightful approval. Insofar as Plato's claim that virtue *(arete)* is knowledge means this, it is an indisputable truth.

(3) Although insight in moral certainty does not affect consciousness as a kind of feeling, it still seems to remain foreign to consciousness because it needs affirmation to become determinate. It does not appear capable of becoming part of consciousness the way something does when it reveals itself to our reflection as the ground of this reflection.

This attempt, however, at delimiting the insight-character of moral consciousness also fails to do justice to the phenomenon of this insight. Although the good does not come into view through a self-reflective act of the individual, it still is a form of self-understanding; indeed, it is a privileged form of self-understanding. Approval, without which the good is nothing, is the expression of the good's obligatory character for the existence of the self. When I know in moral insight what is good, I also know that I understand myself in relation to it, or that I must understand myself in relation to it in order to become a self. The first is the case in substantial moral relations, the second in moral conflicts.

Accordingly, this approval is a spontaneous achievement of the self. We can say that by means of this approval, the self first constitutes itself as a self.[5] For the self of theoretical reflection is as little capable of achieving an act of consent as the *nous* which "touches" the first principles in intuition. Knowledge can only "let be." In insight, in the mere presence of things, or in the process of the movement of its thoughts, the self as self has receded in order to do justice to thought itself. However, moral insight is also part of the self. Without the consent of the self it cannot come to be; and this self is in turn rooted in its approval.

Those who hold the belief that moral insight is a feeling have identified one part of this phenomenon and isolated it from the rest. The fact that this belief is a partial truth is both its strength and its weakness: The self that constitutes itself through approval in moral insight is really more than the *nous* or the theoretical self. The traditional psychology first developed by Plato in the *Republic* differentiated between various faculties of the soul. One of these is capable of insight *(logon echein)*. But moral insight cannot be understood as the achievement of just this one faculty. In approval *(complacentia)* other acts are implied. Although it is originally insight, it is also more than the knowledge of a state of affairs. The self, in the act of identifying itself, is also related to the good in what has traditionally been identified as "feeling." Although the legitimacy of the demand is not founded in a feeling and the approval is not motivated by it, it is connected with it. Traditional psychology transforms the original unity of knowledge and feeling in moral insight into a philosophical problem.

The role of the self in moral knowledge becomes most clear when we differentiate in moral consciousness between the standpoint of the person who judges and that of one who has been called to action. For the latter, insight into the good is at the same time a motive for action and the basis for his conviction that he will prove to be adequate to the demand that he accepts. This motive and this certainty are not forms of knowledge. However, they are aspects of the structure that is called "insight" in moral life. The entire self, as a moral self, is determined by its insight into the good.

(4) We can understand the originally ontological character of moral consciousness from these three characteristics. Although moral insight does not follow from thinking about the structure of the being of beings, it is impossible without such thinking.

This claim may become clear from the following: Moral insight founds the self. Without a complete self, the special traits that differentiate moral insight from theoretical knowledge would be impossible. Therefore, knowledge of the good cannot be isolated from the reality of the self. If we deny this character of our self, then the concept of moral insight also loses its determinate sense. Without approval, motivational force, and the conviction that it is possible for me to be adequate to the good, I cannot recognize the good as good, and I deal only with empty, incomprehensible formulas when I employ the basic concepts of ethics.

The loss of the meaning of "good" is, however, a powerful reality of moral life itself. For the approval of moral insight does not yet guarantee the realization of the good. Guilt and failure are more common in moral life. We would understand the reality of these deficient *modi* of morality insufficiently if we were to believe that they take place in the full light of moral insight. Anyone who proves himself to be inadequate to an accepted moral demand covers up and confuses his understanding of the good. Plato's paradoxical claim that no one freely does evil is quite correct. No one acts contrary to the good without destroying or drowning out moral insight, at least while he is acting. Although it is not necessary to accept Plato's claim that the evildoer considers his action to be good, it is true that the person who acts in an evil way must convince himself that the good, which is contrary to his act, is not really good. This can be done in various ways: He can claim that the good that confronts him is illusory; or he can accept its demand on him but argue that this special case does not fall under it. The given case is an unusual and excusable exception, or it is required by compelling circumstances. However, this covers up and confuses the clarity of moral insight. No action can take place in the full knowledge that "it is not the good," for moral insight comprehends the moments of demand, approval, and conviction that we are able to do what we approve of. The evil will must neutralize at least the third aspect by objecting to moral insight.

All the important theoreticians of moral consciousness agree to this analysis. Plato's theory of moral education presupposes that anyone who knows the good is also a friend of the good. However, knowledge of the good cannot be obtained, or it is lost again, if it is not grasped by the entire soul. Evil is not the conscious enactment of what is not allowed. It takes place when our view of the good has been obscured. Therefore, it is all-important for moral knowledge that the soul learn to enjoy moral action in the right way, and that the forces that can darken moral insight are overcome.[6] Even the theory of the *Nicomachean Ethics* is in this regard quite Platonic.

> For it is not any and every belief that pleasant and painful objects destroy and pervert, e.g. the belief that the triangle has or has not its angles equal to two right angles, but only beliefs about what is to be done. For the principles of the things that are done consist in that for the sake of which they are to be done; but the man who has been ruined by pleasure or pain forthwith fails to see any such principle—to see that for the sake of this or because of this he ought to choose and do whatever he chooses and does; for vice is destructive of the principle.[7]

These four claims contain the Platonic thought in perfect clarity. Aristotle means to show in them that the virtue of moral insight cannot endure without the virtue of a moderate character. The Kantian moral philosophy also sees the concrete phenomenon of evil as a decay of moral principles.

The categorical imperative formulates the demand of the good contrary to all desires that are determined by pleasure. To be able to maintain itself, pleasure must therefore cause reason to prove that the demand is without right and a mere illusion. "Man feels in himself . . . in his needs and inclinations . . . a powerful counterpoise against all commands of duty . . . From this a natural dialectic arises, i.e. a propensity to argue against the stern laws of duty and their validity, or at least to place their purity and strictness in doubt."[8]

Man subtly refines the moral law until it fits his inclinations and his convenience, whether to free himself from it or to use the good for the justification of his own self-importance.[9] Kant considers his entire philosophy an attempt to refute the sophistry of reason that is in the service of pleasure. In this way he also attempts to give firm support to insight into the good against dialectical artifices. Kant differs in this from Plato and Aristotle only in his conviction that education leading to a good character may not use any means other than the "representation" of the idea of the good itself. It has enough power by itself to be reason and motive for action.

The ontological character of this form of knowledge follows from the fact that the reality of evil is a destruction of moral insight. The self confirms the reality of the good in approving it. Where actions do not correspond to this approval, insight is also exposed to destruction. Approval is thus identical with the affirmation *that* the good exists. The practical contradiction of a demand denies its existence. Therefore, moral insight places all of being under the condition that the good is possible in it. Anyone who succumbs completely to his desires understands the world in such a way that the moral good has no place in it. Thus, though moral insight does not entail a fully developed ontology, it is essentially ontological. The Platonic doctrine of ideas is just as much a theory about the possibility of the good as is Kant's limitation of causality to mere appearances. It serves as a foundation for the ontological hypothesis of moral insight and as its defense against the sophistry of the understanding which is ruled by "pleasure."

The experience of moral life confirms the ontological character of our approval of the good. This is most evident when a human being decides to follow the good, clearly grasping it in a situation in which the "natural" morality of personal obligations has lost its orientating force. He then views himself as understanding being as such, and this is basically different from his philosophy for daily life. This "philosophy" is often determined by his interests and the external experience of the futility of the course of the world. His decision opens another dimension of understanding. Now everything seems to him to be designed in such a way that what he finds himself bound to is not nothing but the ground of the entirety of being itself. Plato and Kant reduce this experience to one concept when they say that the virtuous person can lead his life only in view of the idea of the good (Plato), and that the good will can act only under the presupposition of the reality of freedom (Kant).

These four aspects form a whole. They make clear the peculiar way in which moral insight is knowledge. It is the task of ontology to determine the meaning and ground of this form of knowledge. However, it is now clear that ontology undertakes with this question the task that is also given to it by moral consciousness itself. The reality of the good, and that means the true knowledge-character of insight, must be secured in order to save the self-understanding of the good from the dialectical objections of "sensibility." Therefore, though the unity of ethics and ontology is originally a problem of first philosophy, it originates with the same necessity from the basic question of ethics.

III. The Historical Presuppositions of Kantian Ethics

The development of ethics in the seventeenth and eighteenth century was determined especially by the dissolution of scholastic philosophy, in which system ethics possessed a well-defined place. It was part of the teleology of finite and immaterial being. The first attack that Thomas Hobbes leveled against this perspective shook it in its foundation. The view of government that forms the context for his ethics was conceived in accordance with the ideal of geometry. He meant to construe the complicated body of the state from simple elements and thus make it comprehensible. These simple elements were the basic drives of human beings, the most important being the desire to preserve one's existence. This drive for self-preservation is the extreme counterinstance to all anthropological teleology, for it is the only subjective motivational impulse that is by definition without a goal. It forms in psychology the predecessor of Newton's force of inertia *(vis inertiae)*, that is, the force that ultimately liberated physics from the Aristotelian teleology of "natural locations."

The attempts at a foundation of ethics that followed upon Hobbes all refer to him. Even if these attempts reject his anthropological construction on the basis of human self-preservation, their own method was changed by Hobbes's procedure. In this way, there originate from Hobbes two ideas concerning the foundation of ethics: the rational ethics of Clarke, Wollaston, and Wolff and the moral-sense philosophy of Shaftesbury, Hutcheson, and Butler.[10]

The first approach remained essentially teleological. According to Clarke there exist "several necessary and eternal relations by which different things are related to one another." An evil deed does not fit in this relation, but destroys it. Wollaston's principle of truth amounts to the claim that a bad person denies a truth concerning the connection of things when he commits an evil act. Thus the murderer destroys the necessary relation that human beings have to one another (Clarke), and he denies the truth that no one received his life from human hand (Wollaston). These principles can only be applied in a teleological context that teaches us the eternal connections of things. It is also clear, however, that these thinkers were in search of a purely formal criterion of truth that determines the content of particular duties simply by the application of our logical faculty of judgment.

The school of Shaftesbury opposed this idea. The phenomenon of moral insight excludes the possibility of grounding ethics in logic. It is equally opposed to Hobbes's theory, which attempts to reduce moral insight to calculating self-love. We must therefore assume that human nature originally possesses a moral sense, or a feeling upon which all concepts of the good are based.

Kantian moral philosophy united both these moments. It took the formal criterion of the good and the doctrine of the epistemological character of moral insight from rational ethics, and it shared the distinction between moral and theoretical insight with moral-sense philosophy. The connection of these two elements was the problem that fueled its development. Kant achieved a solution to it some years after the publication of the *Critique of Pure Reason,* and he held to it for the rest of his life.

Kant felt it was his special merit that he had justified moral insight as a form of rational cognition. He was convinced that his ethics was the first to conceptually clarify the unconditional demand for action and nonaction that is contained in moral consciousness. He did so with his formula of the categorical imperative, which examines the moral character of an action by means of the criterion of whether it fulfills a rational universality. The rule by means of which moral insight finds its judgment is formulated by Kant in analogy to the law of theoretical reason. He claimed more than once that it is one and the same reason that expresses itself in theoretical and in moral knowledge.

This aspect of Kant's ethics, however, contrasts sharply with his claim in the *Critique of Practical Reason* that the consciousness of the categorical imperative is a *fact* of reason. The concept of a "fact of reason" is apparently contradictory. If reason is defined as a faculty of cognitions a priori, then it is difficult to see how it can contain anything factual. The factual seems to belong to the realm of experience, whereas reason must demand the pure transparency of insight. It appears that Kant's theory does not fulfill its own claim and reveals a lack of development in its main concepts.

For this reason the most important among Kant's followers always found it especially unsatisfactory that he appealed to a fact of reason in the foundation of ethics. Hegel argued against that "cold duty, the last undigested log in our stomach, a revelation given to reason."[11] His antipode, Schopenhauer, went still further than Hegel in his vitriolic criticism. He accused Kant of having capitulated when he faced the question concerning the derivation of ethics from reason, and of opening the door for irrationalism and philosophical romanticism.

> It seems more and more that practical reason and its categorical imperative is a hyperphysical fact for the Kantian school. It is a Delphic temple in the soul from whose dark holiness issue oracular sayings that sadly declare indisputably not what does happen, but what should happen. After the Kantians first admitted that there exists a reason that dictates *ex tripode with regard to the practical,* it did not take them long to take the next step, and to give to its sister—or really its *consubstantial*—theoretical reason the same privilege. They declared it as equally independent. The advantage of this is as immeasurable as it is obvious. Now all the false philosophers and phantasts, Friedrich Heinrich Jacobi, the denouncer of atheists, leading them all on, rushed to this unexpectedly opened little gate so that they could bring their petty wares to market, or that they could save at least some of the most beloved pieces of their inheritance that Kant's doctrine threatened to crush.[12]

Both formulations, which have the laughter on their side, ignore the movement of thought by which Kant was led to his doctrine of the fact of reason. Kant never lost sight of the special character of moral insight, and he conceived his entire theory of morality in accordance with it. The doctrine of the fact of reason forms its conclusion. It leaves intact the epistemological character of moral insight and indicates the characteristics by which it is differentiated from other forms of knowledge. It may be that this theory calls for revisions, and that Kant did not solve the problem once and for all, but he never abandoned it. Furthermore, his doctrine is certainly superior to Schopenhauer's ethics of compassion, which stands entirely in the tradition of the moral-sense school. And compared with the dialectical deduction of morality in the Hegelian philosophy of the spirit, Kant's theory constitutes at the very least a tribunal that has no less weight than the Aristotelian objection to the monism of the Academy.

Kant's system is the first whose genesis we can trace in detail. Its history reaches just far enough into the period of historical consciousness that important pieces of his literary remains are extant. In this corpus we find documents that contain various attempts at solving the problem that correspond more to the demands of Hegel and Schopenhauer than to the final form of the Kantian ethics. This form was ultimately determined by the phenomenon of moral insight, quite contrary to the Kantian attempts at deducing morality during a period of ten years.

Kant became aware of the general situation of ethics in the mid-eighteenth century through the opposition between Wolff's *philosophia practica universalis* and Hutcheson's moral philosophy, and his first independent formulation of an ethical theory resulted from a critique of these two philosophers.

Wolff's ethics, like that of the scholastics, was based on the foundation of an independent ontology and rational psychology. He deduced the concept of perfection and of a will that seeks to realize what is perfect from the essence of the soul. Morality is only one of the ways in which the basic power of the soul becomes actual. This basic power is the *vis repraesentativa universi* which produces new representations in a constant flux. Among these representations, we call "perfect" those that comprehend many other representations in one unity. Perfection is therefore originally an object of a thought that recognizes clearly the unity within a manifold. However, perfection can also be present in intuition. In this case the moments that are united by the perfect are not clearly and distinctly differentiated. Wolff defined "pleasure" as this intuitive representation of perfection. This definition served him as a mediating concept in his attempt to show that the basic power of the soul must also express itself in the form of the will. "Because we now have pleasure in the good that we represent to ourselves, the soul is determined to attempt to create our sensation of it."

If this inference were sound, Wolff would have shown how a relation to pleasure and will necessarily originates from theoretical reason. He would have derived from the representative nature of the soul the two concepts which signify in the tradition what is characteristic of moral life. Moral insight and all its attributes would then be nothing more than a kind of knowledge. However, it is easy to see that Wolff used an ambiguity in the concept of pleasure to create the appearance of a deduction that he never really attempted seriously. Even if we were to admit that pleasure is intuitive knowledge of a perfection that is thought objectively—and thus only a theoretical act—it still would not follow that there must be pleasure (in a second sense) that aims at realizing the pleasing object. Liking as "finding something pleasurable" is not the same as the practical pleasure of "desiring something." If we want to show the connection between the two, it is not sufficient to call them both by the same name.[13]

Kant realized very early that Wolff's reduction of morality to theoretical knowledge did not make comprehensible the nature of moral insight. It was, among other things, Crusius's critique of Wolff that helped him to see this clearly.[14] Crusius had already objected convincingly to the monism of powers in Wolff's theoretical philosophy. He showed in this context that we must conceive of the soul not as a power but only as a "system of basic powers." In his ethical theory he showed in detail why Wolff could not possibly reduce the will to effects of the understanding. He first made clear that it is impossible to understand the way in which the will acts by invoking a flux among the imaginative representations in the *vis repraesentativa*. Then he turned to still more fundamental objections to Wolff's theory. He showed that the concept of perfection important to ethics can only be defined in relation to the will. Goodness "is the relation of an object to a will with which it is compared." The concept of the good presupposes the desire of a goal that makes an action or an object good either immediately or as a means of achieving the aim.

Kant accepted both of Crusius's objections: "Wolff wanted to derive everything from our faculty of knowledge, and he defined pleasure and displeasure as *acts* of our faculty of knowledge. He also characterized our faculty of desire as a play of representations, and thus also as a modification of our faculty of knowledge. Philosophers believed that they had obtained in this way a unity of principle. However, it is impossible in this context."[15] And in reflection 746 he determined the relation between perfection and pleasure in the same way Crusius had: "We must note that pleasure and displeasure are not representations of perfection, but these representations presuppose the former. It is because we take pleasure in an agreement that it is a perfection for us." Thus a moment of striving precedes our theoretical thinking about the good. Therefore it is impossible to derive morality from theoretical reason.

This skepticism concerning a deductive moral philosophy was brought home to Kant even more clearly by Francis Hutcheson, whose moral philosophy was itself already the result of the recognition that theoretical reason taken by itself is incapable of explaining the phenomena of approval, affirmation, and motive for action that are essential for the definition of moral insight.[16] Hutcheson believed that we can make moral insight comprehensible only by assuming a special sense that accompanies "kind" actions of human beings with pleasure. He did not fail to see the seriousness of the objections that Kant later raised with regard to his point of view. He also admits that the foundation of morality cannot be a sense in the usual understanding. And he introduced the moral sense only with some embarrassment and with much sympathy for the attempt to derive morality from reason, being convinced that the reason which Clarke, Wollaston, and Wolff called the *ratio essendi* of the good did not really explain the characteristic nature of moral consciousness. His argument was that we can justify any action in one of two ways: either it is a useful means to one of our aims, or it contains itself the final goal of our actions. Although neither one of these justifications can appeal only to reason, each presupposes some inclinations. The immediate approval that moral actions receive cannot be derived from any judgment that simply establishes a relation between concepts. "Can we then prefer or choose nothing, if there is no inclination? Undoubtedly not, for if we could there would have to be an inclination or a choice preceding any inclination."[17] Hutcheson formulated in this proposition the concept of a "pure practical reason" that means only the "choice that precedes all inclination." However, the concept of reason that he received from the tradition and that signified only our ability to make logical inferences did not allow him to conceive of a rational desire that would precede all inclination. The development from Hutcheson to Kant indeed involved a change in the content of moral doctrine, which amounted first and foremost to a revision of this concept of reason.

The development of Kantian ethics had its beginnings in the context of the presuppositions formulated by Wolff, Crusius, and Hutcheson. This context led Kant to the discovery of the formula of the categorical imperative as early as 1765.[18] The idea of the critique of practical reason, however, is not at all identical with this principle for judging particular duties. In 1769, Kant still sought the foundation of moral consciousness in a *sensus moralis*. Only when he had formulated his new concept of reason in 1770 with sufficient definiteness could he attempt to find the origin of morality in reason itself. At this time he began his attempts at deducing moral insight from theoretical reason. The effects of these efforts can still be seen clearly in 1785.[19] Kant saw then that all such attempts are futile, and only then did he free himself from the methodological presupposition of this—his second—moral philosophy. However, he did not give up the rational point of view in the foundation of ethics. This result constitutes the origin of Kant's doctrine of moral insight as the fact of reason. We can learn most about the problem implicit in the concept of moral insight if we investigate this stage prior to the *Critique of Practical Reason,* which still remains hidden among the reflections of his literary remains and the transcripts of his lectures.

IV. Kant's Attempt at a Deduction of Moral Insight

Moral insight, just like theoretical insight, is no accidental state of being affected that might vary in the degree of its intensity. Like rational cognition, it is aiming at something "true" and "valid," namely, the "good" and the "just." However, as moral insight it also has characteristics that cannot be found in theoretical insight. Because of its obligatory character, the good is immediately related to action. In action we are aware of the necessity that we must follow the demand of the good at any time, under any conditions, and independent of any feelings that we might in fact have. And this demand finds our approval and affirmation. Several such acts that are not purely theoretical play an indispensable role in moral life: our pleasure in a good deed, the rebuke directed at a failure, and the consciousness of our power to overcome all hindrances. The unity of rational and emotional acts is the riddle posed by the nature of morality and moral insight.

Kant himself once called the solution of this riddle "the philosopher's stone." "When I judge by the understanding that an action is morally good there is still a great deal missing concerning the actual doing of the act that I have judged to be good. However, if this judgment moves me to do the act, then we have a case of the moral sense. The understanding can indeed judge, but to give the judgment of the understanding a motivating power that moves the will to do the act, *that is the philosopher's stone.*"[20] In a letter to Markus Herz, written in 1773, Kant formulated the same task as follows: "The highest principle of morality must not only allow of the inference that it is pleasing, it must itself be pleasing in the highest degree. For it is no mere speculative representation, but it must have the power to move us. And therefore, it must have a direct relation to the primary motivating forces of the will, even though it is intellectual."[21]

Even long after the publication of his first *Critique* Kant believed that his new subjective understanding of reason would also enable him to obtain this *lapis philosophicus*. It would allow him to show how a rational idea can originally bring with it both pleasure and a consciousness of the motives that move us to act. The concept of reason that Hutcheson had banished from ethics was still that of formal logic. Reason was for Hutcheson a faculty that established the relations of concepts and judgments, and perhaps also one that could define the basic and universal concepts of ontology. However, Kant's new idea of a transcendental subjectivity, which implies the relation to a given manifold that must be ordered and intellectualized, appears to offer to ethics a methodological possibility that was not an option until then. For if reason constitutes in the theoretical realm the function of ordering given sensations into objective knowledge, then, as moral reason, it might also establish order among the previously given manifoldness of drives and desires. What cannot be achieved by a reason that thinks only logical rules and basic ontological concepts might be achievable by reason as a subjective function. This would have revealed the philosopher's stone in philosophical ethics, and it was this idea that dominated Kantian moral philosophy during the 1770s.

We can reconstruct from Kant's literary remains several attempts at a deduction of morality from theoretical reason.[22] I shall divide them into two groups. One of these groups is formed by direct deductions, the other by indirect deductions. In the first, Kant attempts to show that the theoretical function of reason as applied to the material of action must necessarily bring forth both the affirmation that is necessary for moral insight and the motivating forces of the will. In the second group he seeks to derive essential aspects of moral insight from a presupposition that must be made in ethics, but whose necessity and justification can be made evident only by theoretical reason. The key concept in these attempts at an indirect deduction is "freedom." I would like to present three of these deductions here.

(1) There exists an obvious analogy between Kant's conception of the functions of the understanding and his formula of the categorical imperative. The categories are basic concepts for the determination of objects. They create conceptual unity within the manifoldness of that which is given in space and time. They constitute in this context a connection in accordance with rules that make objectivity as such possible. However, the categorical imperative is also a function of unity, namely, a function of the unity of the will. All moral actions are universal in accordance with their form. We can recognize what is evil by its exclusion of rational universality in action, and by the fact that it leads the will to contradict itself. The rule of judgment of the categorical imperative formulated in 1765 appears to have found its transcendental justification in the concept of self-awareness as apperception that Kant first formulated in 1769. Does it not follow analytically from the concept of reason as a universal function of ordering that if a rational being possesses a will, then the rational postulate of a unity according to rules holds for this being as well? The categorical imperative

appears to be only a special way in which the universal demand for unity is realized.

The first group of attempts at a deductive ethics must be understood as inferences from this idea.

> Pure reason, that is, reason that has been isolated from all sensual motives, possesses legislative power in view of freedom in general. Every rational being must recognize it because without conditions of universal agreement with ourselves and others no use of reason regarding freedom would be possible. However, whatever causes the highest faculty to contradict itself is a natural and necessary object of displeasure. This is just as it is in logic, when reason contradicts itself. (6853)

In a different passage Kant finds: "The understanding takes up all objects that agree with the use of its rule. It opposes everything that contradicts its rule. However, immoral acts are against the rule and cannot be made a universal rule. The understanding opposes them because they run counter to the use of its rule. Therefore, there is indeed a motivating power in the understanding in virtue of its nature."[23] This idea appears to be convincing at first. What makes evil indefensible is the same intrinsic impossibility that also makes a contradictory claim senseless.

However, we can easily show that it is only an analogy that deceives us here. Such a deduction does not pay attention to the special character of moral insight. The understanding demands unity of rule in all assertions. Wherever there is no rule, the understanding is without an object. The faculty of order, *ratio,* possesses a *horror vacui,* a fear of all that is without a rule. It expresses itself in its resistance to hypotheses in the explanation of nature that—once they are assumed—no longer allow the use of reason (as, for instance, the assumption of fate as a determining cause of the history of the world). However, this horror is no displeasure of a moral kind. The resistance of thinking to thoughtlessness also produces a feeling of displeasure among our emotions; and thus a chaotic character and indecisive acting may provide us occasion for uneasiness about a disorderly life. This might have the consequence that the subjectivity of the self attempts to avoid contradiction; and this might lead to a behavior that could be called moral in the sense of the categorical imperative.

In truth, however, such behavior will correspond to the categorical imperative only in a formal sense. It would not originate from moral reasons and motives. It would consist here merely of the attempt to remove the displeasure caused by contradiction; consistent action would not be an end in itself and affirmed for its own sake. Thus, though the action would be morally correct and legal, it would not have been done out of a sense of duty. The categorical imperative would have been followed as a formula, but not as an unconditional imperative.

Therefore, the binding demand of consistency of action cannot be understood through the *horror vacui* of reason. The demand that everything must have the unity of rule is not a demand that reason makes on the will. The wish to remove our dislike and lack of pleasure concerning irregular action might overcome some limited kinds of resistance that other sensual interests put in the way of regular action. However, this wish would never be sufficient to justify the conviction that I must overcome any measure of resistance, no matter what the circumstances or the special case might be, and that I must do so just because I know that I am categorically obligated, having already affirmed the good, and because it is essential for my self. This conviction is part of moral consciousness itself.

Kant attempted a similar justification using the concept of freedom. Freedom, if it is exercised without law, must displease to the highest degree because it is capable of destroying all natural order. "However, the lawfulness of freedom is the highest condition of the good, and lawlessness is the true and absolute evil, the creation of ill. The latter must also cause displeasure to reason even by itself and without restriction; and this displeasure must be greater than that caused by bad luck or mistakes" (7196). Kant is still convinced that theoretical displeasure can explain a moral judgment and a moral emotion.

The transition from knowledge to moral insight that determines the will cannot, however, be found in the concept of freedom. Although freedom without any commitment would be the most dangerous force conceivable in nature, and though there would be more than ample reason to submit it to a rule, this rule of freedom would not be an *imperative* of reason, if we were to regulate freedom only because we fear unregulated freedom. This rule would amount only to a technical institution based upon fear for our safety. Kant still interprets the categorical "ought" that makes our action necessary as a merely hypothetical imperative.

How insufficient this deduction is becomes clearest in reflection 6621: "For if we rely in every case not on a rule, but direct our actions always in accordance with the greatest gain, we will be too fearful and leave our soul always in commotion." However, measuring the validity of an action by an internal criterion is quite different from longing for a calculable life. It is, rather, an imperative, an unconditional demand that holds even when all hope for happiness has disappeared. Kant, in his attempt to find a deduction of moral insight, has only seldom allowed himself to be pushed so far away from the motives that form the basis of his new foundation of ethics, moral doctrine, and pedagogy.

(2) The documents of the literary remains enable us to trace some other Kantian attempts at a deduction. One of these seeks to explain the emotional element in moral insight, the moment of approval that is essentially different from all sensual pleasure, by generalizing sensual pleasure. The universal form of the will enables us to act in the most unrestricted way possible without contradiction. It also affords the highest degree of activity. Kant believes that this optimum of self-actualization also extends all the particular pleasures so as to create a superior form of joy. It is interesting that Kant explains morality here in the same way he later, in the *Critique of Judgment*, explains the pleasure we take in what is beautiful.

In this context it must suffice to sketch briefly another theory, namely, the theory of morality as "worthiness to be happy." In this theory Kant further elaborated his deduction of the emotional act of moral insight from the resistance of reason to rulelessness.

Kant was the first critic of the *concept* of happiness. He differentiated happiness from mere luck. Luck is the uncontrollable success in action and creation, whereas happiness is the consciousness of security that everything will always "happen in accordance with our wishes and volitions." It is the self-assuredness of the person who experiences the satisfaction of all his wishes and who sees all his struggles end. Only the person who sees his entire life as a complete success is happy. The concept of happiness implies, therefore, that it is possible to unite all wishes and desires in such an aggregate. Kant disputed this possibility. He showed that our desires are contradictory, that any degree of satisfaction transcends itself, creating new wishes, and that the sensual motives of our actions contradict one another in such a way that the fulfillment of the one necessarily interferes with that of another. "Happiness is the motto of the entire world, but it can nowhere be found in nature, which is never receptive to happiness and satisfaction with one's condition" (612).

Accordingly, happiness is an "ideal of the imagination." It is thus the embodiment of a whole whose possibility cannot be rationally comprehended. It is still, however, an ideal; and therefore it can only be conceived by rational beings. It has its source in a longing of reason for unconditioned unity even in action. Because this unity cannot be achieved on the basis of content, reason, in order to satisfy its principle, must place happiness under a condition which does not take into consideration the accidental distribution of luck and the contradiction of desires. This condition is that happiness should be distributed only in the form of rational universality for the sake of the idea of universality. Reason places all striving for happiness under the condition that it must correspond to the form of rational order. This is the theoretical reason for the thesis that continually returns in Kant's literary remains, namely, that morality is the worthiness to be happy.[24]

> Nature appears to have subjected us ultimately and for the sake of our actions to sensual needs. However, it was necessary that our understanding also formulated general rules that allow us to order, limit, and unify our striving for happiness, so that our blind desires for happiness would not lead us in different directions. Since these drives are usually contradictory to one another, a judgment was necessary which conceived rules merely through the pure will, without any partiality, and apart from all inclination. These rules are valid for all actions and human beings, and are intended to bring about the greatest harmony of a human being with himself and others. (6621)

This is also a deduction of morality from theoretical reason. Kant applies here the subjective ordering function of the understanding to the ideal of the imagination. He wants to explain the emotional aspect of moral insight by the unification of our striving for happiness in the theoretical self. "Therefore, the good in accordance with these laws cannot be in the same way indifferent to us as beauty can be. We must also have pleasure in its existence, for it agrees with happiness in general, and thus also with my interest" (7202).

But in this way the moral demand is again transformed into its opposite, that is, the hypothetical demand. The expectation of the aggregate of *happiness* is the very thing that motivates me to make the attempt at realizing that order in my actions. The force that motivates my action is not order as such, but my interest in that which is to be ordered.

This account does not explain the moral consciousness that stands under the obligation of the good. This can already be seen from the fact that a rationally regulated striving for happiness causes pleasure to the well-understood interest of sensibility only when there is a prospect that all others will act in the same way, and that God's judgment will compensate for the harm that might be done to me by malevolent human beings. Thus morality becomes dependent on external success. This success is not controllable by the will. The following situation arises: Reason demands without regard to empirical facts that the will be orderly within itself. To realize this order, the will must be interested in it. However, the interest in the rule is superior to the interest of any particular desire only if the rule of universalized happiness promises greater happiness. But this promise is given to us neither by the rule as such nor by our experience of the course of the world. Thus the moral will must obtain its motive from a certainty that encompasses both; and therefore morality as worthiness to be happy gains motivational power for our actions only when it is supplemented by a belief in the divine order of the world. Without such a belief, the necessity of acting would remain an empty representation. "I must recognize moral laws. Thus I must also presuppose as an unavoidable hypothesis all that creates the obligatory force of moral laws for rational beings" (6110). Without the assumption of a world-rule in accordance with an idea, "the moral idea would lack reality in our expectation and would be a mere rationalization" (6958). "Moral laws have in themselves no *vim obligatoriam*, but contain only the norm. They contain the objective conditions of judgment, but not the subjective ones of their execution. The latter consist in their agreement with our desire for happiness" (7097).

This final step reveals that Kant's second attempt at a transcendental foundation of his ethics is not only insufficient but also self-contradictory. The rational law is to gain obligatory force only in moral faith. Conversely, however, this faith, if it is to be conviction and not merely self-deception, must be the consequence of a moral conviction that already exists. It can exist only when someone has accepted the obligation of the good. It is the expression of Kant's decision to view the world in such a way that moral action is not futile or might even contribute to evil. The act of faith therefore presupposes the consciousness of obligation that it claims to establish for the first time. Kant later saw this contradiction himself. However, to remove it means also to look for an entirely new justification of moral consciousness. In such a justification, the theoretical need for rules will no longer be the principle for the deduction of moral insight. We have evidence for Kant's self-criticism in one of his reflections: "If the moral law needed God and a future life in order to place us under its obligation, it would be nonsense to found on such a need our belief in the reality of what can satisfy this need" (6432).

A law that is not binding by itself, but gains binding force only if I am convinced of the existence of an intelligible and original being, does not provide any persuasive reason that would make us assume such an existence. An obligation that we must first create by an act of faith can, for that reason, never exist. The moral demand is real only when it directly concerns the self and the center of subjectivity itself, and not when we must first magically create it by manipulation and imagination. Only when obligation is already real can moral insight be made to accept a theoretical assumption because of its ontological nature and by practical reasons. In his later publications Kant repeatedly warned us not to view moral faith as the foundation of the moral law. "Nor do we mean at all that the assumption of the existence of God is necessary as the basis of all obligation." All passages in which he assures us of this exhibit clear signs of Kant's self-criticism.[25]

(3) In addition to these direct deductions of morality from theoretical reason that he attempted until 1785, Kant also tried to prove the reality of obligation indirectly. The idea of freedom served him as a mediating concept between the understanding and the idea of the good. It seemed that even theoretical reason could not be defined unless it was conceived as spontaneity *per se*, and thus as transcendental freedom. However, the *Critique of Practical Reason* shows that the validity of the moral law follows analytically from the existence of freedom.

In contrast to Wolff's *vis repraesentativa*, Kant understood reason as pure spontaneity. The consciousness of the "I think" already presupposes that I myself am the ground of my representations. To be a self means precisely to be the ground of oneself. The "I" is the unity of all its thoughts. It is not the accidental product of the coming together of many perceptions. The "I think" that must be able to accompany all my representations unites these representations through its own spontaneity. However, "freedom is really only the spontaneity of which we are conscious. If we get an idea of something, then this is an act of spontaneity. However, in such a case we are not conscious of our activity, but of the effect. The expression 'I think' indicates already that I am not passive in regard to the representation, that it must be ascribed to me, and that its counterpart depends upon me" (4220). "The reason for the necessity of a first action that forms the basis of all that is accidental is indeed to be found in reason . . .; for the self proves the ultimate end of all reasons for our actions" (4338). "However, the question is whether the actions of the soul, its thoughts, derive from that internal principle which is not determined by any causes . . . Whether I can think as a soul? Whether I possess transcendental spontaneity or absolute liberty? Here the 'I' must come to the rescue again . . . The 'I' proves that I myself act; I am a principle, not something that is principled . . . When I say 'I think, I act' etc., then either the word 'I' is inappropriate or I am free . . . All practically objective demands would make no sense, if man was not free."[26]

In this argument Kant makes the transition from a theoretical conviction of freedom to the practical sphere. That moral obligation is something real is certain because the consciousness of self in thought, which alone could doubt that obligation, can be conceived only as freedom. The principle of theoretical reason also gives foundation to the possibility of moral existence. We can still hear distinct echoes of this indirect deduction in Kant's late review of the *Moral Philosophy* of Schultz, as well as in the third part of the *Foundations of the Metaphysics of Morals*.[27] The difference in the structure of the *Foundations* and the *Critique of Practical Reason* can be understood only if we realize that Kant did not yet see clearly in the *Foundations* that a deductive justification of ethics must necessarily turn out to be unsatisfactory and contradictory. This new insight also determines the method of his later work.[28]

Kant goes furthest in overstating the analogy between the epistemological self and the moral self in reflection 5441. For this reason the reflection provides a good example of why this analogy is insufficient for the justification of moral insight:

> All our actions as well as those of other beings are necessary. Only the understanding and the will insofar as it can be determined by the understanding are free and constitute a pure spontaneity that is determined by nothing but itself. Without this original and unchanging spontaneity we could not know anything a priori, for we would be determined in all we do, and our thoughts themselves would stand under empirical laws. The ability to think and act a priori is the only condition of the possibility of all other appearances. Otherwise, duty would not have any meaning.

While writing this text Kant obviously still believed that the phenomenon of demand and obligation can be shown to exist in both the theoretical and the moral realm, and that it signifies the necessity of both thinking and acting.

Yet we must make a distinction between the two realms that Kant did not consistently observe even after his publication of the *Critique of Practical Reason*. Substantially, this distinction is implied by the special character of moral insight. Thinking and its laws do not require the approval of the self in order to be evident truth. Approval is the answer to the demand with which the good confronts the self. The certainty that we can do justice to the good in concrete action, and therewith the consciousness of freedom, are grounded in this approval of the good in insight. However, pure thought, though it is thought by the self, does not have selfhood in this sense. I know that a pure thought is true and that the self can verify it at any time, but because this possibility itself is selfless, it cannot provide the foundation for our consciousness of the freedom of the self. The truth of thinking, though achieved within me, does not arise as a demand on me.

It is therefore only the moral insight of the good that is originally connected with an emotional act. It alone contains approval, pleasure, and respect as elements without which it would be unthinkable. The fiction of a pure mind can be consistently thought only within a theoretical context, not in moral insight.

The difference between the "freedom" of thinking and moral freedom can also be seen by comparing the privative *modi* of knowing the truth and knowing the good. If we contradict the laws of thinking, we contradict ourselves. However, we do not experience this contradiction as guilt, or even as failure. We can easily remove the contradiction by correcting ourselves. But if we, as selves, fall short of the good, our subjectivity realizes this in the same way it realizes that the good seen by moral insight halts the excessive questioning of reflection. We do not feel guilty because we have confused thoughts unless we experience the consistency of knowing as a moral duty. (This is experienced by the student who "is to become somebody," the politician who must achieve a goal, the scientist for whom knowledge has become a task.) For humans only moral obligations *must* be followed, not theoretical laws. Therefore we cannot assign to the theoretical subject the kind of freedom that must be presupposed by the self of moral insight in its ontological search for certainty.

Reflection 5442 shows that Kant finally recognized this: "Logical freedom in view of all those things which are accidental predicates. Everything accidental in the subject is the objective freedom of being able to think the contrary. If thought also suffices for the deed, it is also subjective freedom. Transcendental freedom is the complete contingency of action. Logical freedom can be found in rational acts, but not transcendental freedom." Only when thought can realize itself do we find the kind of freedom from which the moral law follows analytically. Although our thinking of the self is based on spontaneity, we do not contradict ourselves when we assume that there is no freedom in the transcendental ground of this action. Kant showed in the first chapter of the "Paralogisms" in the first *Critique* that it might be possible that thinking derives from the intelligible substratum of matter. Just as I cannot infer a substantial self from the unity of the "I think," so the spontaneity of the self does not prove a *libertas transcendentalis*. However, this also means that it is impossible to reach in theoretical thinking the kind of freedom that the self necessarily ascribes to itself in moral actions. Therefore the indirect deduction of morality from the unity of apperception has also failed.

V. The Doctrine of the Fact of Reason

Kant's theory, which appeared contradictory and imperfect to his successors, has its origin in the realization that his indirect deduction had to fail in the same way all other attempts at deducing moral insight failed. If it is impossible to explain moral obligation from the primary certainty of all thinking, that is, from consciousness of self, then it must be accepted as pure facticity. Moral obligation cannot be factual in the usual sense that simply signifies the "empirical," for the basic phenomenon of the moral, the obligatoriness of its demand that almost forced Kant to abandon all deductions, is present only in moral *insight*. Kant claimed that it contains necessity and therefore can be assigned only to reason. The demand of the good is thus the only fact of reason, and it is at the same time the only such fact conceivable. In it we experience rational universality as a demand on the self that possesses insight. Theoretical reason can indeed create for itself a priori an idea of obligation. It can determine the content of obligation hypothetically, for the law of the categorical imperative holds under the presupposition that freedom exists. However, theoretical reason cannot create the consciousness of the obligation to act morally. "If this law were not internally given to us, we could not find it by any sophistry of reason *as such a law*."[29] But the fact of this law leads consciousness of self to the assumption that it is free in the transcendental sense. The theoretical self loses itself in the uncertainty of its origin whenever it intends to think something real beyond the necessity of its own thought. The subject of thinking could also originate from matter.

The moral self, however, can understand itself only as free, even if it will never be able to know this freedom theoretically. Its insight has immediate ontological consequences. The self gains a relation to the intelligible ground of its being only in the practical realm, though this relation itself remains practical. The moral subject can be what it is only by believing in the possibility of being adequate to the demand which it sees. This certainty is formulated in the familiar claim that "ought implies can." It cannot be accepted as a theoretical inference, for then it would amount to knowledge of something that exists, and consciousness of freedom would then no longer form a presupposition that is valid exclusively for moral consciousness. This inference is not a theoretical conclusion but the self-explication of moral insight.

In this way, and after many years of hoping to find the philosopher's stone in a deductive ethical theory, Kant came close again to the moral position from which he started. He raised Hutcheson's skepticism concerning a theoretical foundation of ethics to a higher level. Although the fact of reason cannot be called a *sensus moralis*, Kant's doctrine of the fact of reason describes the relation of theory to moral sense in almost the same terms as the theory of 1765 that was inspired by Rousseau. This doctrine has lost again the "illusory advantage" of being a science.[30] Kant, the man of inquiry, now understands his own value as consisting only in performing the service that philosophy can provide for the moral destiny of humanity. However great the practical importance and however pure the pleasure of the progress of knowledge, science is not an unconditional value. It does not reach the ground that allows human beings to live and that first gives to reason the certainty of truly *existing.*

Kant never hid his inclination toward inquiry and the joy he took in it. He also estimated correctly the significance of science for the clarification of moral self-understanding. All the same, he made it sufficiently clear that "his critical business" was undertaken with the goal of justifying the possibility of moral insight and the reality of freedom. After the failure of his attempts to deduce morality, this significance was merely a negative one. Science removes the hindrances to moral insight resulting from a theoretical reason that oversteps its boundaries. Yet it cannot force the approval and decision of the self by rational argumentation. It cannot show that consciousness of self is essentially freedom and demonstrate *ad oculos* that it must submit to a demand that has been scientifically and deductively proved. The question whether a human being is what he can be, or whether he has missed his authentic possibility, must be answered by him without the help of theoretical thought. Theoretical doubt concerning the reality of the moral law is just as possible as the conviction of its reality. For the claim that the good has on us is as difficult to prove as the sophistic objections to it. In this way, the critical philosopher finally, after a long and circuitous route, confessed that the Socratic question of *ti bioteon* can neither expect nor wish for a theoretical answer.

Kant's new theory of the fact of reason resulted in an important change of his doctrine concerning the emotional element in moral insight. This was his doctrine of "respect for law" as the only legitimate motive of the moral will. It may appear peculiar that this concept, which is as characteristic of Kant's ethics as it is of his personality, was the latest fruit of his philosophical development. However, if we trace the outlines of this ethical theory up to the *Critique of Practical Reason,* it becomes clear that it could not have developed earlier or have taken up the place that it occupied in this work. As long as Kant believed that he could clarify the phenomenon of moral insight by a generalization of sensual pleasure or by his theory of the worthiness to be happy, he could not have accepted as an emotional component in this insight and as motive for the will a feeling that is characterized precisely by its exclusion of all inclination and opposition to any "demand of sensibility." And as long as he believed that spontaneity of thought and freedom of the will were essentially the same, he could not see that "respect for the law" reveals to us the freedom that can overcome any measure of sensible resistance. This freedom is thus not one of a theoretical spontaneity but one which *takes for itself the right* to be active. The concepts of the "fact of reason" and "respect for the law" are the central concepts of the second *Critique*. The one cannot be conceived without the other. They form a correlation that would become meaningless if one of its parts were taken away.

The Idealist philosophers who followed Kant attempted to free his ethics of "autonomy" from these concepts. They saw a contradiction between the free rationality of the good will and Kant's talk of facticity and respect. The latter seemed to them to belong to the context of a "master and slave morality." If this critique saw anything correctly, it was something that concerned Kant's moral doctrine, but it did not touch the theoretical motives that led to Kant's terminology in the doctrine of the "fact of reason." This terminology is not at all a "dogmatic leftover" or a testimony of a reason that still does not have enough confidence in its own ability. A reason that has just elevated itself (in the idea of autonomy) to the absolute is the expression of the latest and most mature answer to the problem of the absolute character of the good and of the structure of moral insight itself.

The methodology of Kant's foundation of ethics is therefore neither the Aristotelian dualism of theoretical and practical reason nor the Idealistic derivation of the one from the other. Kant is different from Aristotle because the fact, or the object, of moral insight is a fact of reason. It is a fact of the same reason that formulates the theoretical concept of the unconditioned. Kant's theory is different from the Idealistic point of view because of his doctrine of the facticity of the idea of the good. The uniqueness of Kant's position is that it moves within a duality that cannot be resolved. This position, however, does not remain unmediated, as it does in Aristotle. For the latter, the moral life is a "second life," apart from the theoretical. In one sense, Kant's theoretical philosophy is an investigation of the universal structures of reason. These are also the structures of the rational element in moral insight. In another sense, his theoretical philosophy is the justification of the ontological hypothesis of such an insight. It must show that the material world can be no more than mere appearance. This method of critical philosophy, which establishes relations between its different disciplines, can best be seen in Kant's introduction to the *Critique of Judgment*. We must admit that Kant hardly ever explicitly reflected on this—certainly not to an extent corresponding to the use he makes of it. And for this reason, the Kantianism that appealed only to the Kantian texts was without defense against the attacks of speculative Idealism that pressed for a systematic and constructive unity of the principles.

Kant's theory of moral insight exhibits to a great extent the same structure that determines the critical system in its entirety. It is certain that an ethical theory based on the doctrine of the worthiness to be happy would have decisively changed the connection among its disciplines. They would have formed a series of deductions and not the referential texture that is known to us.

Precisely because of this form the Kantian theory of moral insight could provide an alternative to the solutions of Aristotle and the Idealists. The unity of ethics and ontology, which is demanded both by the ontological relevance of the phenomenon of moral insight and by the ontological character of this insight itself, must not be established by a reduction of the one to the other.

But it is extremely important that we preserve this unity as a problem. From the fact that we cannot justify moral insight theoretically we should not conclude only that objectifying knowledge reached one of its limits in moral insight. Although this is true, it is not the end of all theory. This observation must form the beginning of another way of establishing the unity of ethics and ontology. *The facticity of the good must itself become the presupposition of a theory of this facticity.*

We can understand Fichte's *Science of Knowledge* as such a theory. However, it is more fruitful to remember Plato's theory of ideas in this context. Plato never—not even in his last dialogues—separated the pure knowledge of the ideas from the problem of moral insight. And the silent presence of Socrates in the dialectical conversations of Plato's later period gives witness to the duration of this connection. For Plato, it also had a significance that no longer existed in this way after the Aristotelian foundation of logic. The illusory art and *pansophia* of the Sophists can, according to Plato, be refuted only by the substantial seriousness of Socrates, which asks for the correct understanding and is moral in its origins. Even the Platonic Socrates is not afraid to use obvious sophistical fallacies when it is his task to lead his partner in conversation to the truth. The Platonic problem of the unity of ontology and ethics, however, reaches beyond the discovery of logic, which, in its beginnings, was nothing but an art of persuading in a dispute.[31]

This aspect of the meaning of Platonic philosophy, however, was at first forgotten. Aristotle still retained the special sense of moral insight, but he decided to remove entirely from first philosophy the problem that it contains. The method of pure theory seemed to him secure because of his catalogue of rules in logic. *Phronesis* (insight into the good) seemed to him of an entirely different nature. And the unity of principles did not appear to him a sensible goal for philosophy. The later Greek philosophers hardly

The Concept of Moral Insight

ever asked the basic question concerning the nature of moral insight in their ethical theories. Christian philosophy also suspended this question. It presupposed from the beginning that God, who was understood as Being itself *(actus purus)*, is also the ground of the good and of our knowledge of the good.[32] In this way ethics became just one discipline in an ontology that had a foundation independent of it. Only in the seventeenth century and with the end of Christian teleology could the question concerning the concept of moral insight and its justification again become a motive in the development of the philosophical problem as a whole. It remained such a motive until the end of speculative Idealism. Today it makes sense again to call attention to this question. For, though it cannot be formulated without a clear phenomenological description of the uniqueness of moral insight, it cannot remain in focus if we restrict ourselves to just such a description. This approach still dominates the ethics of the present, while ontology has already begun to hand back to pure thought its right.

Kant called the answer concerning the question of the significance of the unique nature of moral insight "the philosopher's stone." This stone is apparently buried in a deep well, for philosophy has not yet been able to find it. If we are to begin a new search, we must remember the ways of those who preceded us.

3

Ethics of Autonomy

Translated by Louis Hunt

In order to understand the particular character of the systems of Idealistic moral philosophy it is not necessary to be acquainted with all the intricate details of these systems and their moral doctrines. It suffices to convince oneself that only *one* principle underlies the confusing variety of these systems which demands closer scrutiny, and that the movement in which they follow one another, continually generating new systems out of and in opposition to one another, can be understood as the unfolding of this principle. Thus in the following essay I will present the common element and the developmental logic of Idealistic ethics.

That both must take place at the same time and as a unity implies that this principle was not developed together with an adequate interpretation. For to speak of development makes sense only when nothing is explained by assuming a return to something earlier or a new beginning. Since the weakness of a construction of the history of philosophy in Hegelian triads has become obvious, development cannot mean the consistent explication of the truth of a matter out of the immediacy of its appearance. New fundamental thoughts open up to philosophy possibilities of development which the starting point can essentially lack. The beginning of an epoch of philosophizing usually does contain moments which far surpass its continuation. That does not mean, however, that the starting point was not developed in the continuation or that it is possible to know what took place in the starting point without reference to the continuation. In order to judge the meaning and limits of a principle one must neither ignore the path of its development nor assume from the outset that the later interpretation is the more adequate one. Cogent grounds for proceeding beyond a thought need not always be sufficient ones. But these grounds do prohibit one from becoming set on the interpretation in which that thought had first been formulated, and from avoiding its revision. As long as we distinguish the Idealistic principle from the matter itself, the gain which we can expect from the analysis of Idealistic ethics will be neither the justification of its outcome nor the apology for its beginning. The plan to exhibit the common element and the developmental logic of Idealistic ethics ought not and cannot result in the one or the other.

The principle of Idealistic ethics was first expressed by Kant in the formula of the autonomy of reason. Hegel was the last to make this principle the foundation of his philosophy of morality. Despite the criticisms which recently have been brought against the view that the movement from Kant to Hegel is sufficient for an understanding of Idealistic philosophy, it is still permissible with respect to the foundational problem of ethics to designate with their names the beginning and the end of a development. This development must be understood before one can contrast it with Kant's grounds for refusing his assent to it or the thoughts of the later Fichte or Schelling against it. This understanding must first be acquired. We can contribute to this result if we can make convincing that those who succeeded Kant held fast to his principles and motives even while revising his results; and that such revisions can be understood as a more consistent interpretation of these principles themselves.

In order to understand in what sense a new phase of attempts to achieve a foundation for ethics with the principle of autonomy began, we must abstract from what in this formula belongs to the doctrine of morals and to Kant's appeal to the reason of the rational being to reflect on itself. If one grasps this principle as an expression for a theoretical attempt, this implies initially that it is possible to understand the phenomena of the moral consciousness through an understanding of the nature of reason. This thought is certainly not new. Rather, it appears to be a commonplace of the tradition of ethics, in which in antiquity and the middle ages it already found its expression in the *orthos logos* of Aristotle and in Cicero's *recta ratio*. This formula first gets its importance through a new analysis of the moral consciousness itself, from which Kant proceeds. It emerged in opposition to theories of the seventeenth and eighteenth centuries which had exposed the inadequacy of the rational morality of the tradition and opposed to it an ethics on a psychological foundation. In the period after these theories and with knowledge of their accomplishments, the rational origin of the moral nature of man could only be defended if at the same time the concept of reason was grasped in a new and deeper fashion. This changed understanding of reason, which philosophical Idealism first worked out in ethics, must, however, have been significant for its concept of philosophy as a whole. The range of problems uncovered by the Kantian formula of the autonomy of reason encompasses three regions reciprocally related to one another: a new analysis of the moral consciousness and its forms; a theory about the origin of all these moments in the rational nature of man; and a foundation of philosophy as a whole that incorporates in its concept of reason the orientation by the moral consciousness. For this conception of philosophy the possibility of comprehending morality becomes the criterion by which one decides whether and to what extent a proposed ontology or theory of subjectivity is adequate.

The often-cited identity-thesis of speculative Idealism has its origin in this constellation of problems. Even in its later expositions, which have abandoned its starting point with the problem of ethics, this thesis is at least genetically dependent on these problems: Moral consciousness demands of philosophy that it comprehend such consciousness on the basis of the structure of reason. It is nonetheless possible to differentiate in this consciousness moments which are distinguished from each other in a manner that prevents their reduction to one of them. Yet reason must be comprehended as one. This result can be arrived at by another path. If reason is supposed to explain the moral consciousness, it must be comprehended in a way that is different from the analysis of the knowledge of beings; that is, practical reason must be distinguished from theoretical reason. Their unity, however, cannot be understood as the sameness of one thing.

The phenomenon in which speculative Idealism first established an insoluble unity of moments which cannot be reduced to one another is self-consciousness. In self-consciousness the content of thought and the thinking of this content are at the same time distinguished from each other and one and the same, and this so that their unity can be produced or founded by neither of these two moments.

Self-consciousness and morality are thus the two phenomena which initiated the Idealistic movement and gave the Kantian formula of the autonomy of reason a significance that went beyond that which it initially had in the critical philosophy with its determination of the limits of knowledge.

It is characteristic of Kant's position that he saw and made one aware of these two relations while disputing the possibility of systematically developing these relations in a philosophical theory. He placed the concept of practical reason alongside that of theoretical reason. He also distinguished practical reason from theoretical reason on the basis of moments which are incorporated in an insoluble unity in the moral consciousness and cannot be comprehended separately. The demand that one must be able to comprehend the unity of reason in both functions, and as well the unity of reason and sensibility, can only be derived from the Kantian ethics if one misunderstands the theoretical grounds which oppose such a derivation and precisely define the standpoint of the *Critique of Practical Reason*. The Idealistic ethics too quickly dismissed these objections. It did this, among other reasons, because it was convinced that this determination of limits imposed undue restrictions on the analysis of the moral consciousness. According to this view, Kant had in fact grasped the concept of reason precisely to formulate the problem of ethics. But he was at the same time unable adequately to comprehend the structure of the moral consciousness within the limits which his critique of reason imposed on theoretical insight.

If one takes into account this context, the Idealistic criticism of Kant's moral doctrine, i.e., of the elaborated form of his theory of moral consciousness, acquires its due weight. Once a question has been elaborated in the manner of the Kantian one, criticism of the content of an ethics must immediately lead to criticism of its foundation. As long as the leading idea of this foundation remains acknowledged, however, the attempt must be made to grasp this idea anew and to develop a system out of it in another way. In the various phases which follow one another in Idealistic philosophy, dissatisfaction with Kant's moral doctrine became the occasion for repeatedly tackling the problem of the foundation of ethics while determining anew the concept of philosophy. The claim was also made, continually and quite correctly, that one should not give up what was the starting point and leading thought of Kantian ethics: the principle of the autonomy of reason.

In this essay I propose to give an initial concept of the sense in which the principle of autonomy was maintained and developed, and how in this development criticism of Kant's moral doctrine and the problem of the foundation of ethics worked together. This concept may prove useful to a more detailed exposition of this problem.

I. The Problem of Autonomy

The particular character of Kant's position with respect to the problem of the foundation of ethics can be inferred from the very title of the *Critique of Practical Reason*. Kant defines the concept "practice" not so much in the Aristotelian sense of the word as in the sense of "poesis" as the "effecting of a purpose" which follows on the basis of a representation of particular principles of procedure for effecting that purpose. Practice is to be distinguished not only from a mechanical process but also from the activity of a purposively organized being, whether it is aware of its activity or not. For in this case also the purpose is not actualized "on the basis of" a representation of the purpose and the means appropriate to it. We call the characteristic of a human being through which he is capable of such purposive activity his "will." Therefore "practical" also means everything "which is sufficient to determine the will."[1] Reason is practical then if it contains sufficient grounds for the will to actualize a particular purpose.

It already follows from this definition of practice that only that which contains universal principles of action can be practical. According to Kant, the characteristic achievement of reason is to determine the particular from the universal. It is impossible, therefore, to conceive of practice without reason, although one can conceive of a reason which is not practical but merely investigates purposive activities that factually take place (as in the case of organic natural processes). The genuine problem of a critique of practical reason lies in the question in what way reason is practical. Reason can be practical in two senses, as "pure" and as "empirically conditioned." Empirically conditioned practical reason does indeed develop principles for practice, but only with respect to incentives for action which do not have their ground in those principles themselves; for instance, the principle to make provisions for winter because hunger and cold are adverse sensations and detrimental conditions one would like to avoid. Only a practical reason which sufficed to determine the will to action for itself alone, and without regard to other, external, impulses, would be pure. It is Kant's thesis that such reason really exists. Kant set the *Critique of Practical Reason* the task of refuting those who think that our reason can be practical only if it is at the same time empirically conditioned. Whereas the *Critique of Pure Reason* limits the possibility of knowledge to experience, and is thus directed against a use of reason on the basis of itself alone, the critique of reason in its practical form is directed against precisely its empirically conditioned use.[2] The titles of the two works ought therefore to be read not simply as analogous but rather as opposed in sense. Both pure theoretical reason and empirically conditioned practical reason make unjustified claims and demand criticism.

A further distinction between the two works is this: in the case of theoretical reason Kant draws the line between legitimate and merely apparent knowledge along the boundary between empirically conditioned and pure reason. He does this by revealing the conditions of the possibility of empirical knowledge. For an analysis of these conditions reveals the impossibility of pure rational knowledge without relation to possible experience. The *Critique of Practical Reason,* however, does not reject, through a proof of the same sort, the claim of empirically conditioned reason to be the sole ground of practice. A proof would have to demonstrate the possibility of a pure practical reason. Kant considered such a proof to be impossible, meaning, he thought, that it was indeed possible to know the structure of morality but not its ground. For this reason, Kant is only indirectly able to refute doubts about the reality of morality, through refuting the grounds which have been put forward against it. A refutation of this sort is announced in the very title of the *Critique of Practical Reason.* It is not due to an accidental weakness of our cognitive powers that philosophy cannot advance in this field. It is rather the very understanding of morality on the basis of practical reason that forces us to limit the questions formulated by a theory of practical reason.

The grounds which Kant advances for this doctrine were important as well for the Idealistic systems which followed. These grounds are in part theoretical: if pure practical reason is real, freedom is its ground; freedom, however, is inaccessible to all theoretical insight. In part, Kant derived these grounds from an analysis of the moral consciousness. If pure practical reason is real, it presupposes a unity of reason and motive power which is unintelligible to us. We will start with this second ground.

The principle of Kantian moral philosophy is the autonomy of reason. Reason is only autonomous when it "purely," by itself alone, and without regard to grounds or drives distinct from it, suffices to determine the will. In order for reason to be determinative of the will purely by itself, it must satisfy two conditions. It must ground action in two senses.

(1) Reason must contain principles of action which state *what* the will wills. It must designate specific actions as rational without appealing to grounds other than those which result from the structure of reason itself. Reason is autonomous only if it can supply a ground for knowing the right will before it has acquired knowledge of the structure of being or the fundamental tendencies of action of human nature. There must be a *principium diiudicationis bonitatis* inherent in the form of reason.

(2) Even if reason were capable of this, it could still lack autonomy—if it were not at the same time that which gives binding force to the "rectitudo" of the will. Were reason only to know the right, without at the same time being the ground of its obligatory power, then it would indeed be the faculty through which we came to know the right, but not its origin. There

would be a auto*gnosy* of reason with regard to rational action, but in no sense an auto*nomy* of reason. Autonomy requires that reason have the power to effect actions which take place solely because they are rational. Just as the insight of someone acting on the basis of autonomous reason is not directed to facts distinct from reason itself, the energy of his will does not derive from sources other than this insight itself. He does what is right, not on the basis of an interest which his insight serves, but for the sake of the being of the right into which he has insight. Reason must therefore be supplied with a *principium executionis bonitatis.*

Only these two elements together define the concept of the autonomy of reason. Kant did not always express this point with sufficient clarity and thereby made possible a number of misunderstandings. Nonetheless, the problem of the *Critique of Practical Reason* is contained in this duality. Furthermore, Kant's own development toward the *Critique of Practical Reason* and the movement of Idealistic ethics which took its point of departure from that work have been determined by this problem. In both cases the question of the character and the possibility of the autonomy of reason reads: *How can these two elements be thought together in one and the same concept of reason and how can the moral nature of man be understood on the basis of their unity?* It was the concept of the *good* which first led Kant in the area of this problematic. For the concept of the good, if it is taken in its moral meaning, contains an ambiguity, which approximates that which is found in the concept of the autonomy of the will but is not identical with it. We call a particular deed "good." But we also call someone "good" who does good deeds. Both the doing and what is done, the willing and what is willed, are called "good," and, indeed, we only have deep moral respect for the will which wills that which appears to it as the good, and which does not strive only for its advantage. The act and the content of the act are both designated with the same word, which is nonetheless not homonymous. For what we mean is precisely the unity of both. We miss this sense of "good" if we think of the two separately.

Kant suggested the conjecture that the unity of both ought to be understood on the basis of the act of the will, because our esteem concerns only the will which is directed to the "good," regardless of whether it actualizes the good, or whether stronger forces thwart its intentions. We thus value not the existence of the good which it wills but solely the willing itself. The *Foundations of the Metaphysics of Morals* begins with a reference to this phenomenon, and its opening sentence is well known: We can conceive of nothing "which can be regarded as good without qualification, except a *good will.*"³ This sentence is not merely an expression of moral enthusiasm; it is rather the stimulus for developing a theoretical problem. Kant thinks that the significance for moral theory of this universally admitted judgment of the moral consciousness has not previously been noticed. It is impossible to comprehend why the goodness of the will is unconditionally esteemed, if one proceeds from the content of an action. It is certainly worth attempting to achieve an ethics which is adequate to this phenomenon by assuming that the form of the good will also serves as a rule for its possible content.

The decision to make this attempt is Kant's first Copernican turn, and it had already taken place by 1765.⁴ Long before he had arrived at the thought that the objects of knowledge could also be governed by the laws of our intuition he had noted that the explanation of morality on the basis of determinate objects of the will "failed to make good progress"; and it "went better" if he supposed that the objects derived from the will itself.⁵ The Stoics had already found the goodness of the will in itself to be worthy of praise. "Si desint vires, tamen est laudanda voluntas";⁶ "in magnis voluisse sat est."⁷ Kant repeats their phrases emphatically: "That perfection is absolute which is undetermined whether it effects something or not; it is called 'moral.'"⁸ Incorrect principles of ethics obscure the standards of moral evaluation. If the insight that only the good will is simply good can be consistently maintained, not only will this obscurity vanish, but with it the obscurity which has until now surrounded the foundational problem of ethics.

Kant formulated this thought long before he arrived at the formulation of the autonomy of reason. If one relates the two principles which are intended in this formula, that of judgment and that of execution, to the two meanings of good in the discussion of the good will, it becomes clear that the principle of execution deserves precedence. If the good will is the realization of the autonomy of reason, then a power of acting which develops out of itself is at the same time thought of as the ground for that which is the object of the action. Before the question of the possibility of this power of acting can be posed, both moments must be sufficiently understood separately and in their relation to each other.

Kant's first Copernican revolution initially led only to a solution of the problem of how a principle for the judgment of the good can be found. Only later did he achieve clarity about the degree of difficulty which the problem of the *principii executionis* contained. And whereas he arrived right away at the first solution, he remedied the latter difficulty around 1785, and even then not in a fashion which he could find equally satisfying.

II. The Judgment of the Good *(principium diiudicationis)*

If the structure of the rational will itself supplies an immediate ground for distinguishing between good and bad acts, moral philosophy is freed of a difficulty, which can be formulated in the following way: either one must make the rank of moral culture of a human being depend on the degree of his knowledge of the world, or one must place the ground of moral discrimination in feeling and abandon the doctrine of the rational foundation of morality. If, however, the form of reason itself suffices to know the right way to act, then the "common man" is in no sense inferior to the "researcher" as a moral being. It is no accident that Kant discovered his *principium diiudicationis* during the period of his enthusiasm for Rousseau. For only on the basis of this principle can theory respect human beings as such. In order to know the good, one does not require "vasta astutia et sagacitas consectaria" (great cleverness and exact logical acumen).[9] A good will suffices, along with that natural human reason which easily discerns what is correct in all its actions.

Even before Kant moral philosophers had attempted to grasp concretely the talk about the *recta ratio* and to develop a principle for judging what is good that presupposed no knowledge of the world and yet still allowed for unequivocal decisions. Christian Wolff, for example, claimed to see the formal character of the good in the agreement of all activities to the greatest possible extent. William Wollaston thought one could recognize good actions by their "inner truth," whereas bad actions always implied a violation of an evidently true proposition. Kant's objection to these theories comes down in the end to this: that they do not rest on reason in its practical employment, but that they derive rules for the will from the form of reason merely as a faculty of *knowledge*. In every case these rules contain two errors. (1) They must presuppose knowledge of the world—if only to a limited degree—in order to apply these rules of judgment. The person who claims to judge whether his actions are in agreement must know the nature of human beings. The person who claims to grasp violations of truths must be acquainted with these truths. But then that person has a clearer moral judgment who knows human nature better and knows more truths about things. (2) It is not possible with the help of these rules to decide between opposed actions, of which one is clearly rejected by the moral consciousness. They are therefore not identical with the rule which the moral consciousness actually applies, and are in general tautological: they already presuppose knowledge of the good. The criminal need only be consistent to bring about a unanimity in his nature that formally is in no way inferior to that of a good person (contra Wolff). The thief indeed violates the truth that a thing is not his property. But the person who does not steal violates another truth, namely, that there are a lot of things possessed by others which are more useful to him than they are to them (contra Wollaston).

Kant learned from both of these attempts. His endeavor differed from theirs in that the question how can I know what is good is answered by the form of reason in its relation to the will. The will has "truth" (Wollaston) and "agreement" (Wolff) in relation only to itself, not to dispositions or facts. The evil will cannot be in agreement with itself and with all willing and is, for this reason, incapable of publicizing its maxims. The formula in which Kant expressed the demand of the right self-relationship in the good will is the categorical imperative: "Act only according to that maxim whereby you can at the same time will that it should become a universal law."[10]

Although Wolff and Wollaston claimed to supply a formal criterion for distinguishing between good and evil, they had not yet completed that revolution which we called the first Copernican revolution in Kant's thought. They had not yet made the objects of the will dependent on its own form. Kant had good grounds for the opinion that the incomparable goodness of the will itself could only be understood on this path; only the categorical imperative could avoid the paradox which, since Rousseau, had become offensive—that the scholar as such was also superior in moral judgment—and only the categorical imperative was not an *imperativus tautologicus*. If one views these advantages with Kant's eyes, and against the background of the *aporia* of traditional ethics, it is easy to understand precisely why the doctrine of the categorical imperative has been the most durable of all the theories in Kant's development. This doctrine was formulated sixteen years before the appearance of the *Critique of Pure Reason* (1765) and even in his late works was never called into question.[11]

Soon after Kant this principle of judging the good was criticized as being empty and capable of justifying anything and anyone. This reproach was raised most emphatically, and in surprising agreement, by Hegel and Schopenhauer. This reproach, if accurate, is all the more serious, in that Kant claimed to see his contribution in terms of getting free of the tautologies of Wolff and Wollaston. It can be shown, however, that the objection is not tenable in this form and universality. There is, indeed, much that is justified in the criticism of Kant's successors. But such criticism can only be made productive if the above reproach is first refuted.

To do this one need merely satisfy oneself that the formula of the categorical imperative determines the content of the moral will and in what way it does so. Kant's best example of such a derivation was also the first that he developed, and he noted it in his own copy of a book he had just published.[12] This example examines whether a person of good will can will the theft of grain. According to Wolff, in order to answer this question one would have to investigate whether the drive to acquire someone else's property can belong to a constitution of the soul in which the greatest possible harmony reigned. According to Wollaston, one would have to see whether the act of stealing acknowledged or violated truths about the desired grain. To apply Kant's formula, one need (at least in this case) only examine the intention contained in the will itself to see whether it is adequate to the form of reason, universality, or whether it contradicts this form. This reflection "qua voluntatem"[13] assumes that the thief steals the grain with the intention of acquiring it. "Suppose that I am about to steal the grain of another person. Because I am acquainted with no human being who wants to acquire the property of another on the condition that what he acquired will be stolen from him, I want something for myself, which I cannot want for everyone." The thief also acquires, but without agreement, by merely taking. If everyone who wanted to acquire must presuppose that the property acquired will be stolen, then there would be no such thing as acquisition. In a double sense: one would not be able to acquire property, which the thief would immediately steal; nor would the thief steal, for his stolen property would be lost through the theft of others. The thief cannot suppose his intention is of the sort which can be held quite universally by everyone in relation to everything. The principle which underlies and is inherent in his action cannot even be thought with universality, much less willed by him.

Similarly, if not with the same immediacy "qua voluntatem," one can discover the contradiction in a will which refuses every help for others if it is not in its interest. In this case it is certainly possible without contradiction to universalize the maxim as such, so long as one does not take into account the goal of the person who refuses to help others in all circumstances. He wants only to promote his own happiness. In this place in the Kantian deduction knowledge of the world is of importance, although it is of such an elementary form that the scholar can claim no privilege in the moral life: every human being knows that there are cases in which his own happiness can depend on the help of others.[14] If he himself always refuses to help others, he pursues a goal that, if it were the goal of everyone, would make impossible the realization of his own goal. This cannot be the intention of a rational will, whose maxims always satisfy the form of reason (strict universality).

This second example provides an occasion for some reflections. We must first warn against the misunderstanding that this operation leads to the purported moral demand that one ought, out of consideration for one's own happiness, not entirely refrain from helping others. On the contrary, it leads obviously to the demand that one completely give up the maxim that one should seek only one's own happiness. This new maxim, which can belong to a rational will, is not that of acquiring a claim to the help of others in the interest of one's own happiness; it is never to seek one's own happiness by disregarding the happiness of others. This misunderstanding was made easier by the fact that the categorical imperative was previously always understood to be a principle of choice between already given maxims.[15] If this were the case, given two maxims of the empirically conditioned will, the categorical imperative would reject one and legitimate the other. Here that self-interested maxim would be legitimate which purchased help in need through a helpful consideration for others. This maxim, however, withstands the test of universalization as poorly as the other. For I cannot will that others help me when I'm in need only when their own interest directs them to do so. That maxim, in which my own happiness can be striven for only in conjunction with the happiness of others, cannot be chosen from among already given principles of action, for it cannot be thought of as a result of the natural interests of the will. Rather, it is *formed* by the rational will on the basis of the reflection that none of the maxims of the individual pursuit of happiness results in a rational universality. That is the case even if one presupposes a "natural" inclination to help all human beings without distinction. For the demand on the good will requires giving help without any desire and, according to Kant, without any consideration for the worthiness of the person needing help, when I give help to this or that person. It is simply unthinkable that such a will would arise from an inclination that was only sanctioned by reason.

The relation of what is willed to the good will in Kant's ethics is comparable to the relation of object and understanding in his theory of knowledge. In both cases the content of a body of knowledge (of what is given or of the good) can be derived from a function (of the synthetic unity of consciousness or the universality of reason). In both cases, however, this content is independent not of every relation to givenness, but only of a specific manner of comprehending it. Even the good which the good will wills acquires its meaning only on the basis of a universalization of the matter of the empirically conditioned will. Good is the matter of a will of a specific form, which on its part is the form of an already presupposed empirically conditioned willing.

It is perhaps tempting to interpret the concept of the good either as designating a class of given ways of acting or as a specific content that has nothing in common with empirically conditioned intentions. From Kant's standpoint both possibilities are excluded, for they presuppose that "good" is an intrinsically determinate content. For Kant, however, "good" can only mean a content which belongs to a specific form, a content which is arrived at, not from the form alone, but insofar as one grasps a given content in accordance with this form. Moral maxims are therefore neither natural maxims which have been sanctioned nor maxims which are directed to an object entirely distinct from everything natural. Moral maxims are limits on natural striving and therewith an extension of the object of such striving. Thus in the example of the demand that we make the happiness of others a goal, the content of our maxim is *extended* for the sake of the happiness of others, so that our striving for our own happiness is placed under a condition and thereby limited.

Even if it is not true that the categorical imperative amounts to a mere tautology or a formula for the moral justification of self-love, this still does not answer every criticism of it. The two objections which one can rightly bring against the categorical imperative assert that it does not allow one to derive all those duties which are recognized by the moral consciousness, and that even with those duties which do follow from it, it fails to take into consideration the intention of the moral consciousness.

Kant acknowledges that his ethics must do justice to the "common moral reason of human beings." One cannot even think of another criterion for the reasonableness of a theory of morality. Both objections, although not of a systematic character, conclude that *the categorical imperative cannot be the only or the highest principle of ethics*. They force one to pose again the question how, on the basis of a consideration of the good "qua voluntatem," thus on the basis of the principle of autonomy, a philosophical ethics is possible. Between this principle and the highest principle of judgment in Kant's practical philosophy there must be found intermediaries which he did not himself see.

(1) We already saw that Kant himself first developed the principle of the universalization of maxims with the example of theft. Later the example of embezzlement (of a deposit) took its place. This example always had for him paradigmatic importance, so much so that we know only of a small

number of attempts by him to deduce other duties immediately from the categorical imperative. Kant of course developed other procedures of deduction, but he always maintained that a derivation from the universal principle must be possible.[16]

The derivation fails, however, in all those cases in which the duties to be deduced belong to the class of duties toward oneself; for example, the duty to observe moderation and the duty to develop one's talents.

The maxim to will only the use of those talents which require no cultivation on my part can be thought of without contradiction as a universal law, and even willed universally, as long as one takes into consideration only this maxim. The maxim has indeed the consequence that in many cases my will won't be realized, because it will lack the means to its realization. But this renunciation is contained in the maxim itself,[17] and it does not destroy the possibility of my setting goals which are realizable. The assertion that all striving (every setting of a goal) by a human being is in vain if he does not possess cultivated talents does not rest on experience of the same evidence as the need of all human beings for help.

Even the classical virtue of the sensible observance of moderation has a more determinate content than the demand not, through excess, to destroy the possibility of setting goals. This virtue clearly has one of its origins in the consciousness of the dignity of human nature, of which no one has spoken with more persuasive force than Kant. On the basis of the categorical imperative, however, one can immediately derive only the prohibition against ruinous excess. For the maxim to enjoy as much as possible, so long as one's self-control is not destroyed and the rights of others, as well as the duties toward them, are not violated, can be thought of and willed without contradiction as a universal law.

(2) The second objection was of great importance for the process whereby the Idealistic moral philosophy freed itself from the doctrine of the *Critique of Practical Reason* in the name of the Kantian principle. This objection is directed against the theory of duties toward others and says: Even if one admits that the formula of the categorical imperative allows these duties to be derived, this takes place in a form which must ascribe to the moral consciousness an intention which does not agree with the intention which it actually has. According to Kant, I help others because it is my duty to give up those maxims which do not pass the test of universalization. In the intention of my moral will the other person and his need for help are only a case for the application of a universal principle and an occasion for confirming the rational universality of the will. The moral will takes into consideration the other person in its maxim to promote its own

happiness only because the moral law does not allow the pursuit of happiness without consideration of others. The origin of duty in the limitation of our inclination has the consequence that the intention of the moral will is directed to duty by excluding the required content. The moral will helps another, because it takes an interest in the good, but without any interest in the needy person himself. Hegel described this situation quite accurately: "The defense of one's fatherland, the happiness of others, is duty, not because of its content, but because it is duty."[18]

Kant certainly brought up a series of grounds for the position that the good will must give *disinterested* help. He admitted his sympathy for that philanthropist "whose mind is clouded with sorrow," in whom all interest in the fate of others has been extinguished, who is not moved by the need of strangers but nonetheless helps others merely because it is his duty. He awards the highest rank among the helpers of humanity to the doctor, who sacrifices himself helping the sick even when he finds them repugnant and ungrateful. And he has sharp words for that "sentimental philanthropy" which seeks not to help but to receive pleasant feelings from the thankfulness of others. Such "philanthropy" is inclined not to regard what is right as holy, and also to give away what it rightfully owes to others, thus slighting a strict duty for a broad one. In general, Kant says, we ought to understand favors to others as obligations which arise from the fact that the goods of the world are unjustly distributed, obliging us to make compensation. Also, every offer of help requires delicacy. It must not lessen the needy person's consciousness of being an independent and rational being. Someone who shows interest in another risks harming him more in what is most essential to him than he could ever help him through external favors.[19]

These arguments are as convincing as anything that can be achieved under the conditions posed by Kantian ethics. They are good testimony both of Kant's morality and of his capacity to present his teaching in conjunction with the results of moral experience. One must also admit that they refer to a form of moral philanthropy that has been ignored and slighted by popular moral feeling. Nevertheless, even in Kant's time moral consciousness opposed—and still refuses to accept today—a doctrine which sees the origin of the moral relation to others solely in the limitation of the will to happiness of a rational being through the moral law. The correctness of Hegel's statement that the goodness of the will is defined not only by the circumstance that an action falls under the concept of duty, but just as much by the content of this action, is most evident in the example of the active love of one's neighbors. In this case the moral consciousness *is equally* concerned to do its duty and to help the other person. It recognizes as moral only that satisfaction which is at the same time the consciousness of accomplished duty *and* the joy in the accomplishment of care or regret over its failure. It is indeed true that when, with the best knowledge and the best strength, the proffered help remains ineffective, the good will still "gleams like a jewel." It is equally true, however, that this good will becomes suspect if it effortlessly comforts itself in its association with those whom it ought to help with the reflection that it suffices to strive for what is right. And that is because in the case of a duty to another, the intention of the good will is directed to the other *as such* and sees more than a case of the application of laws. This intention is certainly hard to grasp. One cannot derive from this fact a right to conceal this intention with arguments that take one of the essential traits of the moral phenomenon for the whole. It follows, rather, that the attempt must be made on the basis of the foundation developed by Kant *to reconstruct theoretically the moral consciousness in its entire range.*

It is not surprising that the question how the so-called duties of love are to be understood became the *experimentum crucis* for the most important of Kant's successors when one is acquainted with the difficulties which this question has always caused in the history of ethics. Since prior to modern ethics, whose beginning can be dated with Hobbes, theory has wavered between two possibilities, neither of which does justice to the moral reality: either these duties are to be interpreted as indirect duties to oneself, in which case one misses their intention (for example, Wolff), or they are made into the foundation of all morality, in the sense of the Christian doctrine, thereby disputing away the virtues which preserve the dignity of the rational person (for example, Hutcheson). Before Kant it was impossible to see how one could avoid both errors and still arrive at a theory with a seamless foundation. Since Kant, however, it has become completely clear that it is impossible to solve this dilemma through a decision for either alternative. This insight forced the philosophers who succeeded Kant to think through once more the principles of ethics which he supplied.

III. The Power of the Good *(principium executionis)*

We have thus far become acquainted with only one of the two aspects of the problematic which set speculative Idealism on its path. The objection against Kant which was previously treated was directed against his principle of judgment. It was already more than a critique of revisable consequences of an unchallenged foundation. Its whole weight first shows itself when one sees that it arises in another form in the second sphere of Kantian moral philosophy: in the doctrine of the *principium executionis moralitatis.*

As we saw, the thought of autonomy leads to the concept of a rule which has its origin solely in reason. We also saw, however, that if reason is not able to supply the will with the power to resist all inclinations and motives which stand against the good, this rule cannot establish any duties, imperatives, and obligations, and that this thought does not correspond to any reality. "That through your reason you are able to limit and overcome your inclinations, that is the freedom of the will."[20]

It was first seen clearly in the course of the eighteenth century that an answer to the question about the power of the good to determine the will to actions in a binding fashion must be the most important part of a philosophical theory of ethics.

The British moral-sense school discovered the inadequacy of an ethics that indeed rationally grounded the concept of the good but then simply presupposed that it possessed a relation to the will which would be experienced in the moral consciousness as superior to all other motives. This school restored the connection with the problems of the classical ethics of the Greeks, in which the question of the role of reason in the moral life had already been discussed in a way that had been forgotten in the tradition of Christian moral philosophy dominated by Cicero and the ethics of the Stoics. In the fourth decade of his life, Kant received important stimulus from this school.[21] Although Kant had never been a follower of Wolff's, and thus did not first need to be dissuaded from the Wolffian school, Hume and Hutcheson changed the accent of his questioning and also provided him with distance from the pietistic criticism of Wolff, whose most important representative had been Crusius. From now on Kant was no longer in danger of supposing that ethical theory was concluded with the answer to the question of what the good is. It was for this reason that he was not able to complete his work on the metaphysics of morals until he had worked out his doctrine of freedom, and that meant also the essentials of his theoretical philosophy, although he had promised it since the end of the 1760s. Kant himself once compared the search for the *principium executionis* with the search for the philosopher's stone.[22] With this remark he indicated that a theory of the motivational force of reason would render the whole system coherent and bring it to conclusion.

The particular difficulty of this theory is that it must supply the ground of a relationship which is the converse of an accustomed one: Whereas in cognition a given reality is determined by the concept, in the good, insofar as it has its origin in reason, an idea is the ground of a reality—namely, of the good will, which opposes itself to all the forces and drives which hinder it from realizing its goal, and thus it is already reality and realization. Kant was initially convinced that reason did not intrinsically possess such power of realization. The English doctrine of moral sense seemed to him to be correct insofar as along with the concept of reason, which is logical form, a second concept was needed to explain the phenomenon of morality. Reason did not intrinsically have the power "to carry out an action." Even our approval *(complacentia)* of the good is not an act which can be defined logically. It is, like the former, of an emotional nature. There thus appears to be an *antinomy* whose solution would require uncovering the philosopher's stone: Either ethics preserves the rational character of the moral demand, in which case the motives of the moral will cannot be made understandable, or one proceeds from morality as a power to act, in which case one cannot preserve the rational character of the good.

The doctrine of the good as the inner universality of the will as such was already established as the point of departure of Kant's theory. The solution of the antinomy could be achieved only by demonstrating a motivational power of reason, of whose impossibility the English moral philosophers had been convinced. For twenty years Kant made various attempts to supply such a demonstration.[23] He refused from the very beginning to rely on the obvious, but nonexplanatory, thought: God has joined to the reason, which has insight into the good, a moral motive which is called "moral sense." The question is not how an already determined concept of the good can acquire an additional effective power, but how one ought to be able to think of a concept of the good to whose definition effective power already belongs.

We want not to enter into the particulars of these attempts more closely but to understand the insight at which Kant finally arrived through making them. After a short phase during which he proposed a theosophical interpretation of the *sensus moralis,* Kant arrived at the thought that it must be possible as well to derive the idea of the good in its complete determination from the *spontaneity* of our cognitive faculty. What could not be accomplished on the basis of an analysis of reason as logical *form* could be achieved through an analysis of reason as *act.* This thought was all the more suggestive to him because, since the end of the 1760s, he had investigated the theoretical problem of knowledge, which could not be solved by ontology, or logic, or psychologia rationalis, from the point of view that our understanding must be a faculty of synthesizing given representations, i.e., an act which establishes a unity. The possibility of solving the aporia of ethics at the same time as those of knowledge must have occurred to him. It appeared to Kant that the errors of the Wolffians and the empiricists, whose teachings in theoretical and moral philosophy were equally unsatisfactory, had their ultimate ground in the fact that they did not understand what reason really was, insofar as they defined it only formally and through the results of its efficacy.

The doctrine of the spontaneity of the understanding contained *fundamentally two possibilities for a deduction* of moral motives. Kant could explain the pleasure in the good either on the basis of an ordering among intrinsically conflicting sensible motives or as a consequence of the freedom which also constitutes the nature of the spontaneous reason in pure thought. The process by which Kant came to see the insufficiency for the moral consciousness of both these justifications is one of the most exciting and most instructive in the history of the development of philosophical thought. With astonishing consistency, Kant brought to bear on the moral phenomenon from which he had proceeded when he analyzed the will "qua voluntatem" the theoretical possibilities which appeared to result from the new foundation of his critical system: He saw that neither explanation could arrive at the unconditional character of the moral demand and the incomparable worth of the good will.

The first explanation is fundamentally aesthetic and fails to make understandable how the good will, if it corresponds to the demand of the good, can be effective (a) without any interest and (b) against every opposition of the inclinations. The second class of explanations ignores the distinction between the relation of concept and reality in cognition, on the one hand, and its converse relation in morality, on the other. For the very reason that thinking does not contain any demand for realization and no genuine opposition to reality, its spontaneity should not be confused with the freedom of the *will* "to overcome and limit inclinations." The result of Kant's self-criticism, which reached its conclusion in the second half of the 1780s, is the knowledge that the concept of pure practical reason cannot in any way be understood as an implication of the spontaneity of theoretical reason. The dualism of Kant's concept of reason is thus the result of the failure of his attempts to avoid this result. It is the result of the consistency with which Kant kept in sight the problem of ethics and the phenomenon of morality and with which at the same time he kept his theory of knowledge and self-consciousness within their possibilities, without introducing arbitrary postulates in the interest of the greater unity of the system.

At the end of this development stand Kant's critique of practical reason and his doctrine of respect for the law as the sole motive of the good will.

The first states with respect to ethical theory that morality cannot be deduced from any prior principles. The second formulates the conditions under which the good alone can be done for its own sake; it claims to supply a structure on the basis of which the will is immediately related to the unconditioned claim of the good.

The inwardness and the facticity of the good are thought together in this structure. In respect I recognize a command which is neither foreign to me nor imposed on me by a foreign power. I subordinate myself to this command without being moved to do so by grounds other than those contained in it. To that extent the doctrine of respect takes into consideration the thought of autonomy. At the same time, the person who acknowledges the command on the basis of respect distinguishes himself from the acknowledged power. This power is not foreign to him, but nonetheless it *appears* and *demands* respect. Without needing to specify this phenomenon, one can say that respect presupposes that structure which speculative Idealism attempted to develop methodically as the unity of differences, but that in respect the unity is not itself grasped conceptually, but rather exists factually. Regarding persons, we can say that we respect in them what *confronts* us as the perfected demand of our *own* essence.

This concept of respect concludes the Kantian system of moral philosophy insofar as it allows Kant to unite all its parts with one another and to combine them consistently with the results of the *Critique of Pure Reason:* The doctrine of the unknowability of freedom leads to the theory of the categorical imperative as a *fact* of reason. Whoever grasps its facticity while trying to hold on to the unconditionality and rationality of this fact of *reason* will arrive at this doctrine of respect for the law.[24] For this doctrine shows in what manner this fact can be known by a free being and how it can become the foundation for the determination of his will. Of course, Kant had taught earlier that freedom was unknowable, and he had also spoken on occasion about the moral phenomenon of "respect." That teaching and this concept first became the foundation of his ethics when he abandoned his attempts at deducing the moral law, and when he derived authoritative conclusions for the construction of his ethics from these failures. Since then the connection of these three concepts has been characteristic of the standpoint of Kantian ethics. That this connection stands at the end of a development which began with the analysis of the unconditionality of the good will can be seen as well from the fact that, with the help of this connection, such concepts as "dignity" and "respect" can be defined for the first time. For in these concepts one could always find an expression of the experience which underlies the Kantian ethics, and through which this ethics has been impressively transmitted.

It is this very definition, however, which gives rise to new objections to Kant's ethics, and which first gives fundamental importance to the criticism of the manner in which Kant understands the intention of the moral consciousness. Of course, to introduce a concept and relate it to a phenomenon is obviously not sufficient to make a theory compelling. One must also examine the questions whether the theory allows this phenomenon to be understood, and whether all the determinations which enter into the concept can be developed from it. The emotional factors that in Kant's ethics are connected precisely with the doctrine of respect have so far impeded such criticism.

One must distinguish between what Kant claimed to achieve with his talk of respect for the law and what his theory is really able to achieve. If one does this, it becomes evident that here too his theory cannot explain the intention of the moral consciousness. In contrast to the earlier case of duties of love, this difficulty is merely one of theory, not of understanding the moral phenomena themselves. Whereas in the previous case it was obvious that Kant was in no position to recognize a factor in the moral consciousness as such, in this case a phenomenon is brought forward which the theory does not allow one to understand. In both instances one misses the intention of the moral consciousness, and for the same reason. In the case of the principle of "respect," it is more difficult to discover this fact only because the moral consciousness is not provoked to protest. It becomes all the clearer, at the same time, that the ground of criticism falls away only when one calls into question the essential features of the Kantian philosophy and its theory of subjectivity.

Kant constantly distinguished from each other two acts which together constitute the phenomenon of respect: If we respect something then what happens first is that all "inclinations are *checked*" that lead us in another direction. Before the law of reason, which deserves our respect, all inclinations are "beaten down." Respect is the act in which the law "pushes the inclinations aside" and acquires "repute." In an empirically conditioned faculty of desire this act is merely a limitation and thus negative. In respect the law is, however, also the object of a "positive feeling"—an elevation of subjectivity in the consciousness of its independence from inclinations.[25] A philosophical theory which intends to comprehend the phenomenon of respect must therefore comprehend the unity of both acts.

It may be important to note that the German word *Achtung* owes its second connotation to the use which Kant first made of it. Kant himself once noted that it should be understood as equivalent to *reverentia*.[26] Before him, however, no one ever had in mind this equivalence in the word *Achtung*. In the eighteenth century the fundamental meaning of *Achtung* corresponded completely with the Latin *attentio*. Thus a situation required all one's *Achtung* (heed, *Beachtung*), whereas a book did not deserve any *Achtung* (attention, *Aufmerksamkeit*).[27] The call *Achtung!,* which one still hears at train stations and barracks, was overheard in all talk of respect (Be careful, step back, step forward!). One must say of the person who *deserves* such respect that he receives our *deepest* respect. Kant was the first to incorporate into the meaning of respect the positive relation to something recognized by us, to which we must elevate ourselves. For us who stand in the history of the effects of Kant's ethics, this meaning has become so self-evident that we take it to be the primary one.

Kant's theory becomes problematic because he has to assign the two acts which constitute "respect" to two different "faculties" of the human soul. The limitation of the inclinations occurs in "sensibility" as an incomprehensible effect of the intelligible freedom of the moral being. One cannot, however, say of sensibility itself that it is "elevated." For it is not possible to see on the basis of Kantian presuppositions how sensibility can acquire a positive connection to reason solely because its claims were rebuffed. For this reason Kant understands this elevation merely as a relation of practical *reason to itself.* The removal of the obstacles to practical reason promotes its activity. Such promotion is approved by practical reason and equated with an increase in its energy. This takes place in a "judgment" of reason, thus wholly "on the intellectual side" of the moral life.[28]

It is obvious by now that Kant must at least restrict his declaration that respect is also a positive feeling. "For the law there is no feeling."[29] The positive factor in respect exists for feeling only mediately insofar as humiliated sensibility is the ground of a rational evaluation of worth. The unified phenomenon of respect is supposed to be constituted, not only by two distinct acts, but by acts of different faculties.

Even if we desist from raising principled objections against this theory, it is still obvious that it does not explain the phenomenon of respect. We already saw that respect must be counted among that class of accomplishments in which an identification with something of one's own takes place which is at the same time encountered as the other. When Kant uses the word "respect" he has this structure in view. But his theory dissolves this structure into the interplay of two acts which could equally well be experienced independent of each other. As a rational being I know how to esteem a power which I experience as a sensible being insofar as this power exercises force on me in an inexplicable fashion and hinders the unfolding of my inclinations. My reason experiences an expansion, my sensibility a limitation. Although *I* undergo both experiences, this unity is only a formal summation of acts *which are not at all related to each other.* I must indeed be aware of that limitation in order to be able to esteem it. The Kantian theory, however, does not make it possible to understand anything more than the evaluation of "limited sensibility." The evaluation is thus directed not to the power and the demand of the law which encounters me but to its effect on sensibility. Therewith the intention of the moral consciousness is perverted into its opposite, and indeed in opposition to the intention which was contained in Kant's theory. There is no possibility for this theory to account for a positive relation of consciousness to the law, a relation which would be an act of identification and thus distance and unity at once.

One consequence of this is that Kant also fails to describe the manner in which practical reason experiences the facticity of the good. It is tempting to say, and it has been said, that respect is really the fact of reason. If this solution is seriously accepted, however, the structure of the Kantian theory is dissolved. For respect can only pertain to a law which is experienced as deserving of respect, it already presupposes the "fact of reason." Then one must already be aware of this fact in the "judgment" of reason which "imposes itself" through the synthetic proposition of the categorical imperative. But this solution is also not acceptable. For the moral consciousness is distinguished from theoretical insight because it is at the same time the certainty of a motivation to act, i.e., through the second aspect contained in the concept of the autonomy of the will. If we look for this aspect in the concrete execution of moral subjectivity, it can only be the limitation which sensibility experiences through the law. Without this limitation, however, the moral law is not a law of *practical* reason. The facticity of the moral law can be carried out only in concert with the consciousness that inclinations are limited; for that reason it cannot belong solely to the intellectual side. That, however, is contrary to the presupposition. If both explanations are insufficient, the answer suggests itself that consciousness of this fact is both in one: judgment of reason and consciousness of being limited. Even apart from this being just another way of asserting that respect is the fact of reason, it is merely a formula for refusing to explain facticity as such. Each aspect points to the other as the real locus of facticity. The sum of two bad thoughts is not a better, but a worse, thought than each by itself.

A tenable concept of respect and a persuasive theory of subjectivity as carried out in the fact of reason would presuppose that one could either conceive of a positive relation of feeling (sensibility) to reason or presuppose a reason which was *in itself* capable of carrying out facticity. The content of these two alternatives suggests two distinct theories. These theories were also elaborated, not by one, but by two of the most important successors of Kant—the first by Friedrich Schiller and the second by Fichte. Both presuppose a conceptual structure which cannot be given a foundation without a further methodological revolution in post-Kantian philosophy. It is the same structure which is demanded if one is to avoid the error Kant committed in his analysis of the duties of love and their intention. In each of these three cases (respect for the law, fact of reason, and duty toward others) one is concerned with phenomena which afterward were interpreted with the help of the speculative dialectic. And each of these cases contributed in its way to the development of this new method of philosophical reflection.

Kant started with reflection on how one could understand the unconditional good of the good will. This led him to his doctrine of the autonomy of reason, which in turn found its only possible, and in his system only consistent, interpretation in his subsidiary doctrines of respect for the law and the fact of reason. It is important to note explicitly that this path and connection are not called into question by the criticisms directed against Kant's doctrines of the principles of judgment and the execution of the good. The Kantian conception of autonomy cannot be refuted by the circumstance that the Kantian system did not develop any theory about the inner structure of autonomy in its completed form. This conception of autonomy certainly in part disguised moral phenomena and in part made incomprehensible the phenomena it disclosed. That did not happen, however, because Kant allowed himself to be led by an unusable principle. Philosophical ethics not only enumerates moral phenomena, but it must make their unity comprehensible, and for this reason it requires a method of philosophical reflection and a system of fundamental concepts for philosophy as a whole. In Kant's case his method and system determined both the path and the limits of his explication of moral reality and prevented the principle of his ethics from having an elaboration which would be convincing in all respects. For this reason the task of his successors was to grasp this principle more profoundly and develop it more adequately.

Kant has closed off any return to the old interpretation of morality on the basis of the categories *telos-entelecheia*. For this position is not capable of treating thematically what the disquiet in Kant's ethics had been: the *bonitas solae voluntatis*, the moral consciousness as a self-relation of the rational will. The account, according to which the good is the original goal and only mediately a quality of the will, misses the problem of moral subjectivity. If the relation of the will to the good cannot be understood on the basis of the good will, then much less can it be understood on the basis of a goal which precedes the will and makes demands on it. The moral phenomena themselves demand that one proceed from what Kant calls "autonomy." But this cannot mean, after one has criticized Kant, that he must accept Kant's system or even stick to its letter. Moreover, the moral being ought not to be explained as a *causa sui,* or as a manner of consciousness that intends exclusively itself. Yet every relation to something as the ground of consciousness can take place only *in consciousness* and on the basis of its own necessity, not on the basis of something which is prior to consciousness and could be determined independent of it in pure theory.

These propositions must here remain mere assertions. For to argue for them would mean to determine anew the relation of ontology and ethics, and certainly not as the one-sided dependence of the latter on the former. Idealistic philosophy always saw the theory of moral consciousness as one of its first tasks. This philosophy was convinced that the foundation of philosophy could not occur prior to or independent of moral theory. Therewith Idealistic philosophy renewed a conjunction of problems which had previously, originally, and solely belonged to Platonic thought, even on the basis of quite different presuppositions. The Aristotelian criticism of this position and the dominant place of speculative theology had prevented it from being renewed in later periods. Its renewal had been in preparation for a long time—in late Cartesianism, in the moral-sense school, and in the practical orientation of the Thomasian and pietistic criticism of Wolff.[30] This position finally emerged unconcealed in Kant's concept of practical reason and its autonomy and is connected with the consciousness of modernity in a manner which has not yet been sufficiently thought through. This position not only introduced but also authoritatively determined one of the most important and fruitful periods of philosophical thought.

IV. Theories of Autonomy

The historical investigation of the consequences of Kant's thought shows that the journey from the *Critique of Practical Reason* to speculative Idealism proceeded along three paths. It is well to distinguish between them, even if not always to keep them separate. Reinhold initiated the first path.[31] He began by determining more exactly the coherence of the fundamental concepts of Kantian ethics (will, freedom, faculty of desire, and others). Fichte's practical *Science of Knowledge* stands at the end of this path. The second path began with the attempt of the orthodox theologians at Tübingen to interpret the doctrine of postulates of the *Critique of Practical Reason* in their sense.³² This led to a better grasp of the particular character of Kant's philosophy of religion and to an application of it against orthodoxy, especially in Fichte's *Atheismusstreit*, in Schelling's *Letters on Dogmatism and Criticism,* and in the early manuscripts of Hegel. The third path was that of an investigation of moral phenomena which was critically opposed to the moral ideal defended by Kant. Schiller and the young Hegel performed the greatest service on this path.

It is no longer possible here to investigate these three paths. It would be even less to the point to develop the forms of Idealistic ethics in as detailed a fashion as the Kantian. I intend only to explain the standpoint of Idealistic ethics and to show that the Idealists' allegiance to Kant is neither superficial nor a misunderstanding: The continuity of critical and speculative philosophy is revealed by the fact that both accept the principle of the autonomy of reason and attempt to develop it consistently.

It is therefore proper to proceed from this principle. The problems of the third path of Idealistic philosophy have a particularly close relation to the problems which result from Kant's theory of the *principium diiudicationis*. The reflections of the first path consider the difficulties in Kant's doctrine of the execution of the good and of moral subjectivity in its fulfillment. Certainly, the fundamental insufficiencies which attach to Kantian ethics as a theory were perceived in both of these paths. For this reason more is in question in each than a detail of Kant's moral doctrine, and each leads to the problematic which underlies all objections to Kant. Whereas the former proceeds from the moral phenomenon and its judgment, in the latter the concepts *in abstracto* with which the moral will in its autonomy is supposed to be thought are under discussion. We will portray the characteristics of Schiller and Hegel's efforts in the third path and those of Fichte and Hegel in the first in order to gain at least an overview of the history of the Idealistic principle of autonomy and the two aspects of its concept. These two aspects found renewed systematic unity in Hegel's philosophy of "ethical life," although not at all a final conclusion.

The peculiar characteristic of Schiller's contribution to moral philosophy is that he tried to improve Kantian ethics using Kantian concepts.³³ His importance in the context of the development of Idealistic ethics is to have shown through what he did that the questions which Kant's ethics leave unanswered are not questions about the inner consistency of the system—they are questions, rather, which push beyond it. Underlying all these questions is the same problem: the moral phenomena and the fundamental concepts of Kant's theory of morality imply a unity of acts or aspects which Kant cannot explain. Thus duties of love are a unity of an intention directed to the other and an intention directed to duty; respect is a unity of distance and essential identity; the moral law is a unity of facticity and rationality. Insofar as Schiller addresses these questions, he resolves the problem of what type this unity should be through the demand that law (duty) and *inclination* should concur in it. Concrete subjectivity is thus connected with rational law through inclination and not through a *limitation* of sensibility. Love is thus an inclination to reason that manifests itself in the other. Dualism is supposed to be overcome through a mediation of the same aspects which were definitive of dualism for Kant: through the aspects of reason and *sensibility*. It follows from this that phenomena which in truth belong to reason are brought under the titles "inclination" and "sensibility." This mistake was first overcome by those successors of Kant who no longer followed the Kantian position in questions of foundation. Moreover, the conceptual relations which Kant had developed over decades became disorganized, and the impression arose that Schiller, through the imitation of his doctrine by popular moral philosophy and the theology of love, had muddled Kantian ethics. It is easy to furnish proof of this. Only someone who felt he ought to preserve the Kantian letter and defend Kant's moral philosophy as the truth itself would satisfy himself by turning it against Schiller.

It certainly makes it all the more difficult to understand the fundamental importance of Schiller's dispute with Kant that neither Kant nor Schiller had a correct understanding of its peculiar characteristics during the period in which this dispute was being conducted. Their disagreement therefore appears to be merely one over the application of Kantian theory and the relation of ethics and aesthetics. Insofar as these problems were really intended, Kant was led by Schiller's objections to make more precise and to clarify his theory. Schiller as a result considered the dispute at an end and thanked Kant in a glowing letter, without, however, concealing from others his feeling that an essential disagreement remained untouched.[34] He was never clear in his own mind about the ground of this awareness, which fully corresponded to the actual situation.

Schiller, as is well known, objected to Kant that he did not place a high enough estimation on the role of inclination in the moral life. Morality is complete only where it has also "enlisted the service" of inclination and developed itself "freely," without the resistance of inclination; that is, without any impediment at all. But this talk of the unity of duty and inclination can have several meanings.

(1) Duty and inclination determine the will simultaneously. It cannot

be disputed that this is possible, and it was also admitted by Kant. An action is not bad or without merit simply because an inclination drives one to it. Conversely, an action is not good solely because one forces oneself to do it against every inclination. In each case, certainly, the good will alone deserves moral esteem. But the good will can also be effective where sensible motives alone would produce the same action. It matters only that this action could have taken place without the help of the inclinations, solely for the sake of the good. The good will which knows the seriousness of its task and also the weaknesses of human nature, will not combat the inclinations; on the contrary, it will enlist their help in order that the good be actualized with certainty. But the good will must not, through trusting inclinations, allow its own energy to flag or indeed confuse this with inclinational motives. On this point Kant and Schiller are in agreement.

(2) The performance of a duty is the cause of an inclination. Whenever an activity is frequently engaged in there develop a corresponding disposition and inclination. That is also true of doing what is good. It occurs more easily the more often it succeeds. And the person who is aware that he is gradually better able to achieve what is difficult finds ever more delight in doing it. This delight in one's own skill in doing the good is, however, the same as that felt by the swindler engaged in a cunning deceit. This feeling of delight is estimable not on its own account but because of its cause and its content. It presupposes the good will and arises only where no unfortunate circumstance hinders the good will from fulfilling its goals, at least as a rule. "Only after conquering monsters did Hercules become a friend of the muses."[35] On this point as well Kant and Schiller are in agreement.

(3) The good will as such is determined jointly by duty and inclination. In this case inclination is itself a moral act. And with this Kant is not able to agree; for only the will is *bonitas in se*. According to Schiller, however, not only should inclination proceed in conformity with the good, but it should *count as* the good. That is not to say that the person who has an inclination to the good does not need to overcome any obstacles in his moral act. But his relation to these obstacles is of a different sort. His morality is not defined by the overcoming of the resistance of his inclinations. The intention of his consciousness is not the subduing of inclinations but the fusion with the good in which that opposition is one element, but not, however, the determining one. This takes place not in the moral consciousness but between it and particular circumstances, which cannot touch the unity of consciousness with the good itself.

This fusion of the moral consciousness with its object, which is at the

Ethics of Autonomy

same time its own nature, corresponds to the positive feeling in Kant's doctrine of respect for the law. Schiller clearly noted that neither in general linguistic usage nor in Kant's interpretation can "respect" *(Achtung)* really denote such a positive feeling. What Kant claimed, without making it intelligible, Schiller designated as an inclination to duty, which he can also call "love of the good." "Respect is compulsion, deep respect *(Hochachtung)* [which applies only to persons] already a less constrained feeling. But that is due to love, which constitutes an ingredient in deep respect."[36]

The question still remains, however, whether Schiller can determine the accomplishment of unity in the moral consciousness with the Kantian concept of the inclination to the good. Drives are modes of desire which are by nature directed to certain objects. In this way the inclination to eat results from the drive to combat hunger. The demand of the good opposes the sum totality of these inclinations insofar as they claim to be the exclusive determining ground of the will. There is no dispute between Kant and Schiller about this connection. How should one understand, however, the fact that a new inclination emerges when all the other inclinations are limited and forced to attention *(Achtung, attentio)* for a sufficiently long period of time—an inclination not to mere activity but precisely to doing the good, i.e., to the accomplishment of this limitation? The inclination in which the moral consciousness merges with the good can obviously not be called an inclination in the same sense as the inclination which is rejected by the good will. This can also be inferred from Schiller's texts, in which the Kantian terminology is at last completely inverted quite expressly when Schiller ascribes inclinations to reason itself, i.e., acts which, according to the doctrine he recognizes as Kantian, belong solely to sensibility.

By doing so Schiller himself implicitly recognized that his correction of Kant's doctrine of the self-fulfillment of autonomy cannot be consistently carried out within the Kantian system. Without intending it he demonstrated to his time the necessity of proceeding further along the path pursued by Kant, in order first of all to replace the theory of subjectivity attached to Kantian ethics by one that avoided its deficiencies, without, however, once again losing what had been gained by it.

It was Hegel who took the next steps along this path. In his "Frankfurt Manuscripts" he recapitulated Schiller's position, but articulated it much more fundamentally and in a broader context, so that its theoretical consequences did not remain hidden as they had with Schiller.

We can only mention a small portion of the riches of these youthful writings—only the method with which these writings intended to solve Schiller's problem and thus complete the theory of autonomy. Hegel employs a procedure of completion: one begins with an incomplete and hence inadequate interpretation of a principle to which new aspects are added until the initial thought is entirely determined and thus "fulfilled" (complete). We know that this procedure has theological roots, and that Hegel extracted his concept from the interpretation of the New Testament, primarily the Sermon on the Mount and the Gospel of John. We can leave that aside here. For Hegel's procedure is also suited and determined to present and interpret the path which leads from Kant's principle of autonomy over its incomplete interpretations to a system of morality which is free of contradiction. The moral consciousness is autonomous when its relation to the good is not to something foreign to it and also does not lead it into an obstruction or alienation of its freedom.

The first stage of his explication is the doctrine of respect for the law. For in such respect the good is not an object distinct from itself, but rather it is its own nature. With respect to autonomy, however, Kant's standpoint is in need of supplementation and thus completion. From Kant's point of view, "dependence on my self" takes the place of the determination of the will through something foreign to it.[37] This paradoxical formula portrays quite accurately the situation out of which the *Critique of Practical Reason* arose: the law is indeed a law of one's own will; but consciousness cannot identify itself with it unless it possesses possibilities other than those which Kant's doctrine allows. Thus the law determines the will at the same time from "within and yet from without." This, however, contradicts the inwardness of the good, which Kant himself taught, that the law must be able to be a law of *my* good and *my* will. Respect therefore requires a completion. It is the "being inclined to the good."

Hegel admits that Schiller had achieved the second stage in the development of the principle of autonomy. This does not exclude that his theory is distinguished from Schiller's precisely in terms of its presentation of the morality that is the object of such inclination. Hegel did accept Schiller's terminology. He is, however, perfectly aware that the term "inclination" to the good can only be used in an *analogical* sense and that Kant's psychology does not suffice to grasp what is intended by this term. Furthermore Hegel was not at all of the opinion that this second stage already supplied the complete concept of autonomy. The stages which lead to this completion can here be left out of consideration. They are equally stages of the development of moral *philosophy* and stages in the self-knowledge of moral consciousness. Thus in these stages the history of the interpretation of autonomy has become a process grounded in the moral consciousness itself. Hegel is not the first to arrive at this idea. Schiller had already made occasional use of it, if only in passing.[38] But with Hegel it is the foundation for a complete presentation of autonomy.

We should be reminded that Schiller certainly noticed a defect in Kant's moral theory and that he also saw the limits on the analysis of moral reality resulting from this defect. His objections to Kant indeed demanded a new systemization which provides the means to grasp better this reality; but these means are not themselves capable of accomplishing what needs to be done. And Schiller, who explicitly accepted Kant's foundations, was also unable to do so. The first attempts to provide a new foundation are in Hegel's youthful writings, which, however, contain many unsolved difficulties. Only later did Hegel arrive at a better-elaborated systemization that satisfied him. This systemization presupposes reflections which Fichte alone began.[39] I will only give a preliminary indication of these here.

The principle of autonomy demands that the various moral phenomena be understood as a structure of unity in difference. In the objections of Schiller and the young Hegel we have so far found only a demand for such an understanding. In Fichte's practical doctrine of science the attempt is made for the first time to go beyond this mere demand and exhibit the ground of the necessity of this unity.

His deduction takes the following path: morality is always a relationship of a rational being to itself. One must proceed from the rational being as a self in order to develop morality in its original coherence. One can thereby take for granted as admitted that a moral self is always aware of itself as *real*. Fichte arrives at this principle on the basis of his theoretical doctrine of science. But it can also be appealed to as evidence. For the discussion of "morality" includes that of "willing" and "acting," and that in turn the discussion of "effecting." The first question is: How can an "I" (self) know itself as real? "I" is always a unity of intending subjectivity and intended subjectivity. The second must be at the same time "real" subjectivity. That is only possible if it satisfies the further condition of being subjectivity as such. One must therefore think of something objective (real) which is *as such* also subjective. Such subjectivity is the *will*.

"Will" must be taken here in a quite determinate sense. One cannot mean by this term an act of the will with a determinate content. For such an act could not belong to the "I" itself in accordance with its own nature. It would only be an expression of its will in relation to certain objects. Because the will constitutes the reality of the "I" independent of whatever object it has, it can also not be determined as a mere possibility (as the capacity to will). It must have a content which is at the same time not distinguished from the "I." The will of the "I" qua "I" can thus only be a tendency to absolute independence. In it the "I" as subjectivity and the "I" as real are one.

As "I," however, the self must be able to *relate* to everything which it is, it must have knowledge of itself. For this reason, the second question is: How can the "I" know of its tendency to independence? The answer is clear when one considers that the thought of "I" already contains a subjective and an objective component, but that the "I" can never know this unity *as such*. For while it *is* this unity, it accomplishes this unity always as the determination of a subjective component by an objective one or vice-versa (this am I, I am this). Even the tendency which constitutes its reality can only be known by the "I" in this fashion. Knowledge of this tendency has a dual aspect: I know the real tendency to independence as *my own*. And I know my independence as a *real*, objective tendency.

Translated into the language of Kantian moral philosophy, the result of this deduction means that the independence of the "I" can only be found where *freedom* (subject) stands under a *law* (object) of independence, and a law (object) is only an object of the "I" as "I" if it is a law of freedom (of the subject). The discussion of autonomy already contains both moments *(nomos, heautos)*. For this reason it is a good interpretation of the moral being which knows of its self-activity.

We will not debate here the formal stringency of Fichte's deduction. Despite the usual opinion which in a more or less polite manner declares Fichte to be a sophist and his deductions en bloc to be fabrications, it is both a meaningful and a necessary task to examine them. For the idea on which they are based is well suited to overcoming the difficulties of Kant's moral philosophy by making comprehensible the necessity of those difficulties. The moral consciousness can only relate to itself insofar as it accomplishes a double process of identification with itself. The moral consciousness both distinguishes the fact of reason from itself as reason and unites these two as one. This doubling is unavoidable. It is, however, possible to avoid interpreting this doubling in the terminology of Kantian dualism, whereby the act of unification becomes unintelligible and the positive relation of the self to its moral nature can merely be asserted.

Still, the Idealistic reflection on the foundations of morality did not come to an end with this attempt at a proof—neither for Fichte himself nor for those who followed him. On the basis of the preceding discussion we can at least arrive at an indication of the grounds which furthered this reflection.

If Fichte's proof had been persuasive, it would have supplied the Kantian theory of respect for the law and the fact of reason with the foundation they lacked. When we treated Kant's principle of judging the good, we saw, however, that he also missed the intention of the moral consciousness with his treatment of the "duties of love." On the basis of Fichte's proof we can see how it is possible that the "I" knowingly merges with its own nature. But this would still not make it understandable how the "I" can encounter this nature in other human beings, i.e., how moral insight can be knowledge of law and at the same time knowledge of standing in a relationship with an other which regards him as an other. Such structures cannot be grasped on the basis of Fichte's early doctrine of science. This doctrine takes over the essentials of Kant's moral doctrine and merely prefaces it with foundational deductions.

For this reason Hegel had once more to change the principle of deduction. His philosophy of morality proceeds like Fichte's from the concept of the will. Fichte had incorporated the will as the objective side in the unity of the self. On the contrary, Hegel (for reasons that cannot be given here) was convinced that the will defined the self in its unity of subjectivity and object. The will, then, insofar as it has an object, must have itself as object. What the will as such wills is for this reason not the independence of the "I" to which it belongs, but the *existence* of the self-willing will, *itself* as its object, as reality.

This thought is the foundation on which Hegel developed that system of morality which he later called "philosophy of right."[40] We know that this system understands the concrete phenomena of moral life in a manner which is quite remote from the Kantian position. Our task is completed if it has become clear that this system as well still stands in the succession of Kant's principle of autonomy—a position which it rightly ascribes to itself.

Hegel attempted to make the Kantian thought of autonomy into the foundation of a philosophical interpretation of the Greek and also the Christian moral doctrine, and to turn its truth against Kant's worked-out ethics. It would be a stimulating task to examine the extent to which this attempt has been successful, and whether it has more or less claim to truth than the attempt undertaken by Saint Thomas with the means of Aristotle.

Equally important, however, is the question whether Kant's concept of autonomy, which was the foundation of his system, and which then on the basis of evident grounds set in motion the Idealistic movement, is still preserved and understood at the end of that movement, or whether Hegel's system, which concludes the reflection about this principle, does not at the same time misunderstand it. Hegel's most important students were of this opinion. The effective power of the Kantian thought of autonomy has not been extinguished with the end of speculative Idealism.

4

Identity and Objectivity: An Inquiry into Kant's Transcendental Deduction

Translated by Jeffrey Edwards

I. Difficulties in the Interpretation of Kant

We do not yet know how philosophical texts are to be interpreted. The mastery that a classic figure can demonstrate over his basic plan is in inverse ratio to the significance of his achievement, to the profundity of the changes wrought within traditional theory by his investigations, and to the comprehensiveness and integrative depth of that plan. Innovations of theory demand in each case a new theoretical language. The connections demonstrated in it serve to solve problems which must remain unsolved within the horizon common to all previous theories. The critical consequences and theoretically formative perspectives yielded by such connections can be surveyed at an early stage. But it is never the case that a newly discovered connection can be adequately elucidated from the very outset. To comprehend what constitutes that connection, to grasp what elements come together in it and ascertain how they do so—this itself becomes a new task for philosophical thought. The discoverer cannot have a satisfactory answer at his immediate disposal. At best, he will seek it out with the same lifelong perseverance with which Plato sought to determine the essence of the ideas that he himself had introduced into philosophy. The theory and its new language do not bask in the light that they shed upon the questions they are intended to answer.

Hence, we have to reckon with the circumstance that in the classical texts of philosophy the most important (because ultimately foundational) lines of thought and argument are those that give rise to the greatest difficulties. This is not at all primarily due to the difficulty of the subject matter; nor certainly is it because the discoverers of theoretical perspectives are philosophical heroes of incommensurable insight and intelligence. It is due to the internal makeup of the texts themselves.

To date, there are three procedures of commentary: the paraphrastic-expository commentary, the genetic commentary, and argumentative reconstruction. In exposition the textual inventory of an entire work is summoned up for scrutiny. Genetic commentary sets forth the philosopher's perspective upon his own opus. It shows, therefore, the difficulties and issues from which this work emerged, whereby the commentator must guard against describing the preliminary stages of the theory by means of the concepts intrinsic to the fully developed theory. Expository commentaries are the indispensable minimum for all understanding; genetic commentaries are highly valuable in establishing an independent relationship with a text, for they make intelligible those motives which first brought the author upon the path to his discovery. However, both these forms of commentary demonstrate in equal manner a deficiency: neither of them is able to penetrate the conceptual and argumentative fabric of the text itself. Expository commentary presupposes that this is on principle accessible without restriction in the articulation given by the author. Genetic commentary does indeed bring to light the reasons that paved the way to the text, but it necessarily comes to a halt before the principal texts of the mature theory.

Only the reconstructive procedure actually attempts to lay open the text itself. It first assigns definitions that make ambiguous concepts clear-cut. It then isolates premises and arguments in texts of unarticulated complexity. Setting out from these, it seeks independently to arrive at conclusions corresponding as far as possible to those drawn in the text. Reconstruction along these lines is thus in point of fact the translation of a text into the schema of a truth-functionally conclusive derivation.

It can be affirmed of reconstruction that it really does take into consideration the indispensable requirement placed upon a philosophical text, viz., that it must lead to well-grounded conclusions. But if it is correct to maintain that the innovative texts are precisely those lacking in clarity, then one has to discern in reconstruction merely the preliminary work for an interpretation and not the interpretation itself. It substitutes for the texts the best, the most insightful readings available to the commentator. But it does not lay open the text to the degree in which one can be sure that the results yielded by the reconstruction were really operative considerations in the formation of the text.

Arguments, of course, can also be implicitly present in texts in many different ways. Philosophical authors often pursue materially relevant connections without having them entirely or even incidentally as an explicit topic. A reconstruction can for that reason find some textual basis even when it employs premises that are nowhere suggested in the text under consideration. A reconstruction is not, however, fundamentally in a position also to grasp those peculiarities of a text by virtue of which it is vague and unclear. When a text thematizes various matters at once and in such a way that their mutual relations remain indeterminate, that does not mean that it only entangles and confuses them. Although the text does not make transparent the pertinent relations that actually exist between these matters, it can nonetheless have such relations in view. That, of course, can lead to the circumstance that conclusions are drawn within the text which are indeed yielded by various aspects of the matter at issue, without, however, there being the prospect of any supervision over the arguments at work in the text. Consequently, a text can even contain conclusions having no visible support or include fallacious inferences without the point in question and its foundational significance being truly compromised as a result. As distinguished from expository and genetic explanation, reconstruction cannot even allude to such historical deposits within a theory. At best, it can enter these into the account of the author under discussion in order to lessen a negative balance, a balance which requires that interest be paid in proportion to the amount in which the actual outcome of textual reconstruction remains in arrears with respect to the demands of the reconstructive method.

If, however, a text is not in command of its own theoretical perspective, and is thus also not in a position to draw all the distinctions that need to be drawn, the result can be the superimposition of various courses of argument in one and the same sequence of sentences. The interpretation would first have to determine which one of these can be made internally consistent and which one remains defective even when fully articulated. Moreover, in consideration of the overall content of the theory it would also have to further evaluate which procedure comes closest to the actual intentions of the author as well as the extent to which it gains ascendancy within a given text. To the extent that an interpretation accomplishes all this, it makes the text transparent and brings its theoretical potential to full fruition.

Ordinary language is a medium of very limited power for interpretations such as these. Still, it provides the benefit of productive vagueness for theories that have not yet achieved complete clarification. One can very easily let diverse lines of reasoning slip into a given formulation. But the interpretation must still be able to clearly mark out their common presence. The more a text implicitly encompasses, the greater will be the difficulties for anyone who intends to bring its compendiousness to light; and these are difficulties that arise as a result of the linear form of one's interpretive language. Even the interpretive form of reconstruction must often make use of the form of presentation which, since Aristotle, has been developed for relations of logical dependency. The mere affinity between topics and theorems, however, cannot be portrayed in this way. And it does not allow one to distinguish the various degrees to which thoughts which remain implicit are capable of bearing consequences. As odd as it may sound, it would make good sense to develop a new system of notation in support of verbal interpretations. This system would combine the advantages of the present system of notation for logical dependencies with other elements that find their most likely parallel in the present notational system for music: They would be notations for the affinity between thoughts going into one and the same sentence.

Considerations such as these may make comprehensible why—a quarter of a millennium after his birth, almost two hundred years after the publication of the *Critique of Pure Reason,* and despite the never-interrupted continuity of labor on his opus—our ability to interpret the basic texts of Kant's critical philosophy remains far below all legitimate expectations. Kant himself always complained that he was not in a position to eliminate the obscurities in the fundamental passages of his theoretical philosophy. He at first thought that he could achieve complete clarification through the efforts of a decade. Then he believed himself to have found for the second edition of his *Critique* an easier and more accessible manner of presentation which reduced to a minimum the need for in-depth investigations into the ultimate principles of the system. Finally, he advised that the *Critique* derives its persuasiveness not from investigations that pry into its foundations but from its application in the theory of natural science and morality, as well as in its comprehensive diagnosis of the deficiencies in the doctrinal edifice of metaphysics. Kant found the "apices" of the transcendental deduction, as well the "critique of the subject" upon which they rest, too strenuous for his conceptual powers, weakened as they were by old age. He also considered them dangerous for anyone who happens to embark upon them exclusively or even merely preferentially. Whoever does not restrain himself in view of the consequences of an approach can be driven in almost any direction whatever and will quickly lose his bearings with respect to the entire complex of humanly possible knowledge. Warnings like these, which Kant addressed directly to his most eminent followers, viz., Reinhold and Fichte, were naturally a waste of breath. From the time of his Rousseauistic turn Kant himself had ascribed an ancillary role to transcendental philosophy: It is necessary for the defence of the essential interests of humankind, all of which presuppose that the idea of freedom can be justified. But the person who to this purpose discovered and set foot upon, but did not fully exploit, an entirely new field of investigation attracted those who were theorists out of passion as well as those who wanted to see full light shed upon the contours of the terrain as seen by Kant himself.

Nearly all theorists of importance since Kant have sought to establish a relation to Kant through their own investigations. In this endeavor the prevailing procedures of interpretation have naturally been exposition as well as reconstruction carried out in the vicinity of one's own position. The intense interest in Kant's work has also called forth a genetic form of scholarship which, especially in Germany, has yielded important results in the course of what is now the better part of a century. It is this research which has made largely accessible the documents from Kant's work and doctrine, though at times in unsuccessful competition with the fires of war. Until now, however, Kant's basic texts have become only marginally more fathomable. Expository commentaries, even those extending to several volumes, have not been able to penetrate the conceptual fabric in which numerous lines of argumentation indistinctly overlap one another.

The literature on Kant from the English-speaking world, which has been subject to rapid growth since about 1960, has brought real progress to this state of affairs. It originated in a new interest in procedures of what can be called "transcendental argumentation," an interest which for its part was an internal consequence of Anglophone philosophical debate and the increasingly acute criticism of the philosophical particularism of Austin and Wittgenstein.[1] Its significance, though, has to be explained by the fact that since the beginning of the century Anglophone philosophy has ascribed a previously unknown importance to the powers of conceptual analysis and to exercising analytic control over arguments. Both these factors have been brought to bear upon the reading of Kant's texts, and, for the first time, without an aim toward their destruction, but rather on account of systematic proximity to Kant's position and, consequently, with the intention of finding good sense in his words.

But the success of even this new impulse toward a better understanding of the theoretical processes at hand in Kant's texts has been limited as a result of a number of contingent circumstances: the English-speaking authors remain at a measured distance from the actual movement of Kant's arguments because for the most part they do not have Kant's language at their command, and they are able to survey only a small portion of the thousands of pages of Kant's publications, manuscripts, and notes. Kant wrote at a mature age after a lengthy series of failed attempts at constructing a theory and after a comprehensive analysis of the conceptual configurations of an epoch of philosophy that has been assigned to oblivion by his work. He constantly makes implicit reference to both these factors. Moreover, intent as he was upon not losing his readers, he kept his texts in as brief and, indeed, as abbreviated a form as possible. The texts of an author such as this can be pursued in real proximity only if one is sure of always being able to decide when one is staying within the boundaries of his viewpoint and when one is beginning to substitute these with other (and possibly more convincing) ones. Kant's fundamental ideas will become intelligible only when one is able to bring the weight of argument analysis fully to bear upon textual analysis. If that is not accomplished, the result is philosophical investigations which demonstrate kinship with Kant's thinking and are implemented with Kantian quotations. But Kant's historical attempts at formulating a theory must remain in the semi-darkness from which no one has yet been able to draw them out.

The ensuing investigation can find its proper place in carrying out such a task, but it cannot complete that task. By itself, it is not sufficient to disclose fully the content of a single paragraph in which Kant attempted to expound upon his doctrine of the fundamental conditions of cognition. Still, it is intended to show, in the context of providing support for this theory, a nexus of deliberations that Kant actually had in view. This nexus does not cover the entire range of Kant's basic doctrine. It is therefore only an element, not the whole, of an interpretation of his transcendental deduction. Among other things, it will for this reason have to remain an open question to what degree that nexus came to dominate the texts of the *Critique of Pure Reason*. It needs to be disclosed because it has remained undetected until now, even though without it Kant's most fundamental theses lack any support whatever.

Neither will it be decided whether the arguments that Kant himself could provide are, according to the standards of contemporary philosophy, merely understandable or rather promising and perhaps even adequate. Nevertheless, the peculiarities of Kant's argumentative procedures must be clearly brought out. The authors of the best books on Kant of the past ten years are unclear about them and are, on that account, not even in a position to comprehend unambiguously the status of Kant's theory and its fundamental concepts in comparison with more recent theories of a different kind but with related aims.[2]

II. Object and Judgment

As is generally affirmed, Kant's theory of knowledge establishes the thesis that we can know objects of experience only if we make use of concepts and presuppose principles for all empirical employment, these being themselves not derivable from experience. Furthermore, this theory claims that the necessity which accrues to such concepts and principles can be grounded in the constitution of that self-consciousness which Kant calls the "transcendental unity of apperception."

The apriorism intrinsic to this doctrine of the conditions of possible experience is open to two objections, given the doctrine's systematic make-up. If persuasive, each of these objections would by itself be strong enough to destroy the particular position assumed by Kant. One objection disputes the conception that our knowledge of objects of experience is subject to any presuppositions that cannot be grasped as arising out of experience and its genesis, a genesis which is dependent upon empirical conditions. The other objection places in doubt the notion that a priori presuppositions of our knowledge can (to the extent that one is at all willing to grant them) be clarified with reference to aspects of self-consciousness.

Every interpretation of Kant that seeks to exhaust the potential of Kantian theory must attempt to show the strongest arguments that can, within the framework of Kantian premises, be directed against such objections. It must further show how these arguments are evidenced in Kant's own texts, which, as has already been stated, speak in a merely thetic manner at the crucial junctures, or at best announce and presume argumentative procedures instead of carrying them out. In what follows, this will be done in view of the outlines of Kant's doctrine of objectivity and then in connection with his doctrine of self-consciousness qua principle of identity.

Kant calls an investigation that justifies an empirical cognition—one shown beforehand to rest upon a priori principles—the "transcendental deduction" of that cognition. I will discuss only the most important premises of this deduction.[3] The order of sequence in which this takes place should be understood with reference to Kant's more extended program of proof: Of the two lines of exposition corresponding to the aforementioned objections, we shall begin with the analysis of objectivity, which can be expected to have the more limited repercussions within the framework of a transcendental deduction. We shall then move on to the analysis of the identity of self-consciousness in relation to which it must eventually be determined whether Kant's epistemological program can be made transparent and be sufficiently grounded. The analysis of the concept of an object by itself is in fact enough to refute the empiricist theory of the genesis of knowledge. It is also a necessary condition for successfully justifying the claim to objectivity that is made for our knowledge; the investigation of self-consciousness must itself have recourse to an independent analysis of the concept of the object. Still, the conception that experience as the real knowledge of objects is in general possible can, on Kant's terms, be adequately justified only by proceeding from self-consciousness.

1. Preliminary Considerations on the Concept of an Object

One of Kant's major achievements is to have seized for the first time upon some of the most important aspects of the problematic engendered by the concept of an object. This problematic becomes evident to Kant in connection with one of the elementary assumptions that he shares with the theory of knowledge of his time, namely, that the primary occurrences of the real for cognition are presentations of simple qualities in diffuse spatial juxtaposition. These presentations are thought of as events, which are, however, supposed to consist in nothing other than a particular incident in which a sensible quality is realized or instantiated. In Kant's language, which comprehends all that is cognizably real as "that which is given to the subject," these presentations are therefore termed "sensations."

It is easy to see that a relation to objects cannot take effect through such occurrences alone. Regarding both what an object is and the attitude that makes possible its cognition, conditions are included in the thought of the object which cannot be satisfied by the presentations of sensible qualities as such. Whereas objects must satisfy certain requirements of constancy, a cognition that can be called "objective" can come about only through the successful application of criteria that allow a distinction to be drawn between objects which are merely putatively given and objects which are really given. There is a connection between these two conditions that will soon become evident.

We first conceive as constant the relations between everything that is an object. We would not consider representations which under any conditions whatever occur or fail to occur representations that represent objects. Representations of objects are rather those representations that repeatedly occur—and are in principle repeatable—under determinate conditions. Corresponding to this is the fact that all particular objects which we become acquainted with in such representations are situated in generally characterizable contexts and processes that are in this respect to be understood as "regulated."

Even more essential is the fact that we also attribute constancy to the particular objects themselves. And indeed, we attribute constancy in a sense that at first appears to differ from that of regulation: We hold that objects are those particulars to which continuity in existence is fundamentally attributable. These particulars can be distinguished from occurrences that successively supervene upon or in them without it happening that for any one object another object steps in to take its place. Correspondingly, we can come back to the same object under altered conditions. The cognitive setting and the multiplicity of occurrences through which an object is presented to us can change to a great extent while the object of cognition remains the same.

Such objects obviously can never be mere single representations of the kind of sensations which, according to Kant, make up the first basis of empirical knowledge. Sensory representations can only occur and vanish. It makes no sense to assume that the same sensory representations recur. Once gone, they can be replaced by others of the same kind. Hence, if objects are, fundamentally, constant particulars that can be given in different ways, then it must be inferred that the difference between them and the simple representations of sensation is the type of difference which holds between two distinct dimensions. Representations cannot themselves be the actual objects. Rather, they serve merely to indicate these objects. Even groups of simple presentations by means of which an object comes to be given to us in a determinate cognitive setting are still, in principle, to be distinguished from that object itself. And this distinction remains in effect despite the fact that objects of empirical cognition can always be present, and known, only on the grounds of sensible presentations.

In view of the fact that sensible presentations—and these alone—constitute that which is primarily given, one needs to ask how a relation to objects can take effect at all. The path toward the only possible answer to this question becomes clear when one takes into account a further factor which likewise enters into our concept of an object: We must reckon with the fact that simple representations occur which cannot be assigned to objects and which we must therefore deem "mere" representations. Since these representations are just as much primary occurrences as the representations of objects, we can distinguish between them and the latter only by assuming, and then ascertaining, that representations which indicate objects occur in definite combinations and ruled connections to which "mere" representations are not subject.

It is only on the strength of such combinations that objects can be assigned to the primary occurrences and that the representations of objects can be distinguished from mere representations. And it is, hence, only with respect to regulated appearances that the very thought of an object itself has an articulate meaning.

If it has been shown in this way that important requisites of the familiar concept of an object cannot be satisfied in the dimension of sensations as such, then the following can equally be shown by the same token. If one admits at all the distinction between sensible presentations and objects, then one must derive and elucidate important features of that familiar concept: If objects differ from presentations, they can only be determined by the manner in which presentations occur in combination with one another. For this reason, one can never think of objects as being simple entities beyond appearances. A *multiplicity* of different presentations must always be ascribed to them. In this sense objects either are themselves complexes or, in any event, are complexly characterizable particulars. Because a distinction is to be drawn between them and what is given, it is in principle also possible that the same objects can come to be given through changeable multiplicities of combined sensible presentations. In a different way than these presentations themselves, they can remain the same throughout all change in their mode of givenness. Insofar as many representations bear upon that one factor which is an object, they pertain to those aspects of the object that can be called its "properties" or its "states." Objects are therefore constant conditions of unity in respect of properties and states. In the sense of this formal description, they can be comprehended as "things" or as "substances."

It has thus turned out that the second sense of constancy, which is co-constitutive of the idea of the object, is but a variant of the first: The constancy of relations between different objects and the continuity of the particular object are both equally cases of the ruled combination of sensible presentations. Not only are objects related to each other in a regulated manner, but they are also quite simply defined in terms of complexes of properties and states, complexes which for their part are to be thought solely with reference to the regulated relations effected between them. Both meanings are covered equally by Kant's preliminary and still nonspecific definition of object: "An object is that in the concept of which the manifold of a given intuition is united" (B 137).

In the same connection, one can explain the sense in which we are able to assign to a cognition the property of being "objective." Since objects are not pure presentations, and since one must contend with "mere" representations as well as the presentations of objects, a cognition of objects is a real and not a merely putative cognition only when (i) presentations are assigned to objects in the right combination and (ii) "mere" representations are methodically excluded in the assignment of these presentations. The attitude of the knower toward possible cognition can also be termed "objective" when the knower abstracts from her own interests in order to understand what is real.[4] But the knower can attain a cognition that is itself characterizable as "objective" only on the grounds of the successful differentiation between present objects and those presentations which are mere representations.

2. Functions of a priori Synthesis?

To anyone with Kant's epistemological project clearly in view it will have become apparent how easy it is to move to the Kantian doctrine of synthesis from an analysis of the meaning of talk about objects—insofar, that is, as this analysis also accepts the thesis of the data-sensualism of our cognition. According to that doctrine, the relation of our cognition to objects issues from an activity of our consciousness which combines given representations in conformity with certain necessary rules. Assuming that our most elementary mode of representation—intuition—is an indeterminate multiplicity and sequence of simple particular sensations, connections between these sensations of what is given cannot be simply gathered up, as it were. The sensations appear additionally in a form (that of space), by virtue of which each of these elements can be presented in a likewise indeterminate multiplicity of combinations with other elements. The form as such is not sufficient for there to be determinate relations between the elements. Thus, the assumption becomes unavoidable that such relations in any event cannot come about without an activity of the knower being brought into play with reference to the given manifold. All identifications of regulated configurations and sequences, which pertain to the essence of cognition, are preceded by a process through which such combinations are first produced in consciousness. And since objects are complexes of simple representations, objects of intuition can be yielded only when a type of synthesis is completed which is equally the condition of the possible cognition of objects. The act which precedes the ascertainment of determinate relations between sensations is at the same time the way in which objects take form out of the diffuse manifold. Not only experiential knowledge but also the objects of experience have their origin in a single activity (B 197).

Kant infers further that empirical knowledge and the empirical relation to an object which ensues from synthetic activity can be brought about only when certain foundational conditions and basic rules are available to cognition, by virtue of which data can be brought into relation to one another. In those conditions it is already determined what the basic types are according to which sensations can be synthesized into objects. Kant calls these rules "functions," which is the same as to say "fundamental concepts of relations." They are supposed to be specified completely in the table of "categories." Categories as functions are aspects under which the synthesis of given representations into objects is carried out. Inasmuch as categories can be specified prior to all experience, one must assume that they can also be employed independent of any particularities of what is given; and thereby without restriction and with reference to everything that can possibly come to be given.

To the extent that they pertain solely to the classification of the manifold and synthesis according to determinate concepts of relation, considerations such as these are certainly inferred correctly from Kant's most elementary premises. Yet they are without conclusive force for Kant's actual program of proof. If one accepts the standpoint of data-sensualism, then the acceptance of a synthetic activity of consciousness becomes unavoidable as well. This is an activity which for its part cannot be completed without aspects of unity that define the mode of combination. This chain of inference is already quite extensive, but it still leaves two factors entirely undecided: It leaves unsettled whether the relation to objects comes about at all by necessity in accordance with rules of synthesis. Could it not be that we might find ourselves at least partially limited to the ascertainment of simple data which we cannot subject to rules, inasmuch as they do not lend themselves to being so subjected? Furthermore, in the event that our cognition is able to lay hold of objects with a view toward the manifoldness of the data, it is still possible that we extract the rules by which we think such objects from the factual inventory of appearances themselves. Certainly, it has been shown that objects cannot be taken up intuitively, and it can be inferred from this that an object-relation can be brought about only by an activity of synthesis of what is given. But with this the broader thesis is not yet established, viz., that the rules of the classification of the manifold that constitute the fundamental structure of all objects are also, together with the structure of the synthesis-activity, fixed prior to all experience and independent of it. It remains conceivable that what is established

Identity and Objectivity 135

a priori in this activity is restricted to the ability to explore possible uniformities and to the formation of unspecified concepts of unity. What uniformities are found and what concepts of unity can as a result be framed would be left to empirical circumstances, among which are to be counted the factual dispositions of the individual to grasp similarities. Under such conditions an a priori science of the basic constitution of objects would be impossible. The thought of a regulated process precedes every cognition of an object. However, the determinate content of the rules can be derived from actually observed sequences and configurations of data, and this is so without there being any restriction of these rules to minimal conditions fixed prior to all experience.

When Kant found that necessity accrues to the thought of the relation of our cognition to objects, he believed both of the following to be precluded: that objectivity establishes itself in a merely de facto manner, and that its conditions, viz., the unifying concepts of rules for complexes of sensations, are themselves factual discoveries in terms of their content. Just as it is the case for the basic rules that define the fundamental constitution of all objects, necessity ought to be inherent in the thought and the constituting of objectivity. If one cannot make persuasive the actual progress of the argument that advances to these assertions from the analysis of the meaning of objectivity and from the postulate that there is some kind of synthesis—if, therefore, the delineated alternatives to Kant's theoretic claim cannot be conclusively eliminated—then the position of David Hume, which Kant wanted to refute, is in principle confirmed. Taken by itself, the demonstration that objects are functional concepts remains but a preliminary move in the endeavor to ground an apriorism in the doctrine of objectivity as it was conceived by Kant.

3. Properties of Judgment-Structure

The analysis of the meaning of objectivity does not yet remove the deficiencies in the attempt to ground the necessity of the relation to objects as well as the content of the valid basic rules that apply to this relation. It would seem possible to remedy these deficiencies by direct recourse to the highest principle of Kant's epistemology: the unifying principle of transcendental apperception. The appeal to this principle, one which must in any event bear a heavy burden of proof, is permissible only when all possibilities of supplementary argumentation have been explored beforehand. That holds good all the more when one sets out from the circumstance that an argumentative procedure which takes the unity of apperception as its point of departure cannot avoid laying claim to a number of results which, if they can be secured at all, must be obtained independently in an investigation of the conditions of the relation to an object.

In Kant's analysis of objectivity there is an element that has not yet been treated. It is an element that must even be regarded as fundamental to this analysis, one reason being that it is that element which cannot be substituted in an investigation that proceeds from self-consciousness.[5]

At several important junctures in his reflections Kant makes reference to the structure of judgment. In an excursive note in the preface to the *Metaphysical Principles of Natural Science* he even announces that the possibility of experience can be comprehended "almost by a single inference from the precisely determined definition of a judgment in general."[6] This definition portrays a judgment as "an act by which given representations first become cognitions of an object." The definition of judgment is thereby brought into the immediate vicinity of the concept of an object.

In finding this argument Kant saw one of the most important advances in his understanding along the path from the first to the second edition of the *Critique of Pure Reason*. It is true that the first edition of the *Critique* already offers a theory of judgment upon which the doctrine of the categories is built (A 67ff.). But it was only at a much later date that Kant set down in writing his thoughts on the relations between the structure of judgment and the structure of an object in a way that showed him to be striving toward greater clarity. Thus, one can expect that the argumentation which "almost" amounts to a single inference will not lend itself to being made transparent as easily as is suggested by the language quickened by the joy of discovery which Kant employed when he first discerned the new options available for supporting his position.

Kant's definition of judgment alludes simultaneously to at least three properties of propositions by which we arrive at knowledge of objects. It is crucial to distinguish between these and to establish which of them is of fundamental significance.

3.1 Judgment's Claim to Objectivity

It emerges most clearly from the texts, particularly from the second edition of the *Critique of Pure Reason*, that when Kant speaks of objectivity in connection with judgment he has in mind the truth-claims of judgments [*Geltungsanspruch des Urteils*]. Every proposition [*Satz*][7] can be asserted, at which point there arises the claim that it is true, which means that it is distinguished from merely accidental or arbitrarily given representations. But then criteria must also be specified according to which a decision can be made as to whether the assertion legitimately lays its claim to truth, for it is only with reference to such criteria that the distinction between an assertion and the mere association of arbitrarily given thoughts obtains a definite sense. And it is only in this way that the essential characteristic of a judgment, in which several terms are employed, can be distinguished from the simultaneous representation of the meaning of these terms, a meaning which can be forthcoming on any occasion and without any implication of there being an obligation regarding its correctness. Kant seizes upon this circumstance terminologically when he says that the form of judgment encompasses the idea that the merely subjective unity of representations can be distinguished from the objective unity of the same (B 139ff.; reflection 5934). "This is what is intended by the copula 'is'. . . to distinguish the objective unity of given representations from the subjective unity" (B 142).

The meaning of "objective" as employed in sentences like these might correspond to that of the predicate "objective," which applies to a cognition that, by methodically excluding those representations which are "mere" representations, grasps such real objects as come to be given in a manifold of representations. If this impression were confirmed, then the analysis of the difference between the combination of representations and the meaning of judgment would already ensure the necessity of the reference of all cognition to complexly characterizable objects. From a simple consideration, however, one can see that Kant's epistemological concept of object is not to be obtained in this way directly from the definition of judgment. Any statement, whatever its type, lays claim to being an objective and not a merely subjective unity of representations. Thus, statements about, for instance, logical relations between propositions in which no reference at all is made to objects of experience, and statements characterizing single, undifferentiated sensible presentations are all judgments which pretend to be true [*gültig*] and, in this sense, objective. Their claims are understood in accordance with various criteria, e.g., by the employment of rules of inference or by the determinability of the use of demonstratives and the availability of criteria of similarity between sensible qualities. Objects, which are intuitive manifolds brought under rules of unity, are of no significance for understanding such a sense of "objective." According to this sense of the term, every judgment must be deemed "objective" insofar as it has been formulated in view of the criteria of correctness relevant to the type of judgment to which it belongs.

It thus turns out that the meaning of "objective" employed in the definition of judgment does indeed have a property in common with the objectivity that one can ascribe to empirical cognition: both are opposed to mere representations. But the representations from whose influence objective cognition must be freed are sensible presentations without any possible reference to an object, whereas the subjective factor, which is opposed to the objective unity of all judgments, is the associative combination of thoughts without reference to criteria of correctness. In both cases rules stand in opposition to unregulated incidents. Objective cognition is also a special case of the objective unity demonstrated by all judgments. The objectivity peculiar to it, however, cannot be obtained as an implication of the formal objectivity attributable to statements in general. From the circumstance that all judgments entail criteria of validity it does not follow that any criteria of validity are available for judgments about objects beyond presentations and that, therefore, such judgments are at all possible. (Much less does it follow that they are necessarily possible.) The reference of our empirical cognition to objects as specified by Kant's concept of an object is consequently not to be obtained from the objective unity of judgment.

It remains to be mentioned that the possibility of a procedure of proof begins to emerge with reference to the criteria of validity contained in the definition of the sense of judgment, provided that one already assumes that empirical cognition aims at objects beyond presentations which are fundamentally transitory. Each of these objects would have to be distinguishable from others of its type. It would have to be further possible to come back to the same object under changed conditions. Since Frege, semantic theory has emphasized generally the constitutive significance of criteria of identity for the notion of the particular. One could investigate whether a particular that is merely the instance of a simple quality and that can be characterized by nothing more than this quality is at all accessible to identification. If it could be shown that only complex particulars allow for identification, then it would also be shown that we must ascribe to objects (which are not presentations) the basic constitution of an object advocated by Kant.

Inherently, an investigation which would adhere to this argumentative procedure is highly promising, but in the context of an interpretation of Kant's fundamental arguments it can be omitted. For although the literature on Kant from the English-speaking world lays great emphasis upon the traces of such considerations in the *Critique,* it is nonetheless manifest that Kant wanted to grasp the connection between the structure of judgment and the fundamental conditions of objectivity much more directly than such an investigation would allow. It is solely in the chapters of the

Identity and Objectivity 139

Critique following the "Transcendental Deduction" (particularly in the "Analytic of Principles") that there can be found considerations which should be taken in conjunction with investigations concerning conditions of identification. However, they proceed on the assumption that the apriorism of the doctrine of synthesis as well as of the concept of object has already been grounded. And they remain entirely independent of the theoretical expectation characteristic of Kant's foundational idea: that from the structure of the statement as such, particularly from the structure of the subject-predicate statement-form, grounds can be obtained in compliance with which the claim to objectivity conveyed by judgments of experience can be made good only with reference to complex objects, objects which prove to be dependent upon rules of combination for the given manifold.

3.2 Judgment as Synthesis

Considering the application of the class of statements about objects, one might conjecture that the structure of judgment as such allows something to be inferred about the basic constitution of objects, in which case one's attention can be directed most easily to an aspect of the form of judgment which Plato had already maintained to have fundamental significance for a theory of cognition: the form of the subject-predicate proposition includes a connection between concepts. And since all other forms of judgment presuppose this type of proposition, they too are to be thought only under the inclusion of concepts of synthesis. Certainly, one may not define the statement as such as a combination of concepts (B 140/10). Neither in isolation nor in combination with one another do concepts assert anything. The proper character of the statement lies in its establishing claims to objectivity. Yet it remains characteristic of statements, especially elementary statements, that their claim to objectivity comes about *by means of* a particular combination of concepts. This combination has been called the "basic combination."[8]

With reference to this property of the form of the elementary statement it might now be said that nothing can be the object of statements in which there are not to be found at least two different contents or aspects. For in such elementary statements of subject-predicate form an object falling under the subject concept must be addressed as a particular in a way that it can be distinguished from others. By means of the predicate it is then characterized by a property that it can have in common with others. It seems that elements must go into the meaning of the subject concept that cannot be identical with the meaning of the predicate concept. It would thereby remain a matter of indifference whether it is at all possible to think of the subject without ascribing to it the predicate or whether the predication identifies only a property or a state which exists de facto. In any event, the predicate must be attributed to an object of which something must be thought that (i) is different from what is thought in the predicate concept and (ii) has also already been thought.

If it is to remain within the Kantian framework this consideration must be distinguished from those other considerations which aim at the identification of objects. It can only advocate that the meaning of the subject concept is not exhausted by the meaning of the predicate concept attributed to it. This thesis seems to be strong enough of itself, for statements with the same concept in subject and predicate positions can only be sensibly asserted in rare rhetorical contexts. But then they are merely apparent deviations from the basic structure of judgment, a structure which includes the combination of concepts with different meanings.

The reference to the elementary judgment as the basic combination is, however, insufficient for ascertaining whether the referents of its subject concepts must be complex objects. The individuality of an object can be determined by relations to other objects in connection with deictic expressions. One can point to something given or fix its location in relation to other objects. Demonstratives and relational expressions appertaining to space and time can be comprehended only with considerable effort as predicates, and Kant did not want to admit them as predicates in any event. No particular object can be characterized as what it is by means of them. But we obviously cannot speak of an object that has no characterizing features. Therefore everything locatable must be characterizable in terms of something other than merely the location it occupies. That is, it must be characterizable by genuine predicates. Kant's thesis about objects as syntheses requires, however, that objects always be comprehended as characterized by various predicates. And this thesis appears to be insupportable precisely when it becomes apparent that the meaning of the expression in the subject position can be fixed by demonstratives and relational determinations. If this is possible, then it seems also to be fundamentally conceivable that an object can be characterized by only one predicate.

As always in cases such as these, one can make the point clear by means of the example of a datum in perceptual space. Let us assume that invariably one and only one determinate point of color remains in our field of vision and that it changes only its position. Its conspicuous and singular role might perhaps provide occasion to give it a name. By this name it could be made thematic in judgments in the subject position without there being, for that reason, more than just one possibility of characterizing it by means of a predicate. This predicate could, for instance, be aimed at a color which in principle could belong to many objects, but which actually has always belonged to only one object. In this way its singular character would correspond to its singular role in the field of vision without being derivable from that role.

It is no accident that this example gives the impression of artificiality, for there are grounds which really do establish that objects of singular character are, for us, unthinkable. As soon as all the conditions are specified which necessarily apply to the relation to objects, such an example can no longer be construed. Furthermore, it can easily be shown that objects which are extensive magnitudes, and are perceivable as such, must invariably be comprehended as complexly characterizable entities. The purpose of the example is merely to make clear that when judgment is portrayed *exclusively* as a combination of concepts, no conclusion can be drawn which implies that objects are complexes of properties.

If this can already be shown for elementary subject-predicate propositions, then it is all the more accurate to say that it is solely by fallacious inference that one can conclude, from the general nature of subject-predicate propositions as combinations of concepts, that only complex objects are objects at all. After all, predications arise also from the fact that simple properties are classified. It can be said of the color predicate of our privileged point in the field of vision that it is one of the shades of red, shades which in their turn are shades of color and are, in addition, optical phenomena. By means of such predicates of predicates the classified object does not become a complex object. From the fact that in a judgment a higher-order concept is related as a predicate to a subordinate concept, and is thereby indirectly related to an object, nothing whatsoever is established about the form of that object. Kant incorporated passages seemingly affected by this misunderstanding into the introduction to the metaphysical deduction of the categories (A 68/69).

That properties and objects with their properties can at all be classified already presupposes, of course, a context of unity among concepts. This possibility presupposes further that objects need not be characterized only in each actual experience. Were every datum incomparable with others, and were a thought which holds for us framable solely in the presence of that datum, then concepts belonging to an ordering system could not be obtained. Our judging would then be limited on the one hand to isolated predications and, on the other, to purely formal operating. Given the possibility of thoughts about what is given that go beyond the most elementary statements, it is already guaranteed that the world cannot be mere chaos and that experience necessarily includes regularity. However, this regularity consists only in the circumstance that in unforeseeable sequences appearances arise which can be coordinated with certain other appearances as members of natural classes. But this is possible even when regularities in the flow of appearances or constant combinations of data are never observable. A world that is not chaos need not also be a world of things existing under laws. But then it follows even less from the classifiability of what is given that the rules guaranteeing a constant order among appearances must—as far as there are any such rules—be discernible prior to all actual experience.

A line of argument which remains within the boundaries of the Platonic conception of judgment as synthesis thus does not suffice to eliminate any of the doubts going back to David Hume. If one is unable to discern more about the particular properties of synthesis in judgment, then judgment could remain restricted merely to the ascertainment of simple characterizing features and sequences of sensations. It would have to remain an open question whether these sequences are subsumed under rules; and the rules actually to be discovered would have to be drawn from experience.

3.3 Subject of Judgment and Object

For the reasons just given one must return to a third aspect of the form of judgment, an aspect which Kant has in mind *together* with judgment's claim to objectivity and its formal synthetic character when he designates judgment an act, one through which representations come to be cognitions of an object or are brought to the objective unity of self-consciousness. Of course, in the work which he himself brought to print Kant never did expound upon this feature as a topic of its own and in abstraction from other aspects of his work. Nevertheless, only this feature can lead his theory of objectivity, as Kant conceived it, to success; which is to say, by means of "almost a single inference" as a consequence of the form of judgment.

(a) Judgments do not have to apply immediately to given occurrences. They can also attribute predicates to classes of objects. This presupposes, however, that judgments can also be made about particular objects. Judgments can attribute predicates as well to those subjects which themselves originally have the status of predicates. But such nominalized predicates must in turn be capable of being employed, in elementary statements, in the predicate position of sentences; if this is not possible, then their meaning cannot be determined at all. Up to this point it could not be excluded that these elementary statements apply to simple, internally undifferentiated (though perhaps classifiable) occurrences. But now the question arises whether this possibility can be eliminated when the analysis of judgment takes a different path. Before one can start down this path, though, a number of preparatory considerations are necessary.

Predicates are simple when they ascribe to something given a property which cannot be further analyzed at the level of discourse upon which the predication takes place. Even those predicates which are complex according to their linguistic form can be simple in this sense. Thus, the predicate "blue-green" pertains to a simple color quality, and this is so regardless of the fact that it indicates this quality in terms of relations of proximity within the color spectrum. Most linguistically compound predicates do specify predicates of nonelementary reference (sky-high, wide-awake, rake-thin); others are aimed at complexes of attributes (sweet-sour, good-humored, simple-minded). Complexes such as these can occasionally even be designated by linguistically simple expressions, as when the predicate "beat" is used to connote a combination of the feeling of pain and the sensation of tiredness. The question to be answered now can be posed as follows: can a reason be found which is obtainable from the form of judgment and which supports the claim that judgments of the subject-predicate form must refer to occurrences to be characterized by more than a single predicate—and this no matter what that predicate's linguistic form may be?

There are linguistic utterances which can be true or false and which in this respect must be acknowledged as statements or, in Kantian terminology, "judgments," but which still consist of a single word. If something has a name, then in its presence and with clear reference being made to it—for instance, by pointing to it or by responding to the question "Name?"—one can pronounce its name (or else some other name), at which point agreement (or rejection) can follow. "Godot" or "That is Godot" are examples of statements that do not demonstrate the distinctions presupposed by the subject-predicate form.

Through sentences of this undifferentiated type one can even refer to occurrences that are merely instances in which a simple quality comes to the fore. Such instances of qualities, which one can fix terminologically as a "quale,"[9] will bear a name only by way of exception, and presumably only in philosophical constructions. But in one sense they can be addressed truly or falsely, which is analogous to the designation of a name.

One can best get an idea of what it means for there to be such qualia with the aid of a fictitious psychological experiment in which a person's attention is artificially limited to some diffuse coloration in a foggy environment or to single tones that do not have an identifiable source. Upon being requested to indicate what is perceived, the subject formulates such elementary statements as "Green" and "Green now," or "C sharp" and "C sharp now." The quale which occurs in each case would be characterized truly or falsely in the statement corresponding to it. But insofar as the quale has been correctly characterized, everything would already have been stated that can at all be determined about the occurrence in question. If we were limited in our cognitive activity to making such statements, then we would hardly have arrived at a stage at which the subject-predicate form is applied to a particular.

In his analysis of the forms of judgment Kant did not take into consideration the form of such elementary statements. He supposed that the simplest statements about occurrences already have a subject and a predicate. From a number of texts (these will be cited later) it is unequivocally clear that he further considered such elementary statements necessarily to be statements about objects, and not about those simple occurrences which he called "sensations."

From the perspective of present-day semantics one can discern an important difference between the producing of the correct characterizations in a situation in which what is characterized occurs and predications in the full sense of the term. This difference stems from the fact that it is only in the instance of predication that the generality of the designation, and thereby a predicate in its constitutive sense, is seized upon.[10] In the absence of an articulated conception of what it is that the generality of a predicate consists in, the very notion of the singularity of the particular makes no sense. For one knows of a particular only when one is in a position to draw a distinction between "one and the same x" and "another x." In order to thematize what is particular, there must at least be supposed, and in principle mastered, criteria of identity for the particular, criteria which relate to that range of particulars to which the general predicate is to be applied. It was pointed out previously that this analysis was not available to Kant. To the extent that they do so at all, the texts of the critical philosophy must make convincing in some other way Kant's thesis about the connection between elementary propositions of subject-predicate form and the concept of an object.

There is in fact to be found in Kant's writings a deliberation upon the form of judgment as synthesis that is entirely different from the one Kant shares with Plato—despite the apparent similarity in its literal sense. It is rather of Aristotelian provenience, a factor which comes to be integrated into the new theoretical requirements of a constitutional analysis. Admittedly, this deliberation is adequately indicated only in a few places in Kant's

Identity and Objectivity   145

Nachlass. And the foundational considerations which these passages can be seen to convey cannot be brought to light by way of textual exegesis alone. To do this we must also undertake to expose a number of pertinent connections within the broader context of the subject matter.

(b) It has already become apparent that statement-forms simpler than those of subject-predicate propositions are appropriate and adequate to statements about realized instances of simple qualities (qualia), this being true to the extent that statements about such instances are at all possible. Now if one assumes that these qualia would nonetheless be thematized in the subject-predicate form, he will recognize that the conditions for employing this judgment-form would, in such a context, be entirely different from such conditions in the normal circumstances of its employment.

As regards every simple particular, each correct elementary subject-predicate proposition would also be the *only* one that can be expressed in reference to this particular with a legitimate truth claim. For the subject concept in propositions such as these would designate a particular concerning which it is automatically excluded that with respect to its diverse qualities it can be correctly characterized by various predicates. Consequently, every true proposition to be expressed about such a particular says at the same time everything that can be expressed about that particular as such. Apart from this proposition, only those propositions are possible which locate the particular or assign it to some class of particulars by reason of its single quality or its location.

Such propositions can nevertheless be negated, for an attempt at characterization can completely miss the mark with reference to the particular to be characterized. If there is, in fact, only one possible correct predication, it is still not the case that every actual predication is necessarily correct. By reason of its mode of givenness a quale presumably offers merely the occasion to take into account a comparatively small number of possible predicates which could have application to it. However, its status of being only simply characterizable provides in principle the greatest conceivable number of characterizations which have no application to it. If an actual attempt at characterization fails, then the articulated knowledge of the intended particular is reduced to nought by the negation of this simple subject-predicate proposition. Beyond the inarticulate familiarity with that particular in the perceptual situation, a familiarity stabilized by habit, there is nothing to be thought about the particular apart from a quality which has just been misidentified in a legitimately negated proposition. This quality had been designated by the predicate. As for the subject concept in such a subject-predicate proposition, no further components of meaning are available which likewise include possible characterizations as well as the means by which reference to the particular could be ensured and by which the particular could be comprehended, independent of the failed predication, as the determinate content of a thought. The subject-expression can indicate only a location or an indeterminate element [*Relatum*] of some relation for which there simply is no characterization. For if even one characterization were successful, it would already be complete in itself.

Under normal conditions of the employment of subject-predicate propositions, a different set of circumstances is assumed. It is a peculiarity of this form that it permits fundamentally the same terms to be placed in the subject position as in the predicate position. If categorical statements are statements about the particular, then the concrete subject term cannot, indeed, be transferred to the predicate position. But expressions which themselves have the status of predicates find room within the statements. It is only when the description [*Kennzeichnung*] of a particular contains such elements that the normal instance of a subject-predicate proposition is also given. Examples of subject-expressions of such propositions about the particular are "The man at the wheel . . ." and "The oldest citizen of . . .," or "Fido . . ." and "The pope . . ." However, expressions which are merely demonstratives or descriptions which provide only the specifications of relations are distinguished from normal subject-expressions. "That there is green" is indeed a proposition in which both designation [*Bezeichnung*] and predication are at work. The fact that these two features can be distinguished—that a "topic" is named and a "commentary" upon it given—is the minimal condition for one to be able to speak of a proposition. Nevertheless, this proposition will not be comprehended as having a subject-predicate structure. Neither will the proposition "The x up there on the slope is green" be regarded as a subject-predicate proposition of normal form if it has been expressly determined that nothing more should be presumed and said about the x than what is attributed to it through the predicate. For if the x is to be interpreted as a body, an after-image on the retina or a cloud of smoke, or even as a disjunction between these descriptions, then the proposition is more than just the specification of an empty place in a relation. For it then conveys in the meaning of the subject-expression elements suitable for predication, and it does this no matter how linguistically unarticulated it may be.

If this is typical of the subject-predicate form in its normal employment, then no statements about the presence of simple qualities, or qualia, can, under normal circumstances, be made in such a form. Wherever a predicate characterizes such a quale, it must be presupposed that further predications are impossible with regard to it. But a direct implication of this is that subject-expressions which themselves bear the elements of further predications cannot be used with regard to a quale. Propositions about qualia that, for instance, are formulated in subject-predicate form are made contrary to the expectation which necessarily springs from this form. They cannot, therefore, be the primary—let alone the only—subject-predicate propositions that can, with a truth-claim [*Wahrheitsanspruch*], be formulated about a particular.

It does not follow from this that propositions like these are impossible in general. The propositional form specifically suited to qualia is the one with demonstratives and relational expressions in the subject position. But one must proceed on the assumption that the subject-predicate form is, in its normal application, of such universal significance that even those statements must be adapted to it in which the implications of the form are disregarded. Statements about qualia can have this form precisely because concepts of classes can enter into the subject-expression—classes to which belong the quale that is completely characterized by the predicate. Thus, one can say "This color-quale is green." No element is employed here in the subject position that could be employed for an independent elementary characterization. Moreover, it has already been shown that in artificially devised situations propositions about qualia with names in the subject position are possible. Names, though, can be shown to be comprehensible basically as conjunctions of characterizations. Here, too, it is certain that in sentences about qualia statements are made in a way that must expressly be set apart from the normal conditions of employment of the subject-predicate form if these statements are not to be open to misunderstanding.

This applies in a similar manner even to normal propositions with demonstratives in the subject position. When we say "That over there is green" or "That to the left of the red is green," we assume that we can shed light upon these propositions by the addition of further characterizations; that is, by saying something like "This spot is green" or "That button to the left of the red one is green." Supplementations such as these are excluded for genuine propositions about qualia. Their demonstratives must therefore be of a special type if they are to be freed of the implications of the subject-predicate form. Formerly, a number of philosophers of science purported to detect them in the ostensibly pure protocol language of physics: e.g., "There—a green" or "On the left edge—a bright." It is manifest that genuine subject-expressions do not make an appearance in sentences of this nature.

(c) By definition, predicates applying to qualia characterize these exhaustively. They are incompatible with other predications at the same level. Now among the predicates employed in normal subject-object propositions are those that lay claim to exclusivity. These are predicates by which particulars are assigned to natural kinds. If a dog is correctly described as a poodle, then by this description it is excluded not only that the dog can be characterized as a terrier (that already follows from the incompatibility of the two predicates) but also that the dog can be characterized by any other expression coordinate with the expression "poodle." For every particular, above all every living being, can belong to only one natural kind. The assumption that there are such kinds is, of course, not one that belongs to the theory of logical forms; and besides, it is not permissible to make this assumption with any claim to ontological universality, as if everything particular must be capable of being assigned to some natural kind. The elementary statements about qualia, however, have a status that subjects statements about them to rules which strictly satisfy the conditions applying to natural kinds as predicates. It can never be truly said of a qualia that it is green. The really adequate statement must identify it as "a green." One sees that if a particular has only one character, then precisely for this reason it evinces nothing *in* which a character could inhere. What is said about it constitutes just that which it is, so that there is no room for further attributions.

It follows from this that the distinction between predicates with the indefinite article "a" and other predications cannot be drawn with respect to qualia. Qualia do not allow for the distinction to be made between essential characterizations and identifications of other properties. *All* predicates that can be applied to them must, either implicitly or explicitly, be accompanied by the indefinite pronoun "a." However, this kind of restriction obviously does not apply to predicates involved in the standard employment of the subject-predicate form. The paradigmatic case of such a predication is rather one in which a subject that is already implicitly determined according to its kind is attributed a property: e.g., "The plate is warm" or "The plate is of tin." It can thus be seen in a different way that in the subject position of this proposition a concept must be assumed that can convey possible characterizations.

(d) But we must correspondingly say that in the standard manner of employment the predicate-expression and the subject-expression are separable from each other. And indeed, they are so independently of the indicating function which accrues to the subject-expression. The normal subject-expression has a meaning that can be retained even when the cur-

Identity and Objectivity   149

rent reference to the particular about which something is to be stated has been cancelled. "The pope," "The green cloud," "The man at the wheel," and similar expressions are, independent of immediate references as well as of their being descriptions, intelligible in terms of their semantic content. In statements about qualia expressions of such meaning can appear only in the predicate position. The content of that which is referred to in the statement is to be found solely in the expression occupying the predicate position.

It can be said that in normal subject-predicate propositions something is invariably thematized to which a character is *attributed*. The same cannot be said of statements about qualia, for qualia are nothing but the instance of the character that is to be ascribed to them. This instance can be further determined only by the conditions of its occurrence, but not by anything that there occurs. One can analyze things as bundles of appearances or as substrata with attributes. In both cases the attribution of properties in categorical judgments has a point of reference consisting in something different from the instantiation of just these properties. That is why qualia actually have no properties whatever. They are that which we normally assume to be "possessed." It is in this way as well that the negation of statements about qualia has a specific meaning, for characters cannot really be *denied* to qualia. The only thing a negation with reference to them can do is to simply *annul* a characterization, which is in any case the primary sense of negation. But it is not without cause that negation could be interpreted as denial [*Absprechung*] or dihairesis. Under normal circumstances the negation of propositions about particulars invariably leaves behind unnegated elements of meaning in the subject position.

(e) Propositions of subject-predicate form can be seen to ground and proffer the various distinctions and possible applications that have now been presented, and under normal circumstances of employment these latter are all assumed. Propositions about qualia eliminate them and, accordingly, diverge from the original conditions of elementary statements in a way that calls for explicit restrictions and methodic controls. To the extent that they are at all possible, even statements about so-called sense-data and about what Kant calls "mere" representations must, in the absence of these limiting factors, be misunderstood as statements about quasi-substrata.

But it has been recognized as part of the import [*Sinn*] of the form of an elementary statement with subject-expression and predicate-expression that different elementary statements of this type can be formulated about the same particular. Customarily, one assumes correctly that it pertains to the sense of statements in general that they can be negated. But from the preceding analysis it emerges that not only the negation but also the conjunction of propositions with the same subject concept or a conjunction of various predicates relating to the same subject concept is a possibility necessarily inherent in the form of the elementary statement.

Implicated in elementary subject-predicate propositions is the possibility of a conjunction of predications about the same particular. But this does not mean that in every cognitive situation more than one predicate or more than one group of incompatible predicates must be currently available. For certain particulars it can be the case that at a given time only one predicate can really be applied. Nevertheless, insofar as these particulars are addressed in the form of the categorical judgment, it is *assumed* that they are endowed with more than one character. Even "mere representations," insofar as they are topics of such statements, are first subject to the hypothesis that they are quasi-things and not qualia.

If the particular continues to be subject to the expectation implicit in the subject-predicate form, then, together with this form, a dimension of particulars is invariably brought into play which is distinguished from that of simple occurrences or "sensations." Whoever learns to judge about particulars in accordance with this form is already oriented toward such a dimension in her relation to an object. One can reach this conclusion without having to decide whether the categorical statement-form inherently enforces that object-relation. One can also assume that this statement-form originally belongs to the context of formal operations and that it is only used for statements about the particular because the particular is to be addressed as a particular for other reasons, and thus requires complex characterizations.[11] In such a case the relation to complex objects would not be comprehensible from the perspective of the form of judgment. The ineluctability of this relation would nonetheless be evident in view of the implications which this form has in its employment in statements about particulars.

Thus, there is presupposed in the elementary judgment-form a "putting together" [*Zusammennehmen*] of a kind entirely different from that involved in the synthesis model of judgment which had incorporated Plato's ideas about synthesis. Not only the combining of subject and predicate but also the very thought of the subject includes the notion of plurality-in-unity. The synthesis of which Plato spoke can be a synthesis between a nominalized predicate and a determination which classifies that predicate. The multiplicity of characters that are granted to every object of an elementary proposition about the particular is, however, on one and the same level as that of predications. The determinations with whose aid the particular referred to by the subject-expression can be thematized are, fundamentally, alternatives to the predicate attributed to the particular in the predicate position. They are alternatives to the current predication in the elementary proposition, alternatives which are, therefore, to be linked to the current predicate in a conjunction accomplished at the same level. Socrates is not thought of as a particular by being determined a man, a human being, and a living creature any more than a feeling of wetness comes to be a complex particular by virtue of its classifiability as a tactile and a close-range sensation. Rather, in these classifications he is already presupposed as being a complex particular. But he is a particular insofar as he is wise, snub-nosed, able to hold his liquor and indefinitely more. A "wet" cannot be characterized in this way by a multiplicity of predicates on the same elementary footing.

(f) The investigation of the form of judgment has thus yielded a consequence that could not have been arrived at in any other way: by the mere fact that it avails itself of the categorical judgment-form, the cognition which is called "experience" is necessarily oriented toward a conception of phenomena in which many properties are attributed to a single object. In it, the understanding is always occupied in scrutinizing appearances with the intention of making comprehensible their connection as one of complex particulars.[12] And the understanding finds itself so occupied simply by virtue of its nature as the "faculty of judgment" (A 69). Such experience can never amount merely to the ascertainment of sequences of single data. Much less can it begin with this procedure, for no level of discourse is thinkable upon which fundamentally only simple data are thematized, but in such a way that they are characterized in elementary subject-predicate propositions. If, as Kant assumes is the case, it is not possible to get around the subject-predicate form, then data can be thematized only in connection with complex objects. A theory of mere data or of qualia must invariably amount to secondary knowledge.

This result is interesting enough in itself. And within the context of Kant's theory of knowledge it provides the basis for drawing many other farther-reaching conclusions: we know that Kant considers himself justified in making the assumption that all immediate data for our cognition, i.e., the presentations of our sensibility, are but simple and isolated qualities. They are not, for instance, aspects of complex objects of which we are likewise always conscious. Such objects are not at all encountered in the range and the cognitive phase to which the data belong. But in themselves those data are not possible objects for our cognition, which, by dint of its taking place in judgments, is, to begin with, always oriented toward complex objects. But it follows from this that all objects of our cognition must be *constituted*. Cognition can simply not come about through the fact that it is determined in judgments what particulars really exist in what relations—and this indeed on grounds of the familiarity or direct encounter with this reality, however interpreted. The manifold of given representations must, with direct reference to the possibility of a judgment, be brought into combinations which yield the thought of those particulars that on principle simply cannot belong to the dimension of the given. Given occurrences (Kant calls them "appearances") are, as such, no objects at all; they merely indicate objects (B 235). What they indicate is for its part nothing but the thought of a possible object of a judgment. But inasmuch as we judge, we are immediately related to objects. Hence, the conditions of the constitution of objects are, on the one hand, to be distinguished from the formal conditions of judging; but, on the other hand, they must be conceived as being directly dependent upon these. From the outset we relate to appearances that are simple qualities in such a way that through predicates we attribute (or rather can attribute) these qualities to objects as their properties.

In a manner peculiar to Kant a dilemma is thus resolved, viz., the dilemma at the root of the question whether underlying all properties there are naked, uncharacterizable things responsible for the fact that such properties really exist, or whether particular things are nothing other than combinations of simple qualities. The latter alternative is correct to the extent that only instances of such qualities are really given; these and only these enter into combinations. But neither the simple occurrences as such, nor any combinations of them—combinations which must be produced and which are then themselves given—already constitute the thought of the particular that is posited in the subject position of a judgment. Given manifold qualities must be combined in a special way, and indeed in such a way that they can be comprehended as properties of particular things, things which, for their part, are to be posited beyond the dimension of what can be given. What constitutes a particular is there a product of construction; it is not something given. But in this respect it is also different from the sum of its properties, even though the construction that has this particular as its result can only be produced by properties combined in relation to it.

3.4 Supporting Evidence from Kant's Texts

Only one text documents incontrovertibly that it had become clear to Kant himself which aspect of the judgment-form sustains the grounding of his

Identity and Objectivity   153

thesis about the concept of an object. In reflection 6350, presumably first composed in the summer of 1797, Kant writes:[13]

> What is an object? That whose representation is a complex of a number of predicates appertaining to it. The plate is round, warm, of pewter, etc. etc. Warm, round, of pewter, etc. etc., is no object, but very well warmth,[14] pewter, etc. etc.
>
> An object is that in whose representation various others [i.e., various elements] can be thought as synthetically combined.
>
> In every judgment there is a subject and a predicate. The subject of the judgment, insofar as it can contain various possible predicates, is the object. The predicates are all dependent upon the subject, as warm [depends upon] warmth . . .
>
> Warm, quadrangular, deep are predicates—warmth, the quadrangle, depth are objects—as is the case with reasonable and reason. That which is determinable in a judgment, the logical subject, is at the same time the real object . . .
>
> The subject of a judgment whose representation contains the ground of the synthetic unity of a manifold of predicates is the object.

This passage both demands and deserves extensive commentary in its entirety, but only the most indispensable aspects will be expounded here. For Kant does not limit his assertion about the connection between logical subject and real object to the range of particular things. In his examples he also admits to the subject position concepts of physical mass (pewter), of abstract objects (quadrangle), of the states of physical bodies (warmth), and of faculties of cognition (reason). What is first established for a particular thing (viz., "the plate") is supposed to apply to all of these.

That this plate is meant as a particular can be gathered from its transitory state of being warm. This can also be gathered from its being introduced by the definite article and thus, in a grammatical form suitable for the description of a particular. There are two explanations for the fact that Kant draws the same conclusion for abstract objects and physical and psychological properties and dispositions as he does for the particular. First, Kant is of the opinion that all objects, in the broadest sense of the term, are synthetic unities of a manifold. Second, it is actually the purpose of the reflection to point out anew a distinction which is fundamental to Kant's position and philosophical development. This is the distinction between what is determined purely on grounds of that which is posited in the subject concept of a judgment (and which is thus analytically determined) and something which must be ascertained with a view to the object as such.

This topic requires the mention of all kinds of objects whose concepts occupy the subject positions in judgments. "Warm," when used only as a predicate, thus means in the context of Kant's reflection something different from the physically described state of the warmth of real bodies, this being an object in judgments. What constitutes warmth as such a state cannot be determined by analysis of the predicate "warm." It results from experience and in physico-theoretical knowledge. The fact that the predicate "warm" can be attributed to a body is likewise grounded in experience. But it is not grounded in an understanding of what warmth is. Rather, it results from comprehending that the property "warm," which cannot be further analyzed at the level of the primary experience of the given, really does belong to a body.

It goes without saying that objects such as warmth—objects which are actually structural connections between particular objects or states of particular bodies that are yielded under specifiable conditions—cannot be simple objects. Kant's reflection is noteworthy in the present context only because it establishes the necessity of always determining objects by a variety of predicates (a necessity established not only for physical processes but for particular objects as well), and because it claims that there is a direct link between this internal manifoldness of the particular and the form of the categorical judgment.

The text quoted belongs to the last set of reflections on the topic of transcendental philosophy that have come down to us apart from the *Opus postumum*. These reflections originated in the year after Kant's retirement from academic teaching. As is true for many of them, this reflection has as its context Kant's final attempt to publicly articulate his philosophy with greater clarity and to disassociate it from that of his putative successors and "hypercritical friends."[15] For this reason Kant was once more occupied with providing a series of detailed—and in part novel—argumentations.[16] One could therefore suppose that Kant's ideas and theses about the connection between the subject of judgment and an object were also first put forth during this late period. This supposition is plausible, especially since those ideas and theses have a parallel in the writing by J. S. Beck that occasioned Kant's efforts,[17] and since they are not given such extensive treatment elsewhere in Kant's work. It is therefore of considerable interest to ensure that from the time he began working on his critique of pure reason Kant had in mind the same connection.

The connection is already assumed, even if in an unarticulated form, in a definition of object from around 1775/76: "An object is merely something in general which we think through certain predicates that constitute its

Identity and Objectivity   155

concept" (reflection 4634). From this period onward there are to be found regularly in Kant's work definitions of an object in which given appearances are assigned as predicates to objects: "The appearance has an object when it is a predicate of a substance, i.e., [when it is] one of the modes of cognizing that which perdures" (reflection 5221); "for we cognize an object only as a something in general of which the given intuitions are only predicates" (reflection 5643). These reflections give us to understand, of course, that their evidence is derived not from an analysis of the form of the categorical proposition but as a consequence of the data-sensualism inherent in the Kantian conception of sensible appearance. Nevertheless, the allusion to the categorical judgment-form, the only form in which predicates are attributed to something, is an essential condition of their intelligibility.

We do not know when Kant first worked up this material into a theory sketch that no longer leaves undifferentiated the various aspects of the categorical judgment-form, thereby, so to speak, promiscuously laying claim to those aspects in the doctrine of objectivity. Even if this had first happened during the late period, from which we have the only document demonstrating a reasonably well articulated train of thought, it would still be permissible to appeal to that theory sketch in interpreting earlier texts, in particular the *Critique of Pure Reason*. For the *Critique* requires such a theorem; its place is clearly marked within the theoretical context expressly developed by the *Critique*; the progress made in presenting the theorem (of which progress Kant was fully aware) resulted from the endeavor to bring to bear more fully the definition of judgment; and finally, there are enough texts that can be interpreted only in conjunction with the theorem about the subject of judgment and object. Admittedly, only theses, not arguments, are formulated by even that text which unequivocally ties Kant's general argument about judgment and object to an analysis of the specific relation between the subject of judgment and an object. The required argumentation must, in its entirety, be incorporated retroactively into the frame of Kant's theory.

4. Consequences and Limits of the Argument

Against the claim that one must posit a difference of dimension between appearances and objects (given that objects, but not elementary appearances, must be characterized by various predicates) one can still formulate an objection accordant with the premises of Kant's data-sensualism. There are data which are indeed simple inasmuch as they can be traced back by analysis to no other occurrence, but which nonetheless can, and must, be characterized by various predicates. Tones, for instance, are to be characterized in this way by pitch, timbre, and strength, as are colors by color quality, brightness, and saturation; and this holds true for every instance of their presentation—even if it is assumed that they can be given as not having any spatial extension. If predicates consonant with these three groups are attributed to such a datum, then there occurs a synthesis of these determinations, as predicates, in relation to the referents of the subject concept of [in] a judgment. But a synthesis of various occurrences *into* an object is not at issue here.

There is no indication that Kant himself raised an objection like this. And the objection cannot be weakened by the reference to a synthesis of distinct sensory spheres—a synthesis that takes place when, for instance, visual and tactile sensations are brought—any more than it can be weakened by, say, the fact that different physical processes underpin the diverse characteristics of such sensory occurrences. For one cannot properly speak of processes such as these when one is expounding upon how an occurrence must actually be described as given. Even the difference between the extensivity and intensivity of sensations does not explain the internal complexity of those data to which the objection relates.

If one's intention is to weaken the objection, then one must proceed from Kant's thesis that the notion of a subject in an elementary categorical proposition *necessarily* requires an object with various properties. It is, however, the accidental peculiarity of several types of sensation that they are capable of being complexly characterized, such that this complexity is not only that of the means of description but also that of the characterized state of affairs itself. If there is no reason to assume that all data necessarily demonstrate such complexity [*Komplexion*], then it is also unavoidable that in the relation to objects one will, from the outset, step beyond the dimension of the immediately given and refer what is given to objects belonging to another dimension. Now it really cannot be conceived how an a priori reason could be found for the fact that all data which are not analyzable, and in this sense simple, both require and necessarily make possible complex characterizations. But then the thought of the object as synthetic unity of predicates compels one to bring into play a dimension of objectivity of its own.

If one continues along this line of deliberation, certain results become discernible which go beyond the connection at hand: if sensations are at least in principle simple occurrences, whereas objects are to be complexly characterized, then for all data that can possibly enter into the characterizations of objects, one must assume there is a basic relation (or various basic relations) which permits those data to be set off as particulars from other particulars—particulars which in relation to the same object come to be identified by predicates. A particular that has been constituted from data that at least in principle occur separately must be analyzable into these data; and the thought of such conditions as apply generally to its constitution as well as to its analysis is at least formally implicated in the thought of such an object. Kant discerns in the forms of intuition such general conditions of synthesis and its investigative analysis. These are independent of all special conditions by which certain classes of data or classes of objects could of themselves already be complexly characterizable. It could be shown in this way that the spatial and temporal type of synthesis is postulated in the very notion of the synthesis of predicates (which must be thought in the object of every simple subject-predicate proposition) as a presupposition of the possibility of the synthesis. This implication could be defended even if one takes into account the fact that complexly characterizable data are forthcoming. Regardless of their internal complexity, such data are fundamentally to be thematized as properties or appearances of the complex particular.

But even apart from such far-reaching prospects for introducing the Kantian doctrine of space and time in a new way, Kant's considerations on the specific synthesis-form of judgment have brought about for the first time an argument which, to the degree that it is persuasive, is also decisive against Hume's doubt. Its result can be formulated independent of the specific premises of the Kantian doctrine of knowledge: it is not the case that we must leave it to the factual inventory of appearances themselves to decide whether we are to comprehend objects as complex or as simple occurrences. Neither can it be maintained any longer that nothing whatever can be discerned a priori about the rules to which appearances conform. For insofar as we at all judge in the form of the subject-predicate composition [*Subjekt-Prädikat-Komposition*], appearances are already addressed as complex objects. With that, a basic rule is already in effect as well, a rule which declares that we must address occurrences in such a way that they can in general be characterized in terms of the unity of various predicates. Since we can have knowledge only in judgments, we must from the outset comprehend occurrences as appearances of objects which are particulars and have their properties in such appearances.

The circumstance that a fundamental distinction must be drawn between simple appearances and the objects to which they are assigned confers henceforth a necessary presupposition that objects satisfy constancy requirements for behavior that conforms to *further* rules. Complexes of sensations also can, under regulated conditions, occur and change until they disappear. However, if objects are to be thought not as appearances, but rather only in relation to appearances, then it is incumbent upon us to assume that their existence with respect to their presentation is subject to much more complicated rules. Completely diverse complexes of appearances which have nothing qualitatively in common with one another can, under different conditions of presentation, find their ground of unity in one and the same object. Even various complexes of data demonstrating no manifest continuity with one another can all be the appearances of a single object. Moreover, only objects, not data, can recur after they disappear from our intuition. In this way, too, the analysis of the object as the referent of the subject of a judgment extends the boundaries of the investigation and leads to this question: What basic assumptions about the existential conditions of objects are already implicated in the circumstance that objects are in principle not immediate occurrences but rather the products of construction?

For the progress of Kant's theory toward perfecting a transcendental deduction, questions of this type are of preponderant significance. One may well have determined the aspects under which, even in the most elementary cognitive situation, given "sensations" must be assigned to objects. But one has not at all established thereby *the way in which* we are *successful* in discerning objects beyond appearances, such that the ascertainment of their existence and reliable knowledge about their changes are rendered possible. Taken by itself, the concept of the particular thing, or substance, is the mere *form* of the thought of something real precisely because it specifies no conditions which guarantee the possibility of its employment. Even if objects can be cognized only as complex particular things, this still formulates but a necessary condition for the possibility of a cognition's being objective. And with that, the question of how, and on what grounds, the cognition of objects comes to be an objective cognition in the methodological sense of this term has not yet even been made into a problem.

In coming to grips with this problem, one is constrained to inquire into the objectivity conditions of our natural language (in which sensibly given qualities are properties of appearing things) and about their relation to the objectivity conditions of the scientific knowledge of nature. In the latter, sensibly given qualities are to be interpreted only as effects upon the perceptual apparatus of the subject proceeding from substances of a different kind—substances which for their part might be conceivable even as complexes and sequences of events.[18] Kant was occupied with this question into his final years without, however, undertaking to draw a number of absolutely requisite distinctions. In the investigation into judgment and object there was only one outcome to be achieved, an outcome that must remain greatly inferior to the results obtainable by investigations along this line of inquiry.

There is yet another respect in which the outcome achieved does not meet expectations, even those which a transcendental deduction must already meet by virtue of its highest principle and most general argumentative procedure: Kant always emphasized that the rules to which all objects are necessarily subject can be only formal rules. What constitutes determinate particular objects and objective processes as well as determinate natural laws is essentially to be gathered from experience. It is clear that the concept of an object, which was obtained in view of the structure of judgment, easily satisfies this condition of the formality of a category. But the latitude which Kant leaves to experience is far greater than what he actually wanted to concede. We do, of course, know that as thinking beings we could not even begin to actualize the principles of our cognition in real knowledge if it were not possible to relate appearances to objects in judgments. However, it is perfectly consistent with the sole condition of objectivity specified thus far that any object-relation which we might succeed in establishing could be wholly sporadic. If that were so, then in a vague (albeit colorful) life full of sensations which do not even yield images, objects would occasionally emerge in order, perhaps, to reappear later. It could also happen that each of these objects would conform to certain rules of incidence that largely or fundamentally differ from those of other objects. By reason of the form of their behavior, all objects would then be, in a way, absolute individuals. The rules to which they conformed would indeed be adhered to invariably, or at least in by far the greatest number of instances, so that the essential minimum of universality would be retained by these rules. But there would be no rules that would be universal in the sense that classes of objects, and perhaps all objects whatever, must conform to them. Naturally, under conditions like these, one could hardly speak of the objectivity of a cognition of such objects.

Is it but a fortunate accident that we need not live in this kind of world? Kant obviously maintains that this possibility must be ruled out on principle: objects belong essentially to a world we call "nature." That means that they are all subject to universal laws. It means further that it is fundamentally possible for each particular in nature to be related to every other particular. Translated into the context of Kant's theory of knowledge, this sentence says the following: it is not merely the case that several qualities can be conjoined respectively in the thought of particular objects. Over and above this, there can be thought a necessary combination of all possible objects with all others. For it is not merely de facto the case that we have at our disposal the conditions of unity and the rules for such thoroughgoing combination. Rather, we have these at our command on grounds which lie in reason as such.

But where are we to find the grounds for a thesis that, by the standards of philosophical theory, raises so extraordinary a claim, though it is certainly intended to justify a conviction which we entertain in any event without the trace of a doubt?

One could attempt to push on further in investigating the relationship between the unity of judgment and the concept of an object to try to see whether the comprehensive cognizability of all objects can in this way be progressively substantiated. From this point of view one could analyze Kant's considerations on the truth conditions of judgment forms[19] other than merely the elementary subject-predicate proposition. Above all, one might subject to analysis the "Analytic of Principles" in the *Critique of Pure Reason*.

There is, however, little reason to expect that Kant's wider-ranging epistemological goals can, in the end, be achieved along this path. And there is no doubt that this path alone does not allow one to make intelligible and evaluate the intentions which guided Kant in drafting his theory blueprint. For Kant plainly believed that only the analysis of self-consciousness furnishes the way to establish that objects must be thought to exist in thoroughgoing interconnectedness.

Hence, the investigation of the connection between the form of judgment and the concept of object will now be broken off. It must be followed by the attempt to exhibit Kant's analysis of self-consciousness in a way that this conclusion can be obtained from it: from the beginning, all thought of objects necessarily stands under the presupposition that universal rules guarantee the interconnectedness of all objects.

III. Identity and Self-Consciousness

An investigation which claims to ensure the presupposed connection of all objects as well as possible, and at the same time to make transparent Kant's thoughts about it, is confronted by difficulties greater than those posed by Kant's equivocal remarks about objectivity and by his definitions of "object" and "category," definitions which had been abbreviated to the point of vagueness. In Kant's work one cannot find a single passage that provides a sufficient evidential basis for the illumination of these derivations, which are fundamental to his entire theory. Only when one has clearly distinguished the central problem of his doctrine of self-consciousness from other problems that are likewise of importance in the transcendental deduction, and which must therefore receive their due, does it become fully clear how narrow the textual basis in the *Critique of Pure Reason* is upon which the interpretation is to be supported. And it becomes further evident that Kant never got beyond mentioning or indicating the arguments that uphold the theory he had pioneered. Nowhere can they be found elaborated to the point where single steps can be checked, and nowhere is it possible to decide, on the grounds of Kant's explicit declaration, between a series of alternative readings of the text. As was also the case with the problematic of objectivity, Kant had at his disposal a series of arguments. But he failed, not only consistently and clearly to distinguish between them, but also to expand upon any one of them, even if only retroactively at a later date, whereby he would have given himself the opportunity of distinguishing between his actual proof-intentions and others.

In what follows it will become apparent that there is one Kantian line of argument that stands out to some extent and holds sway over other such lines. However, it is also the one which draws lasting and presumably insurmountable doubt upon itself. But the text indicates other arguments as well. One line of argument in particular is irrefutable within the overall theorematic context of the *Critique*. Moreover, when compared with the prevailing line of argument in Kant's view of the problem situation, it demonstrates the advantage of greater insightfulness. Finally, it is a line of argument that is compatible with the first; it is even imperative that it be consolidated with the first in one argumentative move, given that the first is by itself deficient. Only in this way can the basic doctrine of the *Critique* be adequately articulated and given the persuasive power of which it is generally capable.

In a situation such as this the presentation must be a highly intricate one if it is to do justice to the subject matter. Thus, in what follows a reading of Kant's text is presented first which, even though it is the textually predominant one, does not possess sufficient conclusive force. Next, the second interpretation is worked out and combined with the first to produce a complex line of argument.

1. Unity of Self-Consciousness as Simplicity and as Identity

In the chapter on the paralogisms of rational psychology in the *Critique of Pure Reason* Kant discriminates between four features of self-consciousness, two of which are significant in the present context (A 351ff., 361ff.).

(a) Self-consciousness is *simple*. If one conceives of oneself as the thinking subject of one's thoughts, nothing more is contained in this thought of "I" than this: a thinker is related to all its thoughts in one and the same way. In the mere awareness of thought nothing further is to be discerned about who this thinker is. Consequently, it is part of the thought which the thinker forms of itself that all the properties attributed to a *person* capable of thought do not eo ipso belong to the *subject* without which no thought can, as such, be explicitly thought.[20] The properties can be as diverse as one pleases and can be subject to change. Such properties are not contained in the notion of the subject of thought. Consequently, the question arises as to how the unity of the subject of thought is to be related to the personality of that which thinks. But whatever answer must be given to this question, the subject as such must be thought of as being, as Kant says, "logically simple."

Thus, the subject fundamentally distinguishes itself from the contents of the thoughts with which it is correlated: These thoughts are always manifold or, when taken together, constitute a manifold. For many things can be thought by the subject which, inasmuch as it is itself simple, cannot be added as content to that which it thinks. In the abstract, it is indeed possible to form the notion of a subject which is related to only a single content and which, in this one-only relation, is just as simple as a subject that (as is the case with ourselves) is conscious of a manifold of possible thoughts. Moreover, it is possible (again, merely in the abstract) to form the notion of a subject that is related to its thoughts in each instance on grounds of certain properties that belong to it qua subject. However, both notions omit the characteristic mark of subjectivity that we are conscious of in thought, i.e., the mark of being simple and at the same time related to something manifold.

The two properties imply jointly that our consciousness must be defined as a principle of unity. The unity of consciousness results from its lack of any specific determination in its relation to manifold contents. In simple consciousness these contents are to be comprehended as a sum [*Inbegriff*] of what is conceivable: all thoughts belong equally to the one consciousness that takes form in them. David Hume had in mind this structural aspect of self-consciousness when he ascertained that our perceptions belong, one and all, to a single "bundle."[21] The circumstance that representations occur in each instance in such a bundle does not appear to be purely accidental, but is fixed independent of all experience. For Kant, the simplicity of the subject accounts for its status as the principle of unity for our thought. It does this by means of the additional notion that the simple subject is a subject of manifold thoughts. Consequently, the simplicity of the subject already entails that it must be possible to state that this principle of unity is necessarily one and the same in all its thoughts.

(b) With regard to the following series of analyses it is of considerable importance for one to realize that this sense of unity that has to be attributed to the subject must be distinguished from another sense that can be formulated in precisely the same terms: the subject of thought is a *principle of identity;* it has the property of being numerically identical.

"Is numerically identical" can be translated word-for-word by the formula "is one and the same," a formula which was previously found to be derivable from the unity of the subject. Kant certainly pursues this connection wherever he describes the subject as a principle of unity and then, in the same frame of reference, goes on to characterize it as "numerically identical." By established convention, however, predicating identity of a subject or a person has a further, philosophically well founded sense: identity is ascribed to a particular (or also to an abstract object) when it comes to be presented under varying conditions. Now persons as well as things in space and time come to be presented because they occur in different *states.* As long as the subject is understood merely as "simple," different states cannot be attributed to it. This is so regardless of its having been conceived as related to a manifold of thoughts. It was to be assumed that its relation to this manifold is polymorphous and yet instantaneous, as it were, just as a multiplicity of different relational elements in relations of exactly the same kind can be related to a single element. But if numerical identity in any specific sense is to be attributed to a subject, this picture must be corrected. This must be done essentially by extending its scope. The subject cannot lose its property of being simple within the manifoldness of its thoughts. But the unity situated in this simplicity must also make itself known in the succession of states in which the subject is in each instance related to one definite manifold among others.

Kant based his refutation of rational psychology upon the argument showing that the simplicity and self-sameness of a substance in the succession of its states may not be inferred from the simplicity and identity which accrues to self consciousness. However, he did not thereby claim to deny to self-consciousness the property of being identical with itself throughout a series of states. Rather, he at one point designates with complete explicitness and with greater precision the property of its identity as the identity of "I think" *in every state of my thought* (B 419).

It is as conspicuous as it is remarkable that Kant did not generally underscore the distinction between numerical identity in its specific sense and the unity and self-sameness of the subject. As a rule, he neglects the distinction, even though he explicitly introduces it. One must therefore assume that there were compelling reasons for him to attribute states to the subject and that there were at the same time motives of sufficient strength for him not unambiguously to build the argument of the deduction upon this specific sense of numerical identity. We will be inquiring into these reasons.

The distinction between simplicity and numerical identity is fixed in its essentials and is sufficiently well grounded in Kant's theory. This serves to justify the attempt to work out arguments in support of the theoretical move from the unity of the subject to a synthesis under a priori rules by way of the notions of simplicity and numerical identity. The arguments formulable in respect of these two ways must be worked out separately and in abstraction from each other. It is only in this way that the theoretical potential of the doctrine of self-consciousness will be fathomed and made recognizable in the entangled webwork in which it is enveloped in the *Critique of Pure Reason* as a result of Kant's incomplete penetration of the substantive connections at issue.

2. Simplicity and Combination within Self-Consciousness

The consciousness in which one knows that one can *add* the thought of oneself as a thinking subject to each of one's thoughts is called by Kant the "original synthetic unity of apperception" (B 131). It is not difficult to understand the sense in which this consciousness is original: it demonstrates the evidence of being beyond any doubt and of not being derivable from any other consciousness. It is this evidence which Descartes first claimed for the self-certainty of his thinking substance and which we are on that account accustomed to calling, for the sake of brevity, "Cartesian evidence."

One hardly has any greater difficulty in making clear to oneself that it is a *synthetic* principle, at least to the extent that this is supposed to mean merely that it can be thought in relation to *any* combination that representations enter into: it is the same subject which accompanies all its thoughts—whatever they may be—with the consciousness that articulates itself linguistically in the sentence "I think ... these thoughts." A consciousness which could comprehend itself merely as the subject of a single thought would perhaps be self-consciousness. But it would not be the self-consciousness of a subject that could address itself, by means of the nominalized personal pronoun, as "I." Only by thinking oneself in relation to an indefinite multiplicity of possible thoughts which are, or can be, one's

Identity and Objectivity

own thoughts can one think of oneself as a subject, and in this sense as "I."

If categories are to obtain their warrant from self-consciousness as functions of combination between manifold representations, then it does not suffice to identify which manifold thoughts come together as separate with one self-consciousness. First of all, a combination of these thoughts must be accomplished, a combination that can further be shown to come about on grounds of the categories.

When our attention is redirected from the consciousness of "I think" to the thoughts that can be accompanied by such consciousness, then it becomes immediately apparent that they really are combined with one another—that they *share the property* of being (actual or possible) thoughts. Whatever their content may be, they are all indiscriminately and in the same way the thoughts of a subject.

On this interpretation, "combination" means, of course, nothing other than the membership of various elements in a class as defined by the relations of many elements to a single subject. To be combined in such a way does not, therefore, entail that real relations are at all established between each member of the class to another member. Neither can such combination be comprehended as an activity which, for instance, would have to be performed by the subject. "Combination" designates here nothing more than the condition of belonging, a "*being* together" and not a "bringing together." Moreover, it designates a "being together" merely in an abstract object.

Nevertheless, the relation of the one subject to all its thoughts also cannot be conceived without presupposing that a combination can come about which must be comprehended as a "doing" or "combining." One sees that insofar as any thought whatever is accompanied by the consciousness of "I think," the fact that this consciousness arises from the subject must be charged to the subject itself. For though the thought "I think" does occur spontaneously, it does not occur groundlessly. It must be brought about. And it can very well be ruled out that the content of any thought, as such, could produce the thought "I think." In order for this to occur, an operation which we call "reflection" must be performed. If it makes any sense at all to call the subject of thoughts that which comes to awareness in the consciousness of "I think," then one must also consider this subject to be the initiator of that reflection. To suppose that every thought can be accompanied by the consciousness of "I think" is tantamount to assuming that there is a subject of thoughts capable of reflection in relation to every thought.

A formulation has been achieved herewith that for the first time comes close to Kant's far-reaching thesis about the general possibility of a combination of the given. But at the same time it is also clear that this formulation has a much more restricted meaning. For with respect to both the class of thoughts which really are accompanied by "I think" and the class of thoughts which are merely subject to this activity, there is lacking the single decisive component of meaning for the notion of synthesis within the given and into objects, a component according to which combination takes place when a given element is brought into a definite relationship with another. For in the activity of reflection one can discover nothing that goes beyond the subject's relation to a determinate thought which provides the occasion for reflection. If all thoughts were isolated from one another before reflection takes place, one could find nothing in the structure of the reflective act which would require the termination of this isolation and the establishment of a combination of thoughts. Every thought is related to the subject such that it can be explicitly thought by the thinking subject as its own. Nothing is thereby determined about any combinations which may, or must, exist between particular thoughts, and even between all possible thoughts.

The arguments weighed up to this point were intended to ground the necessity of a combination of thoughts in the proposition that the same subject reflects upon these thoughts and becomes conscious of its self-sameness in relation to them. However, it is clear that the possibility of reflection already presupposes the self-sameness of the subject. This is the self-sameness of a subject which, in advance of all reflection, has made a manifold of the given into the content of its thoughts, so that it can reflect upon these as its own and have knowledge of the possibility of this reflection. For the subject as such can be expressly conscious only of thoughts that really are the thoughts of the subject. It has turned out that the possibility of reflection can provide no foundation for the validation of a transcendental deduction of the categories starting with the unity of the subject. For this reason, it must now seem appropriate to obtain, with reference to that elementary sense of the unity of the subject, arguments in support of the position that a combination of the given in a subject requires a priori functions for a synthesis of what is given.

In all probability Kant, too, was of the opinion that by an investigation such as this adequate support can be found for the proof of the most fundamental and far-reaching thesis of his *Critique*. It is therefore all the more important to achieve clarity about the type of supporting arguments that can be supplied in such a context.

The categories are supposed to be functions of synthesis without which

Identity and Objectivity 167

manifoldly given contents cannot "stand together" [*zusammenstehen*]. They are necessary conditions of synthesis. Arguments which claim to show the indispensability of conditions such as these must refer to the manner in which possibility conditions of the synthesis of the manifold can be operative in the subject. Before the conditions or the grounds for their acceptance can be named, however, one must specify precisely what these conditions make possible, as well as the sense in which they do so. These specifications divide all conceivable grounds into various kinds.

Three such kinds of conditions are distinguishable: (a) categories that are necessary for a given manifold to be at all subject to the possibility of becoming the content of a subject's thoughts; (b) categories that are a presupposition for the conjoining of various contents into particular complex thoughts of this subject; and (c) categories that are the conditions for the subject's ability to recognize different thoughts as its own. These three modes of the conditionedness of self-consciousness by the categories are listed here in such a way that we begin with conditions that precede all current consciousness and proceed ultimately to the designation of a mode of conditionality that is applicable to all the representations of which the subject is conscious. We can now evaluate the strength of those argumentative procedures which claim to find support in such conditions of the unity of consciousness.

2.1 Combination into the Unity of Self-Consciousness

The unity of an enduring [*durchgängig*] self-consciousness must be establishable with reference to everything that is the thought of a subject which achieves consciousness of itself. Whatever is given to the subject in intuition as a possible content of its thoughts can therefore be thought by the subject only when it is capable of entering into the unity of such consciousness. Hence, we have no reason to suppose that this condition is satisfied eo ipso by any given occurrence whatever. To the contrary, we have good reason to suppose that everything given in intuition can be included in the unity of consciousness only when it is subjected to certain processes which permit what had previously been pure givenness to become the conceptual content of a certain subject.[22] What is given does not enter into thoughts as persons enter into houses. The homogeneity demonstrated by thoughts *as* thoughts—as the thoughts of a subject in particular—can only be understood in view of the fact that what is given is subject to functions that are nothing more than the conditions of the possibility of thoughts. Only a given which "submits itself to thought" and which, moreover, can really be "grasped" in thoughts belongs to the unity of the subject. It appears that the functions which make possible such unified consciousness, and which necessarily make it possible inasmuch as this consciousness is in itself necessary, must themselves be comprehensible as necessary functions of combinations and, consequently, as categories.[23] The investigation has thus yielded, for the second time, a formulation corresponding to the standard formulations of the goal of Kant's validative scheme.

But if one scrupulously abides by the premises from which this inference is to be made without letting any allusions to other arguments slip into the conclusion to be drawn, then one must realize that the decisive move in Kant's program of proof (i.e., the move to the justification of functions of a priori combination) remains as yet unfounded. Self-consciousness certainly presupposes a synthesis by virtue of which many thoughts become thoughts in a possible self-consciousness. This synthesis explains, therefore, the possibility of the interconnection demonstrated by thoughts in this consciousness. But so long as the argumentation requiring such an explanation strictly maintains its own course, there is no discernible reason which would compel the acceptance of the idea that this synthesis must be carried out by the subject itself, or at least must take place solely in the realm of the consciousness of the subject. Rather, the synthesis must precede this consciousness, for it is comprehended as the *condition* of that interconnection of thoughts, a condition which constitutes the most elementary unity of the subject. In this case it must indeed be supposed that the synthesis leading to the most elementary unity of the subject is subordinate to some conditions by virtue of which the given is taken up into the unity of the subject. But it must not, and cannot, be supposed that these conditions have the status of a priori accessible rules, or rules which the subject must likewise be a priori conscious of in its self-awareness. The *philosopher*, who deliberates about the possibility of a unified self-consciousness, comes to impute or disclose conditions for the synthesis of the manifold. He is not permitted, nor does he need, to attribute to the subject as such in its consciousness of selfhood the knowledge of these conditions. Kant bases the fundamental argument of his transcendental deduction not upon an incontestable *explanation* of self-consciousness on the part of philosophical theory, but upon the inseparability of knowledge of the principles of synthesis from real and original self-consciousness per se. As Kant repeatedly and unambiguously declares, the mind could not at all be certain of its unity if it did not have, "before its eyes," the function which subjects all synthesis to a transcendental unity (A 108).

Kant had no choice but to express himself in this way. For as soon as it is established that conditions of the unity of synthesis serve only to explain

Identity and Objectivity 169

the unity of the subject, it follows of itself that it is impossible to determine other than empirically what these conditions really are. A subject's knowledge of self is indeed dependent upon experience. But that does not rule out the fact that the de facto possibility of such knowledge is dependent upon processes which are not themselves susceptible to Cartesian certainty. Only as long as these processes take place is Cartesian self-consciousness possible. Its ascertainment alone, not its continued existence under all conditions, has the property of being a priori and beyond all possible doubt. In this connection, it makes no difference whether the conditions upon which the Cartesian subject depends are conditions of its own possibility or conditions of the availability of the given for thoughts. If, therefore, we also assume that the conditions of an inherently Cartesian and, hence, necessary consciousness are indispensable, then they are necessary in a different sense than this consciousness itself inherently is. They are necessarily to be presupposed without, however, being the content of necessarily true propositions.

A completely different situation will, of course, be engendered if the synthesis through which the given enters into the unity of the subject must be described as an *activity* performed by the subject. If the subject is the agent [*Akteur*] of combination it can have no consciousness of self without being conscious of itself qua agent. To carry out an act of combination would in this case be the same as bringing about a consciousness of some given. Kant's declarations pertaining to the question whether the subject is to be conceived as the subject of synthesis in the same way as it must be conceived as the subject of reflection are everywhere inadequately articulated and distinguished by theoretical tensions. But they speak clearly enough for the fact that Kant claimed to comprehend the subject of cognition in principle as the subject of combination. Were the subject correctly characterized in this way, then, insofar as it exists at all, it could guarantee the possibility of combination. Kant may have regarded this as a necessary condition for the conceivability of the self as subject, even though hardly a trace of support can be found for such a conviction in the *Critique*.

Now let us make the additional assumption that all synthesis is established with a view toward some conditions or other which are constitutive of it. It would follow from this that the subject which becomes conscious of itself necessarily as the operative ground of combinations must also become conscious of the conditions in relation to which synthesis alone can come about. It would have to become conscious of these conditions if it is to become conscious of itself at all. And it would always have to do so at the point at which it actually does become conscious of itself. Consequently, the consciousness of conditions would encompass the same necessity that distinguishes self-consciousness as such.

To achieve this outcome—which must prove most desirable to Kant—one would again have to avail oneself of the premise asserting that a synthesis presupposes conditions of unity that can still be distinguished from the unity of the subject itself. This assertion, however, was originally found to be persuasive in a context entirely different from the present one: previously, synthesis was understood as combination toward a unified connection in which the unity of the subject showed itself for the first time, a connection which therefore must be preceded by a synthesis. In this situation the synthesis must, in all reasonable likelihood, rest upon conditions out of which the unified connection first emerges and which must for this reason be distinct from the subject's own sense of unity, even if they serve as the conditions of the realization of its unity. The circumstance that conditions of the unity of the synthesis leading to the unity of the subject can, and must, be distinguished from the unity of the subject itself presupposes that it is not the subject which at the fundamental level produces and ensures its own unified connectedness in relation to what is given. Meanwhile, however, we went on to treat the attempt to discern, in the subject, the subject of the act of combination as well. The requirement to distinguish yet further conditions of unity from the unity originally grasped in [the subjects's] consciousness is thereby provisionally set aside. The subject is *in any event* a principle of unity. Because of this, one must proceed on the assumption that it is also an adequate ground of unity for synthesis leading to the unity of consciousness so long as no new reasons are advanced in favor of the proposition that the subject's thoroughgoing unity of consciousness can be conceived and engendered only by means of further conditions of unity.

Until now the unity of the subject has been (and for the time being will remain) defined in terms of the simplicity and singularity that the subject is able to bring to mind in the consciousness of "I think." But this unity seems to suffice entirely for establishing the possibility of the combination of representations. And it appears to impose no further conditions upon the representations that can enter into such consciousness. Whatever thoughts are possible must be capable of being made known as thoughts of a subject. The singularity of a subject is therefore an effective principle of unity, inasmuch as it excludes from the synthesis all thoughts that cannot be brought into a connection in relation to which the subject can become conscious of itself as a single subject. Many representations for that reason may be incapable of becoming the possible thought of a subject.

But any circumstance whatever can stand in the way of representations becoming thoughts. Insofar as they occur at all, the subject would immediately take them into account in view of the unsurrenderable unity of itself, and would enforce this unity over and against the occurrence of such representations. But the requirement of unity at hand in the very concept of the subject is already an adequate guarantee that this will happen. The form of unity per se is the condition of the unity of the synthesis. Additional concepts which would serve to combine all given representations in conformity with rules can therefore be dispensed with. Consequently, categories cannot be derived from the unifying concept of simplicity on grounds of the premises that have been available up to now.

2.2 The Unity of Complex Thoughts

Until now, a priori rules have been regarded as principles for bringing about the connection of representations in self-consciousness. It has become apparent that a persuasive argumentative procedure cannot be instituted on this basis. The unity of the subject in relation to the manifoldness of its representations can, however, be viewed from a different angle, whereby the question arises whether this view makes evident a real prospect of grounding the a priori concepts of combination.

The subject not only must be able to think of itself as being one in relation to an indeterminate multiplicity of thoughts, but it must also be in a position to bring together many kinds of contents into particular complex thoughts. The consciousness of "I think" is not merely one thought in relation to all possible thoughts to the extent that these are in each instance particular thoughts. It is also the consciousness of the one subject of a particular thought, insofar as this thought contains, for purposes of its conceivability, the possibility of a multiplicity of thoughts that are distinct from one another. Conjunctions, disjunctions, all thought of relation, and—as has already become apparent—even the thought of each particular as an object are such complex thoughts. To be sure, they are particular thoughts in the sense that a thought is in each case a single thought. But they would be unthinkable were it not the case that the possibility of particular thoughts about their constitutive elements is conceived along with them.

Now the conditions constituting complex thoughts must surely be distinguished from the conditions of the mere copresence of thoughts in the consciousness of one and the same subject. Otherwise the thought of a complex set of circumstances would be nothing other than an aggregate of thoughts—something which can well be counted as being clearly false. It follows, therefore, that a subject which becomes conscious of itself as a particular subject in relation to the elements of a complex thought must further be conscious of the way in which these elements are represented together within that complex thought. However, the way in which elements such as these go to make up a complex thought can be properly comprehended only as a rule for the formation of complex thoughts. Consequently, the consciousness that a subject has of itself appears also to include an awareness of rules for the combination of thoughts, and it does not appear to be possible apart from such awareness.

A concise argument for assuming a priori rules as conditions of the possibility of self-consciousness could be obtained from this consideration if it could be shown that the thought of the possibility of complex thoughts is a condition sine qua non for every possible thought of self-consciousness. However, the line of argument that has been sketched out does not reach this far. It can only ensure that self-consciousness must be able to ascertain its particularity in relation to each complex thought *as such;* which is to say, in relation to its constitutive elements. The possibility of self-consciousness as a presupposition of the possibility of complex thoughts is thereby made comprehensible. But with regard to this self-consciousness itself, it has merely been asserted that, insofar as complex thoughts are supposed to be possible, self-consciousness must be possible under certain conditions that differ from the general conditions of the possibility of self-consciousness: it must be possible in relation to the elements of such thoughts and, at the same time, in relation to the complexes themselves. In short, it must be possible in relation to both at once. What has not, and cannot, be shown so long as the program of proof makes exclusive reference to the particularity of the subject is the imperativeness of the reference to complex thoughts for the possibility of self-consciousness per se. However, if consciousness of a particular subject is possible apart from its happening with reference to the possibility of complex thoughts, then also the conditions upon which complex thoughts, as such, depend are not necessary implications of the thought of the particular subject. The situation would have to be entirely different for one to be able to demonstrate, for instance, that the thought of the subject includes the thought of a priori rules for complex thoughts. Consequently, by virtue of its particularity self-consciousness contains no resources for the a priori specifiability of the conditions of complex thoughts. If they are at all to be specified a priori, then they can only be so specified for reasons that cannot be derived from the particularity of the subject.[24]

This program of proof, too, has come to nought. Nevertheless, one can

Identity and Objectivity 173

still maintain that it could be complemented if the subject could be attributed the necessary property of being able to develop complex thoughts. The way in which this might take place cannot be read off the as yet entirely vacuous concept of "complex thought." Still, no other program of proof has led us any closer to an argument that could be successful as a transcendental deduction.

2.3 The Unity of the Subject in Its Representations

The same cannot be said of the only remaining member of the group of arguments that find their support in the particularity of self-consciousness. This argument can be constructed along the following lines: It is determined that the subject must set itself in relation to all its representations in precisely the same way. Inquiry is then made into the way in which a subject can become conscious of its representations *as* its own. Because the representations have entirely disparate contents, their belonging to the same subject is not to be determined on grounds of their content. But since they belong to the subject, and since, by virtue of their belonging to something particular, they constitute a single representational connection, there must also be conditions by virtue of which their connection can be displayed to consciousness. And these conditions must differ from what is immediately displayed to consciousness in the consciousness of the subject. Inasmuch as the subject is one and the connection of representations in it corresponds to its particularity, these conditions must be such as to guarantee the connection of representations as a particular and unique connection in that subject. Moreover, since Cartesian certainty accrues to the subject, these principles must be accessible a priori in one knowledge.

As was the case with the preceding arguments, it cannot be denied that this argument, too, has suggestive force. Neither can one rule out that it had a role to play in the network of theoretical associations which influenced Kant in the actual composition of the transcendental deduction. Nevertheless, when taken by itself it must be seen to rest upon a fallacy. For were the subject not in a position to bring to awareness that representations belong to the complex of its thinking in relation to itself as a subject as well as to every single thought, then it would be incapable of recognizing as the correlate of its singularity the connection between its representations that is established on grounds of certain combinatory functions. From the general availability of certain combinations it can at best make clear to itself (though it cannot, for instance, originally disclose) that the thoughts at hand in this combination are *its* thoughts. What first makes this function into a correlate of unity is the relation of the combinatory function to thoughts which the subject can in each instance have knowledge of as its own. Thus, the subject must already know of this function in order to be able to comprehend the combination as the correlate of its unity.

Accordingly, the argumentation presupposes what it disputes: it is only in relation to itself and without reference to the determinate structural properties of its thoughts and representations that the subject is able to understand that these representations belong to the sum-total [*Inbegriff*] of its representations. And this totality is conceivable as the thought of the multiplicity of representations which a subject attributes to itself as its own, apart from any relation to further properties that the elements of this multiplicity must have in common or which bind them together in one-to-one relations. If there are any compelling reasons for all the subject's representations having to submit to rules, it is under such rules that the subject will become conscious of these representations. If these reasons cannot be found, then the relation of representations to a single subject is a sufficient ground for comprehending them as representations that can be related to one another in one consciousness. It can thereby remain an open question whether this consciousness already implicitly accompanies every representation, whether it is merely a consequence of the reflection by virtue of which the consciousness of "I think" occasionally makes its appearance in addition to the consciousness of representations, or whether the consciousness of the connection of representations can be described adequately as a consequence of the ever-current consciousness of the possibility of reflection. In no case can one obtain a connection of thoughts still distinguishable from their connection in the subject from their relation to the knowledge which that subject has of them as its own thoughts.

3. Identity and Combination within Self-Consciousness

The approaches to a transcendental deduction starting from the notion of the particularity of the subject alone appear now to have been exhausted. They have led several times to formulations corresponding to Kant's thesis about the dependency of self-consciousness upon the possibility of a priori combination. However, if one pays heed to what these formulations really say, it is not difficult to discern how vast the distance is which separates them from Kant's thesis. Several of the arguments evaluated came down to imputing to Kant a capital logical fallacy. Others were able to demonstrate theoretical potential but were by themselves inadequate for actually executing the decisive move in a transcendental deduction: the grounding of the categories as principles of necessary combination prior to all experience.[25]

All the arguments considered thus far have been structured and formulated in such a way as to preclude any reference to self-consciousness as a principle of identity. But in the few brief texts that must figure as key passages for the interpretation of the transcendental deduction, Kant notoriously, and almost without exception, avails himself of the "numerical identity" of self-consciousness. It is not determined whether Kant everywhere explicitly gave this term a specific meaning. Nonetheless, the text of his *Critique* gives good reason for us to expect that what has remained unattainable with reference to the particularity of self-consciousness can be achieved with reference to this special sense of identity. Here we have compelling reason to develop and test the arguments pertaining to the identity of the subject in the same way we did for the arguments concerning the subject's particularity.

To attribute identity to the subject is to ascribe to it a multiplicity of different states, in each of which it comes to be conscious as the same subject. It has already been shown that Kant unequivocally (even if not in all cases) attributed such states to the subject and that he defined the meaning of its identity with reference to these states. The kinds of states which Kant needed to suppose can remain an open question for the time being. However, we must note to begin with that it is impossible to ascribe a number of states to the subject without simultaneously thinking of it as submitting to a *process*. The subject must be able to *progress* [*übergehen*] from one state to another. And it must be able to do this in such a way that it is able to think of itself as the same subject both in relation to its states and in relation to the process of transition.

Thus, as soon as the notion of the unified subject is introduced as being equally the notion of the identical subject, it will inevitably be understand falsely, if one takes it as implying that all thoughts convene in the subject in a single thought of overwhelming richness in content, or as implying that the self is the subject of an aggregate of different thoughts in a single state of consciousness. The identical subject is the subject of *one* thought at a time or of several among many possible thoughts. It is the same subject insofar as it is conceived as that which can always in the same way think different thoughts as its own thoughts, and insofar as it is conceived as that which really does think many thoughts separately. Thus, from the outset the subject is thought of in such a way that it is adjoined to certain representations, or that it produces certain thoughts which can only be thought insofar as other thoughts are *not* thought. Nonetheless, it is also thought of in a way that the very same thing can be said of these other thoughts, for they too are real thoughts of the subject in a different state. And inasmuch as they are currently thought by the subject, other thoughts are excluded from the actual thought of the subject. Moreover, if the connection of thoughts in the subject is grasped in this manner, then the transition which takes place in consciousness from one thought to another is correlatively thought of as well. And this transition can be conceived without our having to draw upon the specific properties of any temporal sequence. The complicated formulation of the preceding sentences was chosen to ensure this possibility.

On the strength of these considerations we can achieve an overview of the arguments to be investigated with regard to the identity of self-consciousness and with the intention of establishing the necessity of the categories. They can be divided, first of all, into two groups: There may be arguments which are related to the concept of transition implicated by the identity of the subject. These are arguments which exhibit their validating procedure solely in view of this implication of identity and not in view of identity per se. Other arguments will make direct reference to self-consciousness as a principle of identity. On grounds of a more definite interpretation of its identity, they will seek to make evident the necessity of the categories. But before we can enter into arguments like these we must investigate the different accounts of the numerical identity of self-consciousness. We shall begin with the arguments that pertain solely to the consciousness of transition, since they include but a small group and are of lesser importance.

3.1 Transition in Self-Consciousness

Transition in self-consciousness combines particular thoughts with other particular thoughts. If "synthesis" is to be neither merely the name for the juxtaposition [*Zusammensein*] of representations in one consciousness nor the name for an activity that has this as a result, if it is rather to designate an event or act in which, or by virtue of which, one representation is in each instance added to another, then transition in consciousness is the minimum condition for an interpretation of synthesis such as this. Since this synthesis has turned out to be the implication of the identity of self-consciousness, no self-consciousness is possible if the synthesis does not take place.

It is, of course, obvious that this does not prove that such synthesis necessarily comes about in accordance with well-determined and unchangeable laws. At this point, a conclusion bordering upon an assertion of the opposite is far more plausible. That is, if the subject can accompany all its thoughts by the consciousness of "I think," then the way in which one thought comes to be related to another is of no import. In each instance

Identity and Objectivity

the subject can pass from the one to the other in the awareness of being the same subject. It can be determined entirely through experience which thoughts actually occur, as well as the circumstances under which they do so. Thus, for the present, the synthesis lacks the property which is decisive for the constitution of the object, i.e., the property of placing the transition from one representation to another under universal and necessary conditions.

In the first edition of the *Critique of Pure Reason* Kant worked out, in connection with his theory of the synthesis of recognition (A 103ff.), an argument which in a sense forces us to think of all transition in consciousness as being regulated transition. Transition in consciousness is distinguished from change as an objective sequence by the circumstance that in the consciousness of transition the past must still be present if change as such is to be experienced. Kant appears to proceed on the assumption that we relate ourselves to past representations by means of a representation of the past which we currently have. If one grants him this premise, it follows that we relate ourselves to past representations by thinking one of our current representations as being the same as one we ascribe to our past representational state. But then one must be able to state what it is that allows us to know of the self-sameness of two representations under entirely different conditions. Knowledge like this is possible only when we are also in a position to characterize past and currently nonactual representations. We store them, as it were, under a description that applies equally to a current representation by means of which we keep present as our own the past representation. If all this is correct, then it would be shown thereby that transition in consciousness is the recognition of what is past, and that it consequently involves the use of concepts. However, concepts are rules of combination. More precisely, they are rules of combination in the sense that they encompass manifold representations as instances of the same kind, and that they consequently link the occurrence or recurrence of instances to the satisfaction of a set of defining marks.

This argument may be taken as a prelude to fundamental considerations on the theory of the categories, for the possibility of the relation to what is past is constitutive for the structure of our consciousness. This possibility allows a priori principles of the basic constitution of this consciousness to be inferred. But from it one cannot ground the necessity of the Kantian categories, since basic concepts such as these are certainly not to be comprehended merely as a type of rule under which past representations are convened. Through the categories we conceive the conditions for consigning to the same class of representations those future representations to which the description thought in the category applies. However, the necessity of employing concepts, which could be detected, for instance, in Kant's argument regarding recognition, is confined to the lasting presence of past representations in the transition to new ones. This does, of course, make the possibility of advancing to new representations dependent upon the circumstance that rules are in force. Still, these rules hold not for the transition to new representations but merely for the storing of those representations in relation to which other representations can be forthcoming as something new. Representations can thus arise in relation to past representations in an entirely arbitrary manner, even when it is impossible to represent those past. From the circumstance that recognition is subject to conditions, nothing is settled about the fact that the fundamental aspect of synthesis, i.e., the progression to new representations, also requires the *precognition* of the progression's conditions. But the question about rules for synthesis in consciousness concerns rules of progression in precisely this sense.

The analysis of recognition shares with other arguments the drawback of merely postulating rules in general and, consequently, of not being in a position to show in detail what rules make possible the transition in consciousness. If that is the final word, then the rules that allow us to retain in awareness what is past must be gathered from experience. But even if Kant's intention to achieve a priori rules for recognition could be realized, the fundamental weakness of his analysis of recognition would persist as long as it is not integrated into the broader context of other lines of argument which alone can decide Kant's problem of the deduction of the categories.

It cannot be excluded that other arguments can be framed which describe and ground the categories as necessary conditions for a transition in self-consciousness. However, the argumentative scheme actually furnished by Kant is inadequate, and his texts suggest that his argument must be referred specifically to the identity of self-consciousness. There is thus reason to place greater hope in the investigation of argumentative procedures of the latter type.

3.2 Two Concepts of Numerical Identity

From the whole of possible consciousness "numerical identity is inseparable" (A 113). The term employed in this and other passages (A 107, 108, B 113)—and which is not always strictly distinguished from the unity of self-consciousness that derives from its simplicity—was familiar to Kant from Leibniz and the debates among the Leibnizians.

According to Leibniz, two objects are numerically identical when they have exactly the same properties. Such objects can be deemed identical by reason of being in truth but a single object regarded from different viewpoints. Particular objects which differ in number can be identical with each other only in kind or species. Numerical identity is total identity; it is the identity demonstrated by the particular qua particular: "The same in number is in truth that which can be affirmed of itself, or which is opposed to existing as two. It is also called 'the Same itself.'"[26]

Identity is attributed to such a particular insofar as an observation similar to a comparison has been made with respect to it. Of course, only what is really different can be subject to comparison. But since difference [*Verschiedenheit*] is the concept opposed to undifferentiatedness [*Unterschiedslosigkeit*], and since the latter in its strict sense determines the meaning of numerical identity, this identity, too, can only be asserted with reference to something which likewise can be addressed on the strength of possible difference. Baumgarten, a disciple of Wolff's, underscored this connection by treating identity as a relational concept (*Metaphysica*, §215ff.), and Kant securely established it by comprehending identity as well as difference not as concepts of objects but as concepts for the comparison of objects (B 319ff.).

From the circumstance that every particular must be attributed numerical identity, Leibniz drew a far-reaching and astonishing conclusion: If identity is a property that presupposes different states, and if a particular (i.e., a substance) can demonstrate identity only when it is in itself completely the same in every relation and under every condition, then it seems to follow that a substance must at all times possess all its different states. Otherwise it would not be one substance, but rather a sequence of different substances. It can further be inferred from this that substances can only be Leibnizian monads: all states of substances are present in them from the beginning onward; they can neither be brought to new states by external influence, nor can they spontaneously generate states. The only real changes in a substance are changes in its self-comprehension.

The foundation of Leibniz's theory of substance is thus to be found in the theoretical operation by which he exploits the tension that exists between the two aspects of the meaning of "identity," a tension necessarily engendered by the way in which he defines this concept. Leibniz acknowledges that without states which demonstrate real differences, identity loses its sense. But at the same time he grasps the meaning of identity as restrictively as possible. He treats it in such a way that it requires the exclusion of every difference, including even the difference between varying states.

The attempt to make both warrantable at once inevitably results in the theory of substances as monads. It is probable that there are no possible means of making this theory consistent, but this issue can be disregarded here.

Leibniz's strict concept of numerical identity was criticized at a very early date, by Crusius among others. The criticism of it is also easy to substantiate, for Leibniz's definition deliberately overburdens and overextends the genuine meaning of the concept of identity. Since this concept is expressly aimed at different states of the same particular object, it cannot be redefined to the effect that the change of states is excluded by the concept itself. Particular things can remain the same throughout change in their states as long as several of their constitutive properties remain unchanged or as long as the thing in question endures through the continuous, but never total, change of its states. Let us call the concept of identity defended against Leibniz along these lines the "moderate" concept of numerical identity. We shall oppose it to Leibniz's concept of "strict" numerical identity.

At this point, two questions naturally present themselves with reference to Kant: Which of the two concepts of identity should be imputed to the text of the transcendental deduction? Which of them furnishes the means for formulating a deductive procedure which really does achieve its intended goal?

Kant rejected the strict concept of identity as a general ontological principle. The observation that things sharing the same properties can nonetheless differ from one another according to their position in space and time belongs to his best-known and simplest arguments against the Leibnizian philosophy. But even if it is probable that Kant wanted to conceive of numerical identity in terms of moderate identity, it cannot be directly inferred from his customary arguments against Leibniz that he could not—even in the special case of self-consciousness—have thought of identity in accordance with the strict concept. For precisely that which applies to things as appearances does not apply to self-consciousness, viz., individuation by the form of appearances. In opposition to this is grounded the tendency in Kant's theoretical approach to comprehend self-consciousness as something "pure, original, unchangeable," as the "fixed and abiding" self (A 107) beyond all flux. Kant follows that tendency without hesitation and, as will become apparent, conforms to it even more emphatically than the general thrust of his approach ought to allow. For this reason, it is not at the start pointless or far-fetched to explore the feasibility of a transcendental deduction that is provided by the concept of strict numerical identity.

3.3 Strict Identity and Rule of Combination

Let us therefore assume that Kant attributes to the transcendental subject the property of numerical identity. Insofar as the transcendental subject partakes of identity at all, states must also be distinguishable with reference to this subject. Kant does not have the option of conceiving (according to Leibniz's example) all these states as being incorporated in the definition of the essence of the subject, for the states of the representing subject are dependent upon what is given to it in intuition. They cannot be attributed to the subject in the same way as the inner make-up of its consciousness and activity. Consequently, Kant would have to seek another avenue of escape from the theoretical tension between identity and sequence of the states of a particular which is necessarily generated by adherence to the strict concept of identity. Such states appear to rule out further conceiving the subject as being in the strict sense identical in its states. In any event, they do this unless a mediating principle can be found by virtue of which changing representations can be seen to belong to the same subject while the subject remains inalterably the same in relation to them. The subject must be related to changing contents; it must be present in them; yet it must be inalterably the same. How is a mediating principle like this to be conceived?

To pose this question within a Kantian framework is already to propose an answer: the subject can be present in changing representations by the way in which these representations are represented in a combination. In this case, the representations qua representations are not ascribed to the subject qua subject. But they are that by which one representational state distinguishes itself from another. Conversely, the way in which different representations are combined with each other in this state is determined by the subject. Indeed, it is so determined once and for all independently of all given contents. Representations can be representations of the subject only when they comply with the conditions prescribed for them by the unchangeable constitution of the subject's unity.

States will therefore be attributable to the subject only in view of the circumstance that it enters into relations. However, the subject remains completely unchanged in the representational states resulting from the entry of the given into the numerically identical form of the subject-combination [*Subjektverbindung*]. Hence, the difficulties incurred by Leibniz, when he described the progression in the consciousness of a substance as the consequence of a process of its self-clarification, do not even arise. Through such a process the substance seems in turn to become involved in a sequence of states, each of which modifies the substance as such. To be sure, they are distinguished from one another not by the contents of representations intrinsic to the substance but by the varying degrees of clarity of those representations. They are thus states of a different kind from those which Leibniz had attributed to substance. Nevertheless, they are similar to these inasmuch as they are in principle modifiable states of substance. In view of a theoretical predicament such as this, the argument that Kant was able to make use of appears in a favorable light. Kant could conceive of representational contents in such a way that the subject is related only to them and that they nonetheless lend meaning to discourse about states of the subject. But they do this for discourse about states which do not detract from the strict identity of the subject. Regardless of its other merits, this Kantian argument nearly resolves Leibniz's dilemma.[27]

The assumption from which this argument proceeds may appear quite odd, but its conclusion is nonetheless compelling. The step by which it passes from the constancy of the identical subject to the constant form of combination cannot, of course, support itself. But it becomes mandatory when one bears in mind that other, more elementary investigations of self-consciousness already had established that combination is the way in which the subject is related to what is given to it. It is also legitimate to comprehend a constant form of combination as a rule that in the actual course of synthesis must be, and always is, taken into account. Kant's concept of a rule is formulated in such a way that he also designates as rules relations of conditionality which by no means may be violated: "Now . . . the representation of a universal condition according to which a certain manifold can be posited in a uniform manner is called a *rule,* and when it must be so posited, a *law*" (A 113). The normative component of meaning according to which rules are instructions subject to violation is no longer taken as basic on this definition, and in all probability it can even be eliminated. A rule like this can be the constant pattern of a relation of conditionality which must always be taken into account when the identical subject comes to be related to changing contents.[28] The possibility condition for the identical subject to enter into such relations would be located in the identity of the rule. Its identity would consequently correspond to the identity of the subject and would be derived from it.

Still, one does not wish to attribute to Kant a strategy of proof which by a coup de main, as it were, resolves the problem of understanding or construing the connection between self-consciousness and the categories in terms of a definition of identity. That identity can be grasped only in this way has not been made evident. And the philosophy of the final third of the eighteenth century both contains too many objections to this defi-

Identity and Objectivity   183

nition and points out too convincingly the absurdities to which it leads for one to be able to maintain that Kant could have made the success of his deduction dependent upon such a line of argument.

Even more important is the circumstance that Kant is compelled by reasons intrinsic to the *subject matter* itself to apply the moderate concept of identity to the unity of apperception. For he could not get around ascribing to the subject states which cannot at all be interpreted according to the model just presented, by which states are interpreted starting from strict identity. It was thus constitutive for the notion of the transcendental unity of apperception that the consciousness of "I think" can at all times be adjoined to every representational state of the subject. This consciousness must further be comprehended as the result of an activity called "reflection," which must be exercised by the subject and which consequently can be exercised at all times. Hence, for any representational complex, if the consciousness of "I think" (this representational complex) really occurs, then the total state of the subject is thereby altered. It is altered not only by the circumstance that certain representational contents are replaced by others, but also by the way in which the subject is related to constant contents. Reflections must therefore be acknowledged as real changes in the state of the subject qua subject, but as changes which nonetheless leave its identity untouched. But then the identity which accrues to the subject must be identity in the moderate sense of the term.

Yet another line of argument founders on the necessity of conceding this point. It is a line of argument which is actually to be found in Kant's texts and which makes clear how susceptible his entire train of thought was to the temptation of becoming involved with the concept of identity in the strict sense. In the chapter on the paralogisms of rational psychology in the first edition of the *Critique,* Kant explains that the self may not be regarded as permanent. This is owing to the circumstance that permanence must be thought in relation to change, but that all change takes place *in* the self and not in relation to it, since time is nothing but the form of intuition (A 362ff.). Were one to take this argument as Kant's final word upon the question of whether states can be ascribed to the self, then it would indeed amount to saying that the transcendental subject must demonstrate identity in the strict sense of the term. In truth, though, it suffices only for distinguishing between the enduring character [*Ständigkeit*] of the self and the permanence of substance. The sole thesis in which rational psychology was interested, i.e., the thesis that the self has necessarily to be conceived as unchanging, has thereby already lost its evidential basis. But even a self which does not endure in time like a substance is comprehended by Kant as a source of acts, among which are to be counted those acts of reflection which alter the state of consciousness. This does not rule out that notions of unchangeable self-sameness and necessary unity are also included in the concept of the subject. They constitute what can doubtlessly be called transcendental unity of apperception in the "logical" sense of the term. However, Kant's transcendental subject is not merely a logical condition of possible self-consciousness. It is, rather, just that which real consciousness knows to be the subject of all possible real consciousness. Even if it cannot be thought apart from concepts of unity and identity, and if, indeed, it must be thought primarily through these concepts, it is still no abstract or formal object. Rather, it is, among other things, the real ground of reflective acts (and according to Kant, also of synthesis). In the concept of the subject both aspects are necessarily correlative. And no philosophical reason stands in the way of comprehending a principle defined under the necessary inclusion of formal concepts as a real principle, and even as a real particular.

One might remain unconvinced by these arguments against interpreting Kant's texts on the deduction of the categories as proofs carried out in terms of strict identity. If so, then a different argument against such a strategy of proof will presumably be persuasive: in all key texts Kant emphatically maintains that the transcendental deduction cannot dispense with premises asserting that the transcendental unity of apperception is an a priori principle. In the validation of the deductive procedure one must lay claim in equal measure to aprioricity and identity: "For the mind could never think the identity of itself in the manifoldness of its representation, *and indeed think this identity a priori*" (A 108, italics mine).

Now the conclusive force of the argument that makes use of strict identity is entirely independent of whether or not the subject is an a priori principle. If self-consciousness is (for whatever reasons) attributed strict identity, it follows directly that constant conditions of the combination of given representations must be locatable within its structure. It may indeed be necessary to return to the Cartesian status of self-consciousness in order to be able at all to ensure its identity. But the way in which inferences are drawn from identity is of no significance for the way in which identity is ensured. Consider a subject with which we are acquainted from experience and to which we must, for one reason or another, attribute strict identity—for instance, because identity has only the meaning of strict identity. Even this subject would have to produce combinations in a definite, unchangeable manner if it were at all to serve as the ground of combinations.

Now by these considerations a criterion has been achieved according to which the success of the analyses still outstanding can be judged: in what follows, we must examine those deductions based on the concept of moderate identity. A deduction of this type, however, will appear convincing as a proposed basis for interpreting Kant's thoughts only if it is grounded in *both* the moderate identity of self-consciousness *and* the aprioricity of its certainty, these being taken as two independent and indispensable premises.

3.4 Moderate Identity and a priori Rule

One can expect that arguments relating to moderate identity are greater in number than those permitted by the notion of strict identity. Nevertheless, this number is already greatly reduced owing to the fact that from now on we have at our disposal a criterion which allows for the selection of arguments having a genuine prospect of success. As a matter of fact, arguments not satisfying this criterion can be entirely disregarded. In the following, though, two of these will at least be mentioned (a, b), inasmuch as they appear to play a role in the latticework of the Kantian texts. After that (c), the only argument that completely satisfies our criterion, will be expounded upon.

(a) It might seem that a subject which is expressly distinguished from a substance can be characterized as a particular by nothing other than the rules in conformity with which it acts. A self, however, must be a determinate self by reason of some kind of constitutive properties. Consequently, it would simply be inconceivable without rules of its synthesis.

This argumentative attempt is manifestly untenable. According to Kant, synthesis is for its part conceivable only when it is taken in relation to the thought of the same subject. Thus, this subject must be thinkable in advance of all rules of its synthesis or the rules themselves will turn out to be unthinkable. Furthermore, no subject can be thought as a definite, particular subject by means of the notion of rules in general. Rules can be employed by many particulars. Whenever the employment of rules characterizes a particular, there must be the possibility of thematizing the particular as such in a different way and in advance. Now in its self-awareness the subject is immediately conscious of itself as a particular, and it conceives the rules of its synthesis with reference to this particularity. A condition which would precede this consciousness, and by whose satisfaction it would first become the consciousness of a particular, cannot be assumed within the framework of an analysis that adheres to Kant's attestations.

(b) Kant occasionally describes the synthesis of the subject as an activity through which the self ensures its unity or by which it puts this unity, as a product of its own activity, *to the test* in relation to given representations. According to this portrayal, the subject is a principle of independent self-ascertainment. The synthesis according to concepts is the way "in which alone apperception can demonstrate its thoroughgoing and necessary identity" (A 112). And the subject appears to be the principle of unity that it is by reason of its being furnished with the instruments which allow it to *achieve* its unity by imposing that unity upon given representations. As a matter of fact, representations of the independence of human beings which make possible epistemological metaphors such as these can be found in many passages in Kant's work. But quite apart from the fact that they support a conception of independence which for anthropological reasons must be considered dubious,[29] they are also unable to attain their argumentative goal. For the expectation that the subject can, by its own activity alone, guarantee its unity through its synthesis can be seen to be groundless for the simple reason that the continuance of its activity is in any event not dependent upon itself. Certainly, the subject will exercise its synthetic activity as long as it exists. And the unity of the subject may actually be established within that activity. The activity may also be necessary for the subject to have any acquaintance with itself. Reasons for this being the case have not yet been given, but they can only be theoretical conditions of the subject's self-certainty. The connotation of self-generation must be eliminated from the notion of self-certainty. It has its legitimate place in practical philosophy, which, however, presupposes for its part a tenable concept of self-consciousness.

(c) After these two weak argumentative attempts, I shall now articulate the argument without which Kant's multiform considerations can yield no coherent picture. It will become apparent that this argument can be linked to a number of Kant's other argumentative procedures which remain inconclusive when taken by themselves. It will further become apparent that this can be done in such a way that these procedures receive their proper role in a strategy of proof to be framed solely in view of Kant's key argument.

The key argument has its point of departure in considerations on the identity of the subject with which we are already familiar: self-consciousness demonstrates the aspect of simplicity just as it does that of identity. Identity must be taken as identity in the moderate sense. At the same time, it must be referred to self-consciousness as a principle of Cartesian certainty. Now identity entails a sequence of states of the same subject. It is only in the transition from state to state that the subject can at all be the same; it is only with reference to this transition that the subject can grasp itself as being the same. However, since the subject is cognizant of itself in its Cartesian certainty, and since the knowledge of its numerical identity is included in this certainty, everything that is necessarily entailed by the notion of numerical identity so as to constitute the meaning of this notion must be known together with, and in, the a priori knowledge that the subject has of itself. It follows from this that the subject must have in advance of all experience a knowledge of what it means for it to pass from one representational state to another.

This raises the question of how it is possible to know something about a transition taking place under the subject's identity conditions without being able, in this knowledge, to refer to any definite transitions in which the subject has found itself. For even if the knowledge which the subject has of itself can in fact occur only together with the experience of real transitions, the content of this knowledge is, by virtue of its apodicticity, still independent of all cognizance of any definite transitions.

To this question, too, Kant nowhere expressly responded. In only a few passages (ones that remain entirely unelucidated and which, so to speak, sit tight in an underbrush of related considerations) does one find fragments of an answer, fragments which for their part need to be fit together and supplemented by independent considerations. Even the most important text is crammed and overloaded. But it still enlarges upon Kant's theoretical association more amply and is more accessible than Kant's other texts: "For the mind could not possibly think the identity of itself in the manifoldness of its representation, and indeed think this identity a priori, if it did not have before its eyes the identity of its act which subjects all synthesis of apprehension (which is empirical) to a transcendental unity and thereby renders possible its connection according to a priori rules" (A 108).

The train of thought in this passage will later be analyzed in a separate section. We shall here consider the reasons for Kant's thesis that the mind can ascertain its identity solely in view of a regulated synthesis.[30]

As long as transitions in consciousness are to be noted only as *facta*, it is unintelligible why they must be subject to rules of strict universality. But knowledge of the transitional activity of the subject must enter into the a priori knowledge of identity. That which is known in this knowledge is not that through which one transition or another really has, or will, come about. The knowledge of transition seated in the Cartesian principle of identity can no more derive from experience than it can be a forecast of future transitions. Only so much of the transition can be implicated in it as is required for the *intelligibility* of the meaning of the subject's identity.[31]

But it is impossible to conceive of a transition at all without at the same time conceiving the manner in which the transition takes place. I can, indeed, abstract a general concept of transition from many particular instances. But I cannot understand what transition means without referring, with some definiteness, to a transitional activity. It makes no sense to assume the notion of a transition without any specification and in advance of all experience. It makes no more sense than wanting, for instance, to speak of color in general in advance of any definite perception of color. To the extent that it is the notion of the identity of the subject in the transition from state to state, the notion of subject identity must for this reason also be that of definite *modes* of transition. And since this last notion is the indispensable condition for the form of that knowledge which the subject has of itself, the notion of transition that is codeterminative of the meaning of subject identity can only be that of *constant* modes of transition. These must be constant, because it is only in this way that they are suitable for rendering possible, independently of all experience and in unconditional universality, the knowledge of the subject's identity, which is at all times possible.

Because of this, the knowledge of transition of a principle of identity that is known a priori is different from the knowledge of identical objects based on experience. It differs not only in its degree of certainty but also in its structure and content. The modes of transition of empirically cognized identical objects can change, because all knowledge of these objects derives in any event from experience. We can thus assert their continued existence under altered conditions by reason of the adaptation of the level of our knowledge and criteria of identity to real developments. An a priori principle of identity fundamentally rules out such adaptation.

The modes of transition posited in the concept of the identical self have been spoken of in the plural. That does not rule out the possibility that a single mode of transition could satisfy the conditions of self-consciousness. If, however, as will become apparent, a number of modes are included in the concept of self-consciousness, then they are all subject to the constancy postulate just established. It is unthinkable that one could take the place of another. They are several, because they fulfill various *functions* that are coconceived in the notion of the ego as a principle of identity. However, because of the aprioricity of the ego, one, and only one mode of transition can be conceived with reference to each function.

Knowledge of constant modes of transition is thus presupposed wherever the subject thinks itself a priori under the aspect of its identity. Wherever transition occurs in such a subject, it must take place in accordance with those modes. The modes of transition are necessary by virtue of the aprioricity of the knowledge of the subject, something which, according to Kant, is prior to all knowledge of logical principles (B 134, note). Under circumstances like these it is neither difficult nor dangerous to interpret the knowledge of the constant conditions of transition as a knowledge of *rules* that apply to all possible transitions from one state of the subject to another. To define a mode of transition is to specify the conditions according to which one state is replaced by another. It is, in addition, to determine which states can occur in relation to which others. However, it has already been shown that rules cannot be comprehended as instructions. The concept of rules is appropriate even in those instances in which it is unavoidable for conditions to be satisfied, because a principle a priori (and, hence, reason) guarantees their satisfaction. "But now the representation of a universal condition according to which a certain manifold can be posited ... is called a *rule,* and, when it must be so posited, a *law*" (A 113). This definition, incidentally, follows (with changed application) that of Baumgarten: "A proposition enunciating a determination conforming to reason is a norm (rule, law)."[32]

At this point, the suspicion might arise that too many implications have already been packed into the notion of a mode of transition, implications that are simply unobtainable from a completely formal principle. As a condition for the possibility of a concept of subject identity, the mere thought of a sequence of states should already suffice, for it might seem that the temporality of consciousness provides an adequate basis for the thought of the identical subject of consciousness. Two different factors are overlooked in this objection. First, time-sequence too (especially time-sequence in consciousness) is a relation of conditionality. For any present temporal phase occurs only through the disappearance of another; and, as the analysis of recognition has shown, the awareness of the sequence presupposes possibilities of describing what is past. Second, one must take into account the Kantian position that time-sequence is not an implication of the subject's sense of identity. This thesis is not absurd, as it might seem, for undoubtedly one must admit that there are nontemporal sequences such as logical transformations. This is not yet to say that with reference to these sequences one can speak of the identity of, for instance, concepts, through a series of transformations. Nevertheless, it surely presupposes subject identity in discourse. The transformation rules entailed by the concept of the identical subject in consciousness must be comprehended as modes of transition in analogy with rules of such logical derivation.

This analogy has not yet been made sufficiently clear, since our remarks have been concerned merely with the states of the subject, and not with states of contents. Still, these states must from the outset be reckoned among the *representational* states in which the subject is related to contents that are given to it. The circumstance that the sequence of these states is regulated means also, therefore, that the contents represented by the subject can only be represented in such a way that the representations of them always make (or allow to remain) possible that transition from one representational state to another which is codeterminative for the thought of subject identity. Consequently, the rule for the sequence of representational states is equally a rule for the possible occurrence of representational contents.[33] This argumentative procedure can be supplemented and strengthened by means of two further arguments.[34]

(a) The following distinction must be drawn between the identity of the person through the sequence of his states in time and the identity of the subject of thoughts: the sequence of states of the person is defined by his life history. It is indeed possible to survey the stages of life and to add these together. But in this summation [*Inbegriff*] the sequence of transitions between the stages nonetheless remains inalterably determined. The representational states of the subject are related to the subject in a different manner. Something is the representational state, and thus likewise the representational content, of *one* subject only when it is known as that to which advancement can be made starting from *every* representational content. In logical derivation and in inference, as well as in the clarification of recollections or in articulate attention, the subject can pass from each and every representational state to any other in its own total complex [*Inbegriff*] of representations. The principle of the universality of possible transition is established together with the notion of an identical subject of representations. Now the manner in which transitions between elements in the total complex of representations of *one* subject take place in conformity with this principle cannot only be that of the succession of states. Modes and rules must already be in place by virtue of which each representational content can be the content of a representational state in a way that permits a transition to be made from it to every other content while it maintains its own determinateness. Rules that specify conditions such as these must be distinguished from rules for the simple transition between given states. Nevertheless, they presuppose such simple rules, so it follows henceforth that the validity of a plurality of rules of transition is implicated by the concept of the identical subject.[35]

(b) In the knowledge of its identity the subject is therefore related to a total complex of *possible* transitions. Only the modes of these transitions,

Identity and Objectivity 191

not their sequence, are determined by the concept of this complex. It follows from this that the possibility of initiating such transitions can also be fundamentally attributed to the subject. The indeterminateness of the transitional sequence is, of course, merely a necessary, and not a sufficient, condition for such an assumption. Nevertheless, the subject has already been shown to be comprehensible as the agent [*Akteur*] of an activity for other reasons: from the subject there proceeds the activity of reflection by virtue of which explicit self-consciousness (and, consequently, the consciousness analyzed here) can at all come about. If the ego [*das Ich*] is an agent, it is all the easier to ascribe to it a further activity, namely, the activity by means of which transitions between representational states are *initiated*. A transition between such states is also a synthesis with regard to that which is represented in them.

Kant teaches that *all* synthesis must be performed by the subject. Although the problematic resulting from this thesis will not be taken up in this investigation, we have touched upon a point that can be linked to it.[36] Kant's thesis cannot be upheld in the degree of generality that claims to trace back all synthesis to acts of the subject. Nevertheless, it can be shown quite handily that the subject, *inasmuch as* it reflects, must at the same time engender certain acts of synthesis. Even if not all synthesis is subject-dependent, synthesis is still *available* to the subject. The possibility of carrying out such synthesis is included in the latent knowledge of the possibility that the subject has of always being able to reflect upon itself. This possibility, however, must be understood in relation to the total complex of representations toward which the subject, qua principle of identity, is in any event oriented. It further follows that the subject must be aware of the possibility of initiating transitions and combinations with reference to this complex. The fact that transitions which are *occasioned* must be occasioned according to definite modes, and hence rules, seems to be even less dubitable than that the mere notion of transition in a total complex of representations entails as well the notion of modes and rules. Starting from the second supplementary argument, Kant's inference from self-consciousness as an identity principle to the necessity of the categories can be developed with even more direct persuasiveness. Of course, this argument does employ a premise which we have not been able to test and develop.

In any event, though, Kant's claim—one which must be defended at the very outset of a transcendental deduction—can now be regarded as guaranteed by an argument that is the best one, and indeed the only one, which could have been achieved within the framework of his theory: the identity of self-consciousness which we actually think a priori could not be conceived in this way if it did not include the thought of necessary rules to which all appearances are subject insofar as they are to be thought at all.

At this juncture our attention has still to be directed to several merits of Kant's argument, inasmuch as we must show it to be a convincing means of interpreting Kant's texts: (a) The argument is the only one that satisfies the criterion of success for a suggested reading of the text of the transcendental deduction, for it is based both upon the aspect of self-consciousness according to which this serves as a principle of identity and upon the circumstance that this identity and its implications are recognized a priori. If either of these two elements were missing, the argument could not be carried out. This coincides with Kant's own view of the evidentiary situation of the transcendental deduction.

(b) A reason for the miscarriage of one important attempt at developing the transcendental deduction out of the notion of the simplicity of the subject was that it permitted only the assumption of principles of synthesis which in advance of all consciousness make possible the integration of given intuitions into the unity of the subject. It did not require the further assumption that the subject has knowledge of those principles. But Kant's formulations show clearly that he was of the opinion that self-consciousness comes about only in conjunction with the consciousness of the synthetic functions of the subject. The philosopher, therefore, does not discover the fact that self-consciousness presupposes necessary thoughts other than the elementary thought of its simplicity and identity, as when one discovers a treasure hoard as yet unseen by anyone. The philosopher illuminates only the connection between the unity of the subject and the unity of nature that is to be conceived by means of the categories. For in truth, the mind could not even think its identity without having its act "before its eyes ... which first renders possible an interconnection according to rules." Thus it is that the most important textual support for Kant's unexplicated considerations about the transcendental deduction (A 108) describes the inner dependency of the consciousness of the subject upon the consciousness of the rule on the part of that self-consciousness which the philosophical theory analyzes. This dependency is made understandable by the argumentative procedure last elaborated upon, and by this alone. For the notion of moderate identity, apart from which the notion of our self-consciousness cannot be understood, can only be applied to this self-consciousness in advance of all experience when it is at the same time attributed to an a priori knowledge of rules of combination. This is knowledge in which self-consciousness makes reference to possible experience prior to all experience.

4. Identity and Unity of Self-Consciousness

Kant nowhere succeeded in distinguishing between the design for a transcendental deduction starting from the simplicity of the subject and the design starting from the subject's identity. In all textual passages in which one could expect any clarification, elements from both schemes are run together without any well-elaborated plan. What allows these texts to be placed in this condition was previously described as a theoretical context of associations. A context such as this is already provided when various and mutually exclusive argumentative procedures are alluded to at the same time. Numerous associations of this type can be found in Kant's texts.

Now that the designs for a transcendental deduction have been isolated and weighed in detail, one can also envisage another option for interpreting Kant's texts. The fact that in them argumentative procedures come to be confounded could be justified (albeit only partially and retroactively) if these procedures are integrated in a way that, *taken together,* they yield the best form of transcendental deduction for which resources have been allocated within the total context of Kant's theory. In this case, not only the competing designs, but also the component arguments for a complete deduction would be mixed together. This deduction would have the form of a complex argumentative procedure. It would combine the elements of the attempts at deduction from the simplicity of self-consciousness (attempts which by themselves remained unsuccessful) with the successful deduction from the moderate identity of self-consciousness.

In investigating the designs for a deduction on the basis of the simplicity of the subject, two results were seen to emerge. By themselves, these results do not constitute a deduction. But they are suitable for completion as a transcendental deduction; or at least they could play a role in a complete deduction. In the first result it was shown that all real self-consciousness must be preceded by a synthesis which, it must be assumed, is subject to rules. It could not be shown that these rules necessarily had to be brought to awareness or that a priori knowledge of them is possible (2.1). In the second result it was further shown that complex thoughts can only be formed by reason of certain rules of combination, although it could not be shown that self-consciousness is not at all possible apart from complex thoughts (2.2). Now that a proposal for a deduction that can lay claim to being conclusive has been put forth, an attempt will be made in addition to connect these results (for they were results, even though they could not support the burden of proof of the entire deduction) to the deduction from the identity of self-consciousness.

(a) Regarding synthesis prior to all consciousness, it follows directly from the circumstance that if all transition in consciousness is subject to rules the synthesis which first brings given intuitions to awareness must *likewise* be subject to rules. For the transition is transition *in* consciousness, whereas the synthesis is combination *into* [*Verbindung zum*] consciousness. The rules of this synthesis regulate a process that precedes all transition. But they regulate it in a way that transition in consciousness must at all times be possible with reference to its result. Hence, even if the rules are not real conditions of possible transition, their structure is nonetheless determined by rules to which the transition as such is necessarily subject. This needs to be shown in greater detail.

The rules under which a manifold that can be accompanied by explicit self-consciousness first comes to awareness [*kommt*] are best comprehended as rules for the formation of *perception*. For perceptions are actually elementary states of consciousness, and they are described as such by Kant. Of course, Kant does not have at his disposal a consistent theory of perception. In certain contexts he sees in perceptions the simplest forms of the constitution of an object. In other contexts they are taken as being merely subjective and as those states of consciousness in relation to which the constitution of an object must first be set in motion. If one wanted to eliminate the difficulties with which Kant has to contend in the attempt to provide a theoretical interpretation of perceptions, one would have to embark upon a new and extensive investigation. That is not possible in the present context.

Still, it can be foreseen that the differentiation between various arguments within a transcendental deduction provides important foundations for a theory of perception. If perception is the product of synthesis prior to all consciousness, then the necessity for regulated transition between states of consciousness yields conclusions about certain basic structures that must be demonstrated by all perceptions. In the first place, they must be so constituted that a transition from one perception to another must be possible at all times. Since, however, perceptions are *in themselves* the unity of manifold occurrences, it follows that it must be possible to pass from every element present in a perception to every other element in a manner subject to the same rules as the transition from one perception to another. For self-consciousness must be in a position to recognize in conscious representations a united manifoldness as such. And it must thus be in a position to represent the elements of the manifold separately and, consequently, to proceed from one to another. The consequences yielded for the structure of perception by the necessity of possible transition do

Identity and Objectivity 195

not entail that the process whereby perceptions are formed must be identical with, or even merely structurally congruent with, the process of regulated transition in consciousness. Perceptions may come about in a way that differs either entirely or to a large extent from the way in which conscious transitions between representational states take place in the subject. Self-consciousness, qua identity principle for transitions, requires only that the structure of perceptions is such as to permit a *reconstruction* that is accomplished in a sequence of conscious states of a subject. But precisely this is required of a convincing theory of perception: it must admit particular processes of the constitution of perceptions, but it must nonetheless subsume these processes under universal conditions of the possibility of higher forms of discourse and synthesis.[37] The articulated and, hence, necessarily complex form of Kant's transcendental deduction opens up a promising perspective for such a theory.

(b) Although it does not suffice for a transcendental deduction, the second result, which was yielded when the investigation was confined to the aspect of the simplicity of self-consciousness, concerned the particular mode of self-consciousness that must be presupposed by the consciousness of complex thoughts. The simplicity of self-consciousness provided no reason for having to make any assumption of complex thoughts with definite content which are still distinguishable from the total complex of what is known by the subject or which are exhibited to awareness in self-consciousness. Such complex thoughts and their nexus are certainly, and most obviously, fundamental assets of our conscious life. What previously had to remain undecided was not whether they are real, but whether they are implications of self-consciousness on the description given by Kant. Owing to the consideration that the possibility of the transition from state to state is included in the notion of self-consciousness, however, this situation is already modified. This transition must be one that takes place in consciousness and does not result only objectively in relation to consciousness. Consequently, in the state of consciousness to which the transition is made, the relation to the state of consciousness from which the transition resulted must be sustained. But that means that *every* transition is also a transition into a state of complex consciousness. It coincides with this that when Kant speaks of synthesis, he fundamentally ascribes to the so designated state of affairs two structural aspects: "combination" is said to be the transition from one representational state to another; and "combination" is at the same time that unity of a manifold which shows itself as the result of the transition within the resulting state of consciousness. Combination can only be spoken of where a process leading to such a result takes place. Thus, all those rules on the strength of which complex representations are possible must also be operative in every possible act of self-consciousness.[38]

It was not possible to develop Kant's theory of perception, and neither is it possible to construct in detail the theory of combinatory consciousness [*Verbindungsbewußtsein*] derivable from Kant's premises and to determine its relation to a theory of thought. In turn, it must suffice to keep in mind that the transcendental deduction from the identity concept of self-consciousness must bear fundamental consequences for that theory. It shows that no self-consciousness is possible without complex thoughts of its representational states. And it subjects these thoughts to the same fundamental conditions which apply to the a priori consciousness of the form of progression [*Verlaufsform*] of transitions and which thus apply to the structure of perception.

In the development of Kant's key argument (cf. note 34), a combination between the aspects of the simplicity and the identity of self-consciousness began to emerge in another and more fundamental way: the deduction from simplicity had to take up all representations as elements of the comprehensive complex of representations, the sole subject of which is conceived in self-consciousness. The analysis of identity broke down this complex and recognized in it the contents of a sequence of representational states in which the unity of self-consciousness is preserved. Nevertheless, in this sequence the unity that had to be inferred from the simplicity of self-consciousness cannot be lost. The complete unity of all representations in one and the same subject must also be assertable in relation to transition in self-consciousness. That is a subject whose unity can for this reason be described as "thoroughgoing" (A 112). Because this unity comes to stand out with reference to the possibility of transition, it is placed in a new theoretical perspective, a perspective which is both changed and deepened in comparison with the way in which it was first thematized. The thought of the identity of a subject in all its representations must also, from the outset, be formulated with reference to the unity of all its representations. It knows itself as the identical subject only when representational states replace other representational states. However, it is the subject of representations, all of which it knows to be its own only if it is equally conscious of the mutual referability of the contents of its representational states. In this awareness it has original cognizance of the simplicity and the identity of itself in equal measure.

From the beginning we had to proceed on the assumption that simplicity and identity alike are original aspects of self-consciousness. When the warranted move from the analysis of apperception to the doctrine of the categories was at stake, the moment of identity played the key role. For only on the strength of this moment is it evident that a conscious self-relation of the subject could never come about without the inclusion of a priori knowledge of the rules of combination. The logical order of the sequence of arguments in which identity takes priority should not be mistaken for the coordination of the structural features of the subject itself. The concept of identity does not, for instance, draw merely in its wake the concept of the simplicity of the subject. One cannot obtain it as its derivative from the thought of identity. One must, rather, lay claim to it and, hence, presuppose it in order to be able to fully articulate the notion of subjectivity.

By combining both aspects in the notion of universally possible transition in the subject, a conclusion can be obtained that is of decisive importance for a theory of the categories: the rules which apply a priori to transitions determine not only a form of progression with which all transitions must comply, but they must be rules which from the outset determine each transition in relation to all possible transitions. For this reason the table of categories must be comprehended as a system of rules that guarantee a priori this universality of possible transitions. Each category regulates a certain mode of transition. But it does so in such a way that its meaning is fully determined only within the complex of all categories. In turn, the systematic nexus of all synthesis and the unity of a sum total of the given (i.e., the unity of nature) is encompassed by that complex.

The various attempts at developing a transcendental deduction are consolidated into a single theoretical context under the key argument from the identity of self-consciousness. Once the foundational argument has been established, the various fragments of theories which had been abandoned along the way quickly fit themselves into this context. At the same time, the perspective is opened up toward a series of further developments and applications of the notion of a completed deduction. And it is only from this perspective that the thematic of the Kantian theory of knowledge is once again posed in its entirety, a thematic which ought to be constructible in accordance with the ground plan of the transcendental deduction. The associative nexus of texts which had to be broken up for the sake of transparent interpretation can only be achieved again after the analysis has made its return from lengthy, though necessary, detours. But, of course, it can be achieved only to the extent that Kant's textual inventory can at all be justified by a line of argument that finds good support within the framework of his premises.

Not all the arguments that enter into Kant's texts can be granted a place in the transcendental deduction which refers at once to simplicity and to identity. Many of them have proven erroneous. But those arguments that can be linked to the key argument from identity yield an order of argumentation that already demonstrates a high degree of comprehensiveness and complexity.

Kant was unable to cope with the intricacy and comprehensiveness of this argumentative nexus. It is all the more astonishing that he tapped its resources and (though inarticulately and insecurely enough) held tight to it, thereby circumspectly preserving the entire inventory of problems implicated by it. Seen within the horizon of the epoch in which his education took place, Kant's train of thought is wholly original. It is also highly productive as far as the development of a philosophical systematic is concerned. Moreover, it is exceptionally convincing—the presupposition being, of course, that one sees in the notion of the ego [*im Ich-Gedanken*] a consciousness which demonstrates the highest degree of certainty and which is, so to speak, a priori superior to everything.

It was already reported that Kant was under the impression that he was unable to carry out successfully, with complete clarity, the analysis of the ultimate grounds of our cognition. As far as possible, he freed the new version of the transcendental deduction in the second edition of the *Critique of Pure Reason* of this burden. It has often been maintained that the obscurity which Kant confessed to be present in the first edition is prevalent only in those passages in which he attempted to describe the particular forms and conditions of synthesis (A 98ff.). But once the attempt has been made to interpret the meaning of the statements at the core of Kant's entire theory, one must say that even in this domain he would have been justified in complaining about the obscurity of the only texts for which he claimed success. The main problem of the *Critique*, i.e., the problem of how the connection between consciousness of self [*Ich-Bewußtsein*] and consciousness of rules is to be understood, was affected by so many other problems, and was posed under so many different alternatives, that Kant really could not be successful in treating it as lucidly as he did the fundamental principles of mathematical physics, of metaphysics, and of morality. Schopenhauer said that when one reads a page of Kant it is as if one were stepping into a room full of light. He was right in regard to the texts in which Kant applied his principles. However, when reading Kant's chapters on the deduction, one feels as if one were sauntering through the dim and labyrinthine catacombs of a treasure house.

As stated before, Kant attempted to structure the second presentation of

Identity and Objectivity 199

the transcendental deduction in such a way that subtle distinctions concerning consciousness of self and consciousness of rules are made dispensable. The plan and the success of this attempt must remain open issues here. That he made the attempt was reasonable enough, for the obscurity of the deduction drew the criticism of his opponents upon him, just as it later sparked the efforts of his disciples, whose lack of prudence he feared. But the obscurities of the texts are themselves not completely lacking in justification. When a philosopher is unable to master the complicated strategy which alone could lend full persuasive force to his theoretical design and to the ideas developed in it, then it is better for him to set forth global argumentations and to maintain his reserve vis-à-vis fully articulated analyses than to ground his ideas in particularized analyses which manifestly cannot support the entire framework envisaged. Global argumentations are legitimate as long as they maintain contact with a properly cultivated stock of problems, and as long as they do not serve merely the pretense of insight and subtlety. Were such argumentations never ventured, one would never arrive at fundamentally new blueprints for theories and methods. It is merely that the assertoric force of their programmatic character may not be confounded with the force of fully elaborated arguments. Often, such arguments succeed only after a lengthy period of time and for a later generation.

5. Identity of Self-Consciousness and Identity of Act

Up to now, the deliberations of this chapter have been developed in appreciable remoteness from the text. They have been restricted to assigning to the text a consistent [*durchgängig*] and tenable theoretical framework and also to acknowledging in the text the beginnings of arguments which, owing to their fallaciousness, must be eliminated from that framework. For this reason the considerations thus far cannot claim to represent commentary. They are intended merely to furnish the means for possible commentary upon several central segments of the transcendental deduction.

Nevertheless, the previous deliberations were to a large extent supported upon just one of these segments, one which has been cited repeatedly. It may thus be of interest to treat this segment in detail and to show, even if merely in outline, which subterranean conceptual movement is to be assigned to the relevant text, as well as the extent to which it reaches beyond the arguments for which it can serve as support. Let us recall here the text at issue: "For the mind could never think its identity in the manifoldness of its representations, and indeed think this identity a priori, if it did not have before its eyes the identity of its act which subjects all synthesis of apprehension (which is empirical) to a transcendental unity and thereby renders possible its connection according to a priori rules" (A 108).

Several of the essential characteristics of this passage have already been underscored: it grounds the derivation of a priori rules in the identity of self-consciousness; it emphasizes that such a derivation is successful only when this identity is known a priori; and it makes clear that ordinary self-consciousness can come about only with explicit reference to a priori rules.

Kant's formulations, however, contain peculiarities which cannot be clarified by means of this investigation without further effort: they employ the concept of identity a second time, applying it to a particular act which is distinguished from the act of synthesis itself and whose *result* is those a priori rules according to which every synthesis obtains its connectedness. The act that is attributed an identity that is manifestly supposed to derive from self-consciousness is spoken of only in the singular, whereas rules of synthesis are spoken of in the plural.

Instead of the identity of an act, Kant writes several lines beforehand of the identity of a "function." Function is for Kant "the unity of the act of bringing various representations under a common representation" (B 93). Hence, function also denotes the unifying aspect of the kind of act that establishes specific relations between our representations. This concept of function can be applied to the "a priori rules," i.e., the categories. A few pages after the passage under consideration Kant actually writes of "functions of synthesis" in the plural, and he does so in a way which makes unavoidable the comprehension of these functions as categories.

Kant does not apply the concept of identity to the categories themselves. As rules, the categories are formal objects. To that extent, they too can be ascribed an identity. However, this identity must be distinguished from the identity of self-consciousness. Only the identity of the ego [*des Ich*] has those particular characteristics which constitute the self-sameness of a particular through a series of states and which are familiar to us from the identity of the person over time. However, the text to be interpreted advances quite abruptly from the identity of the subject to the identity of an act.

When one speaks of an act by virtue of which the subject subordinates the synthesis to unity, and when this synthesis is ascribed an identity, it is thereby presupposed that such an act must take place. And that presupposes in turn that the unity of the subject is not thinkable without the synthesis in consciousness being conceived under rules. In Kant's text no reference to any argument can be found by means of which a connection between the consciousness of the identity of the ego and the awareness of a priori rules can be made intelligible as a necessary connection. Only necessary conditions which this argument must satisfy are named. They are those conditions which have been utilized for the success of a transcendental deduction. The argument itself had to obtain from the ego-identity a priori knowledge of the synthesis and, from this in turn, the conclusion that the synthesis must be known to be regulated. Only thereafter, if at all, can it be said that these rules emerge from an act to which identity must be ascribed. Kant's text, therefore, actually thematizes only the indirect consequence of a line of argument which is itself not elaborated. Its linguistic form suggests, however, that the step can be taken from the identity of the subject to that act directly and without recourse to unarticulated arguments.

That Kant in fact makes this mediate inference, and that he thus places it in the foreground of his endeavor, can be gathered from a tendency evidenced everywhere in the *Critique*. It is a tendency which had appreciable, and for the most part unfavorable influence upon Kant's various strategies and outlines of proof. In the transcendental deduction (the only one of these that withstands the test) the connection between the identity of the subject and the constancy of rules had merely the character of a logical derivation: if the ego is a principle of identity, then there must *be* a priori rules for the transition between its states. Inasmuch as Kant writes of the identity of an *act* which subjects appearances to rules, he at the same time comprehends the sequence of logical derivation as a context of *real* constitution. Now the subject is certainly the agent [*Akteur*] of a number of activities. It can invariably reflect upon itself and initiate syntheses. But even when one takes both premises together—that is, when one assumes that the subject is both agent and the "highest point" in transcendental proofs—it still does not always follow that it is in the subject and its acts that the ground must be sought of all the conditions without which the concept of the subject cannot be thought and without which the subject could have no knowledge of itself.

If one grants Kant's conclusion pertaining to the theory of constitution, his talk of the "identity of an act" admittedly does become legitimate and unavoidable. If the subject is not only inconceivable apart from rules of appearances but is also their real ground, then one must assume an activity which has as its consequence that every synthesis is subject to such rules. Just like the forms of synthesis themselves, this activity must have its own ground of unity, and therewith perform a "function." It is understood that the ground of unity would be located in the universal unity of the ego, which subjects all appearances to this function. Such an act, function, or activity can only be spoken of in the singular.

Furthermore, identity must accrue to it: it is the same, because it prescribes for every synthesis in every transition the same universal conditions of unity. The type of rule which applies to the respective synthesis finds in these conditions its systematically determined place. And in this sense the identity of the act corresponds to the identity that was to be ascribed to the transcendental subject.

Now it is interesting to note that the identity of such a singular act would have to be not the identity of a formal object or the moderate identity of the subject in transition, but rather strict identity. It would be an act which cannot change and which cannot end. If it is, then, the sufficient reason of formal objects (of a priori rules), it is only in that capacity that it could guarantee the continued existence of these objects. But then it is at least likely that even the identity of the subject as such must be conceived in accordance with the strict concept of identity. For if the identity of the act deriving from it is a strict identity, then particular reasons must be meticulously brought to bear in order to secure for the subject another concept of identity. It was shown beforehand that Kant must reject the strict concept of identity for self-consciousness as well. In the textual passage at issue, however, one of the reasons becomes apparent which could nonetheless make Kant disposed to assuming this concept or to making use of a language which entertains associations from the domain of this concept. The various elements which go into, or can go into, a transcendental theory are related to one another in materially pertinent combinations. These are combinations which do not lead to unwelcome consequences only when supervision over them is complete.

Another implication of Kant's language pertaining to the theory of constitution has still to be mentioned: the deduction from the transition in identical self-consciousness was able to leave open the question of the source from which those rules emerge in relation to which a constant form for the transition in consciousness can be thought. The deduction postulates merely that such rules must in general be conceivable a priori and that they permit the transition between every state of consciousness and every other state. Also, different systems of rules that accomplish this are, consequently, admitted by the concept of the identical subject. But if one refers to an act of the subject which guarantees the regularity of appearances, one cannot in the end avoid deriving the rules themselves from the structure of self-consciousness. For such a program of proof the *Critique of Pure Reason* nowhere offers any theoretical means that stand a good chance of success. It can only specify conditions which every system of rules must satisfy. Information about what the rules are that actually determine the connection of our synthesis must be obtained from independent

Identity and Objectivity   203

premises. In the *Critique* these are yielded by the analysis of judgment and its forms that is developed along the guidelines of those necessary conditions. But the elemental facticity of judgment and, consequently, that which is called "understanding" must already be acknowledged as a basic fact alongside that of self-consciousness.

In order to find in Kant's text a conclusive thought at work, as it were, one must abstract from the associations going back to his opinion that the subject is generative even with respect to the rules by virtue of which it is itself possible. But an even more conspicuous feature of the text than the presence of such associations is the fact that Kant moves with the greatest facility from the subject as a principle of identity to the assumption of a priori rules which apply to all apprehensions. That can only be the result of his having in mind entirely different arguments which adequately ensure that he can, in every instance, assert the connection between ego-consciousness and the consciousness of rules. It was previously ascertained that Kant really does consider arguments from the simplicity of self-consciousness to be validations sufficient for this purpose. It can also easily be made clear why he had to be disposed to attributing to them, over and against the arguments from identity, an importance that they in truth did not deserve: as soon as one speaks of a sequence of states, the danger arises of subordinating self-consciousness to the consciousness of time. One must take precautionary measures which allow sequences of states to be conceived in abstracto without comprehending them as including the characteristic properties of time. The concept by which self-consciousness is defined solely by its simplicity is not exposed to this danger. The same applies to a concept of synthesis by which the assemblage [*Zusammenkommen*] of the manifold is thought in an entirely general manner, without reference to the way in which any particular datum comes to be related to another.

Nevertheless, this merit is just as pretended as a good many others which had raised hopes for an easy solution to the problem of a transcendental deduction. For apart from the circumstance that a deduction from the simplicity of self-consciousness alone cannot be made conclusive, even that process which Kant wants to describe as synthesis in a subject is not at all understandable solely on grounds of the simplicity of the subject. Whoever intends merely to describe this synthesis must pay heed to the fact that it is a process which relates on a one-to-one basis what is respectively given. He must also bear in mind that relations such as these can come about only in view of a complex [*Inbegriff*] or system of relations in which everything given is conceived as being in the comprehensive unity of the subject.

Synthesis as a process takes place on the strength of synthesis as a complex. However, this complex can for its part be conceived only in reliance upon the notion of synthesis as a process. And every particular connection represented in relation to the total complex of everything representable has necessarily to be thought as the possible outcome of a synthesis. The materially pertinent connection which dominates both senses of synthesis is also simplified when grasped as a mere correlation. What constitutes this connection is illuminated by the complex proof-procedure of the transcendental deduction, which must make reference first to the identity of the subject, but then, necessarily, to its simplicity as well.

Kant tended to restrict himself to an argument based solely upon the simplicity of the subject. This notwithstanding, he did not permit the tendency to prevail at the decisive junctures of his text. Its result would have been the simplification of his theory as well as feebleness of its most important proof. But the tendency was nonetheless strong enough to prevent the transcendental deduction from being constructed with complete explicitness upon the identity-aspect of self-consciousness. Had Kant ever been able to render an account of the difference between possible strategies of proof, he would perhaps have convinced himself that his theoretical program must be freed of several connotations operative even in the passage being interpreted here. Only then would he have been able to make his program generally recognizable as successful. He could have done this by including, but not relying solely upon, notions which within his texts appear to be both fundamental and sufficient.

Kant did not furnish this account; nor could he furnish it, considering the comprehensiveness and complexity of the problem. Thus, within the text of the *Critique* certain arguments come to achieve dominance, and sometimes even an exclusiveness which they should not be allowed. Against such tendencies, however, Kant did bring to bear with sufficient force the complex interconnection of the principles of our knowledge that he had discovered. In its key passages the text of the *Critique* makes clear reference to those principles without which a transcendental deduction cannot be accomplished, and it describes the synthesis in a way that can be justified only with recourse to those principles.

IV. The Principles of Identity and Objectivity

By way of conclusion, we must demonstrate a link between Kant's analysis of identity and his analysis of objectivity. In the analysis of objectivity the notion of objects distinct from appearances was clarified in terms of formal conditions of judgment. In the analysis of identity it became apparent that ego-consciousness is consciousness of rules. But nothing was determined about what the actual rules are by virtue of which the consciousness of "I think" anticipates a priori all transitions between representations. All the presuppositions are thereby given for attempting to show that the form of judgment which grounds objectivity is exactly that rule presupposed in the consciousness of the identity of the subject.

Much can be said for the idea that it is the forms of judgment that satisfy the conditions which obtain for rules conceived in connection with an a priori principle of identity for transitions. In judgments, too, transitions from one notion to another are thought. But they are thought in such a way that both notions at once compose a single state of affairs. The rule determines from what element to what other element advancement is made. It also determines that in the transition from one element to another all elements remain held together. Thus, forms of judgment are in fact rules that can be described as rules of a synthesis in accordance with the twofold meaning of "combination," even if this description does not suffice to define the essence of judgment.

Kant could not have meant, nor did he ever claim, however, that the structure of judgment could be derived by a formal method of ratiocination from the structure of subject identity. A transcendental deduction is successful even when it first achieves merely the thought of the rule of synthesis and then shows it to be legitimate to grasp that rule more specifically as a form of judgment. That there is no alternative to this specification cannot be proved immediately.[39] But the structure of judgment is nonetheless of such indisputably fundamental significance for our knowledge as to ensure sufficient plausibility for the claim that one has to discern the identity conditions for self-consciousness in it, and in it alone.

Taken by itself, the analysis of objectivity could not show that all appearances can be combined with all other appearances. It could be based only upon the form of categorical propositions. And for that reason it turned out that this analysis also had to leave open the question whether the combination of particular objects (each of which conforms to its own rules) could possibly be brought to the unity of one nature. But Kant's analysis of identity was capable of supporting the burden that the analysis of objectivity was not able to take on. For the consciousness of rules, without which the identity of the subject cannot be conceived a priori, involves identity in all possible representations. Consequently, it involves the notion of those rules which make possible the thoroughgoing combination of all thoughts with all others. But if the consciousness of rules in the identity of the "I think" guarantees thoroughgoing combination, and if these rules can be interpreted in consideration of the form of judgment, then it follows that, besides the form of the categorical proposition, other forms of judgment must be available as well. There must be as many of these, and they must be of such a kind, that the thoroughgoing combination of all possible consciousness must be secured in relation to objects distinguishable from appearances. It is in relation to this manifoldness of fundamental forms of judgment that the collective unity of objects in One Nature must be thought.

We have thus come to the point at which we can survey a sequence of considerations fundamental to Kant's theory. Once it has become clear which problem and which argument it is that determines the possible success of that theory, we can take a further step back from the theory as a whole. From the distance of two centuries, and from the perspective of the present, we are able in conclusion to single out several peculiarities of the theory.

Nearly all the arguments having exploratory import within Kant's transcendental deduction must to a greater or lesser degree be developed independently by the interpreter. But such an interpretation can ensure that it really does keep within the domain of those notions which Kant's theory permits and which were weighed (however inarticulately) by the historical Kant. Once these notions are developed, it turns out that they contain a surprising number of features corresponding to analyses first worked out in the course of recent decades. It also becomes apparent that Kant's notions not only anticipated these analyses but that in many respects they also go beyond them in a profound way. However, it is clear at the same time that the context of a foundational philosophical theory within which these notions were set forth differs in specific ways from the basic problematic within which it would have its place today. Thus, Kant based his definition of objectivity upon a doctrine of judgment that is still tenable. Crucial steps in his theory of the object, however, can only be taken within the framework of the data-sensualism and data-atomism of his theory of knowledge. Some of the most important philosophical efforts of this century have been directed against theories of this type.

It is also true that Kant's doctrine of the unity of the subject both allows and enforces distinctions which suggest and even foster a projection toward contemporary positions. But Kant set out from the premise that self-consciousness is not only the ultimate reference point of all certainty but also the self-sufficient principle of philosophical analysis. The concepts of unity which he applied to this consciousness he also wanted to obtain from it. For that reason he maintained that the task of investigating basic logical functions was subordinate to the task of disclosing the fundamental aspects

Identity and Objectivity   207

of self-consciousness. Today, one will most likely seek in this the reason for the weakness from which many of Kant's arguments suffer, even after they have been fully worked out. Once it is established that semantic analysis must be the method of prima philosophia, it follows that the arguments of a theory based upon the principle of self-consciousness must always falter when they are intended to obtain from the characteristics of consciousness the logical characteristics of rules, or even to gain insight into the necessary validity of rules.

When presented in this way, Kant's theoretical program almost appears to be a historical counterproject to, and the most significant opponent of, semantic theory. But in truth it is merely the necessary corrective to the latter. If self-consciousness turns out to be not at all understandable as the mere implication of a referential context of propositions, if we know rather that it occupies a constitutive and original function within the reference system of language,[40] then once again that task is posed which Kant inquired into when attempting to make comprehensible that self-consciousness and the consciousness of rules stand in an incontrovertible (even if not logically derivable) relation of mutual dependency. The contemporary relevance of Kant's theory is, in any event, assured insofar as the interpreter is able to disentangle it from its tendency toward a constitutional Idealism.

In this frame of reference an old question arises anew: What is the actual status of the principles upon which Kant's transcendental deduction are based? Even during Kant's lifetime controversy took shape over the way in which the arguments he provided ought to be understood, as well as over the direction in which they out to be further developed. For more than a hundred and fifty years the basic alternative in this question was between a theory of purely formal principles of knowledge (which can also be called a logical theory of experience) and an investigation which anchored, more resolutely than Kant himself had done, the critique of reason in a scientia realis of the principles of knowledge. Now for Kant the basis of all his ultimate arguments is the consciousness of "I think," and this according to the description attained in the course of the present investigation. But it has become clear that the entire conclusive force of Kant's theory would have been lost had he chosen either of the two sides of the alternative forced upon his opus by his disciples.

For the subject of the consciousness of "I think" is certainly something particular and spontaneous, and is thus something real—whatever kind of reality it may have. But one will have a decidedly false understanding of that subject if one overlooks the fact that knowledge of the conditions of its identity must be ascribed to it, conditions which can only be described as logical, and are, in fact, so described by Kant. Neither of these two aspects may be disregarded in the attempt to ground Kant's theory of knowledge. Starting from the fundamental notion of the spontaneous and reflectively acting subject, one can ground the validity of necessary rules for all appearances only by means of the other basic notion of the formal and a priori principle of subject identity.

At the ultimate source of all his arguments Kant cannot at any price distinguish so purely between the logical and the factual, as was required of him for many decades by his successors. In our time it has again become easier to stipulate philosophical reasons for the idea that the theory of knowledge and the theory of the knower can only be developed in a single movement. To that extent, the constellations favor the endeavor to take up the subtlest of the historical Kant's theoretical blueprints, which he had to hand down to us in the form of thetic and hermetic texts. It is up to us to attempt to free them and translate them into completely articulated, and hence philosophically disputable, arguments.

Notes

Sources

Acknowledgments

Index

Notes

Introduction

1. "The French Revolution and Classical German Philosophy: Toward a Determination of Their Relation," in D. Henrich, *Aesthetic Judgment and the Moral Image of the World: Studies in Kant* (Stanford: Stanford University Press, 1992), pp. 85–89.

2. At Marburg, Henrich began his Idealist studies with leading representatives of neo-Kantianism Klaus Reich and Julius Ebbinghaus. His interest in finding a "systematic" Kant was already a departure from this tradition. But the most important formative experiences in Henrich's early studies were his encounter with Max Weber's work and his training in the rigorous scientific methods of *Urgeschichte* in the school of Gero Merhart von Bernegg, the teacher of most German scholars in this field.

3. "Die deutsche Philosophie nach zwei Weltkriegen," in D. Henrich, *Konzepte: Essays zur Philosophie in der Zeit* (Frankfurt a. M.: Suhrkamp, 1987), especially pp. 47–55.

4. For criticism of society based on self-preservation alone, see D. Henrich, "Nuklearer Frieden," in *Konzepte,* pp. 103–113, especially pp. 105–107.

5. See Chapter 1 and M. Heidegger, *Kant and the Problem of Metaphysics,* 4th ed., trans. R. Taft (Bloomington: Indiana University Press, 1990).

6. D. Henrich, "Was ist Metaphysik—Was Moderne? Zwölf Thesen gegen Jürgen Habermas," in *Konzepte,* pp. 11–43. For Henrich's claim that Descartes' beginning in subjectivity is "vindicated," see D. Henrich, *Fluchtlinien: Philosophische Essays* (Frankfurt a. M.: Suhrkamp, 1982), p. 144.

7. J. Habermas, "Rückkehr zur Metaphysik: Eine Tendenz in der deutschen Philosophie," *Merkur* 439/40 (September–October 1985): 898–905; D. Henrich, "Was ist Metaphysik?"; J. Habermas, "Metaphysics after Kant," in *Postmetaphysical Thinking: Philosophical Essays,* trans. W. M. Hohengarten (Cambridge, Mass.: MIT

Press, 1992), pp. 10–27. Recently Habermas has conceded that the problem of subjectivity may have to be reconsidered, and not simply viewed as superseded by the "paradigm-shift" to language, in *Vergangenheit als Zukunft* (Zurich: Pendo, 1991), p. 152.

8. J. Habermas, "Rückkehr zur Metaphysik," p. 903.

9. Henrich has also been engaged in a controversy for many years with Ernst Tugendhat about the semantic reducibility of self-consciousness to the rules of use for the first-person singular pronoun. See E. Tugendhat, *Self-Consciousness and Self-Determination,* trans. P. Stern (Cambridge, Mass.: MIT Press, 1986); D. Henrich, "Identität—Begriffe, Probleme, Grenzen," in O. Marquard and K. Stierle, eds., *Poetik und Hermeneutik,* 8 (Munich: Wilhelm Fink, 1979), pp. 133–186; and D. Henrich, "Noch einmal in Zirkeln: Eine Kritik von Ernst Tugendhats semantischer Erklärung von Selbstbewusstsein," in C. Bellut and U. Müller-Scholl, eds., *Mensch und Moderne: Festschrift für H. Fahrenbach* (Würzburg: Königshausen und Neumann, 1989), pp. 89–128. See earlier essays by Henrich cited in note 18 that are the background to Tugendhat's critique of him. M. Frank provides an account of the debate as well as support for Henrich in *Die Unhintergehbarkeit von Individualität: Reflexionen über Subjektivität, Person und Individuum aus Anlass ihrer "postmodernen" Toterklärung* (Frankfurt a. M.: Suhrkamp, 1986).

Henrich has engaged in extensive dialogue with and discussion of English-language writers, including D. Davidson, S. Shoemaker, J. Perry, D. Lewis, H. N. Castañeda, J. Searle, P. F. Strawson, W. Sellars, W. Alston, W. v. O. Quine, R. Rorty, and others, who have played various roles in debating the Idealist themes of subjectivity, intentionality, self-consciousness, and self-reference within linguistic-analytic discourse. Notable have been the critical yet sympathetic engagements with R. Chisholm in "Zwei Theorien zur Verteidigung von Selbstbewusstsein," *Grazer Philosophischen Studien* 7/8 (1979): 77–99, and the review-discussion of T. Nagel, *The View from Nowhere,* in "Dimensionen und Defizite einer Theorie der Subjektivität," *Philosophische Rundschau* 36, 1/2 (1989): 1–24. Otherwise Henrich sees a positive relation between his conception of metaphysics and the renewal of traditional metaphysical themes and questions (if not traditional approaches) in Rawls, Putnam, Rorty, Kripke, and Nozick; cf. "Wohin die deutsche Philosophie?" in *Konzepte,* pp. 66–75. Accordingly, Henrich accuses Habermas of having a rather outmoded conception of the analytic tradition, which the latter appropriates for the purposes of his theory of communicative action; see "Was ist Metaphysik?" in *Konzepte,* especially pp. 22–24. It is not impertinent to say that Henrich (who taught for a number of years at Columbia and Harvard), Habermas, and Tugendhat have been rivals in developing the most adequate appropriation of analytic philosophy in Germany.

10. J. Habermas, *Postmetaphysical Thinking,* pp. 17–18.

11. Henrich (*Konzepte,* p. 16) discusses Kant's objection to the "indifferentists" who reject all metaphysics. See the passage in *Kants gesammelte Schriften,* Royal Prussian Academy of Sciences edition (Berlin: W. de Gruyter, 1902–), vol. 29. 1, 2, p. 765: "For these questions are so interwoven in the nature of reason that no one can be free of them. Even all the despisers of metaphysics, who wish to appear

to have clearer heads—even Voltaire—have their own metaphysics. For everyone will think in some way about his soul."

12. Kant employs the language of "ascent" *(Aufstieg)* to characterize philosophy in a late sketch (1800) for the prospectus to his student Jachmann's examination of his philosophy of religion. Kant here proposes a kind of antimystical Platonism in which human reason, starting from an "earthly" standpoint, never loses sight of itself "as its own final end" (thus ascending toward a "science of the final end of human reason"), instead of pursuing an "alchemical" *inspiratio* from higher realities. Henrich published the neglected sketch and discussed it in "Zu Kants Begriff der Philosophie: Eine Edition und eine Fragestellung," in F. Kaulbach and J. Ritter, eds., *Kritik und Metaphysik. Heinz Heimsoeth zum 80. Geburtstag* (Berlin: W. de Gruyter, 1966), pp. 40–59.

13. Henrich (contra Strawson) argues for the need for a revisionary and not merely a descriptive metaphysics which at the same time is not explanatory. See "Selbstbewusstsein und spekulatives Denken," in *Fluchtlinien*, pp. 125–181. Henrich makes use of the connotations relating to death or mortality present in the word *Abschluss*. He thus expects a modern metaphysics to take on some of the functions of religion—a role which Habermas expressly denies to rational philosophy and its function in society.

14. D. Henrich, *Konzepte*, p. 65.

15. "The Basic Structure of Modern Philosophy," *Cultural Hermeneutics*, 2/1 (1974): 1–18; "Über Selbstbewusstsein und Selbsterhaltung," in D. Henrich, *Selbstverhältnisse: Gedanken und Auslegungen zu den Grundlagen der klassischen deutschen Philosophie* (Stuttgart: Philipp Reclam, 1982), pp. 109–130. See also *Fluchtlinien*, pp. 151–159, and *Konzepte*, pp. 34–43.

16. Although irreducible, self-consciousness is not for Henrich simple or nonrelational. Rather, it has an internal complexity unanalyzable as a construction from simpler elements. Thus self-consciousness is not a monadic quality attached to relations; nor is it *merely* relational, as in "neutral monist" theories, since the distinctiveness of conscious relations is not translatable into language about relations as such. See D. Henrich, "Self-Consciousness: A Critical Introduction to a Theory," *Man and World*, 4 (1971): 3–28.

17. See J. Habermas, "Rückkehr zur Metaphysik."

18. See D. Henrich, "Self-Consciousness"; "Fichte's Original Insight," *Contemporary German Philosophy*, 1 (1982): 15–53; "Fichtes 'Ich,'" *Selbstverhältnisse*, pp. 57–82. Henrich argues that Fichte discovered the circularity in every attempt to account for self-consciousness self-reflexively, that is, in terms of the self's becoming aware of itself as an object. For any such process to occur, the self would *already* have to know itself, i.e., be self-conscious. When Fichte then tried to replace the self-reflexive model (dominating the philosophy from Descartes through Kant) with a self-positing model, the same circularity emerged. Henrich describes how Fichte, experiencing the failure of all discursive descriptions, struggled to devise a metaphor for self-consciousness that would not encounter this problem—but in vain.

19. D. Henrich, "Selbstbewusstsein und spekulatives Denken"; "Grund und

Gang spekulativen Denkens," in D. Henrich and R. P. Horstmann, eds., *Metaphysik nach Kant? Stuttgarter Hegel-Kongress* (Stuttgart: Klett-Cotta, 1988), pp. 83–120; "Dunkelheit und Vergewisserung," in D. Henrich, ed., *All-Einheit: Wege eines Gedankens in Ost und West* (Stuttgart: Klett-Cotta, 1985), pp. 33–52; "Gedanken zur Dankbarkeit," in R. Löw, ed., *Oikeiosis: Festschrift für R. Spaemann* (Weinheim: Acta Humaniora, 1987), pp. 69–86; D. Henrich, "Was ist Metaphysik?"

20. See M. Frank's discussion of this point in "Ist Selbstbewusstsein ein Fall von 'présence à soi'? Zur Meta-Kritik der neueren französischen Metaphysik-Kritik," in D. Henrich and R. P. Horstmann, eds., *Metaphysik nach Kant?* See also M. Frank, *What Is Neostructuralism?* trans. S. Wilke and R. Gray (Minneapolis: University of Minnesota Press, 1989).

21. D. Henrich, *Konzepte*, p. 53.

22. Through this view of metaphysics Henrich's project is related to Thomas Nagel's.

23. "Art and Philosophy of Art Today: Reflections with Reference to Hegel," in R. E. Amacher and V. Lange, eds., *New Directions in German Literary Criticism* (Princeton: Princeton University Press, 1979), pp. 107–135. It is worth noting that the term *unvordenklich* is used also by Schelling.

24. I. Kant, *Logik,* Einleitung III, "Begriff von der Philosophie Überhaupt," *Kants gesammelte Schriften,* vol. 9, pp. 21–26.

25. D. Henrich, *Konzepte*, pp. 11–16.

26. Ibid., p. 61. Some remarks specifically about the scholarly and historical accomplishment of Henrich's Kant-studies are in order, although this introduction is concentrating on their philosophical import. (1) As already mentioned, Henrich's readings of central Kantian texts are analytical reconstructions exposing possible lines of argumentation permitted by the text, from among which Henrich selects that one best corresponding to Kant's theoretical intention as well as to the content and detail of the text. This approach is not the critically disintegrative analysis which assumes that Kant's premises must correspond to the intuitions and common sense of late-twentieth-century scholars or otherwise be judged defective. Rather, it helps the original text to speak more clearly by bridging the gulf between the concepts and premises of eighteenth-century philosophical argument and those of the present, and it presumes a fundamental openness to the text's theoretical intent. (2) The uncovering of Kant's philosophical development and the emergence of the characteristic "critical" complex of questions, methods, and ways of argumentation have been the subject of many of Henrich's studies, such as "Das Prinzip der kantischen Ethik," *Philosophische Rundschau,* 2 (1954/55): 20–38; "Hutcheson und Kant," *Kantstudien: Festschrift für H. J. Paton,* 49 (1957/58): 49–69; "Über Kants früheste Ethik," *Kantstudien,* 54 (1963): 404–431; "Über Kants Entwicklungsgeschichte," *Philosophische Rundschau,* 13 (1966): 252–263 (which also discusses the methodology of the research into Kant's developmental history); and "Kants Denken 1762/63: Über den Ursprung der Unterscheidung analytischer und synthetischer Urteile," in H. Heimsoeth, D. Henrich, and G. Tonelli, eds., *Studien zu Kants philosophischer Entwicklung* (Hildesheim: G. Olms, 1967), pp. 7–36. The first three essays in this volume also contribute to the understanding of Kant's

philosophical development; the second and third particularly illuminate changes in Kant's program for a deduction of the moral law. (3) Henrich has sought to offer an orientation in the comprehensive, systematic project of critical philosophy and to keep that project in view while engaging in exegetical, argumentative, and analytical discussions of particular theoretical issues, problem areas, and texts of Kant. His very detailed argumentations both start from and return to the larger context of Kant's primary philosophic intentions, in a fashion that has not often been characteristic of Anglo-American analytical writing on Kant.

27. These phases can be compared with the account of seven phases of "speculative thought," especially of German Idealist philosophy and most particularly of Kant, in "Grund und Gang spekulativen Denkens," pp. 104–120; in the same essay Henrich discusses "Kant's concept of philosophy," pp. 92–97.

28. "Grund und Gang spekulativen Denkens," pp. 91–97.

29. Kant indicates a dual structure (in reality a tripartite structure, as is clear from reflection 6612, *Kants gesammelte Schriften,* vol. 19, p. 110) in the numerous contrasts in the *Nachlass* of a propaedeutical or skeptical phase with a teleological or dogmatical phase of metaphysics. See R. Velkley, *Freedom and the End of Reason: On the Moral Foundation of Kant's Critical Philosophy* (Chicago: University of Chicago Press), pp. 111–116.

30. See D. Henrich, "Zu Kants Begriff der Philosophie," especially the statement on p. 58, where Henrich discusses Kant's account of freedom as the "keystone of the arch" of reason: "Freedom is not externally related to reason as a problem to be solved . . . Freedom is for Kant the concept which makes possible the clarifying of the inner structure of reason." In the same context he notes that Kant owes to Rousseau his "insight that reason—and with it philosophy—has a practical vocation."

31. See D. Henrich, "Hegels Grundoperation: Eine Einleitung in die 'Wissenschaft der Logik,'" in U. Guzzoni et al., eds., *Der Idealismus und seine Gegenwart: Festschrift für W. Marx* (Hamburg: Meiner, 1976), pp. 208–230. Henrich proposes a significant reinterpretation of Hegel involving criticisms of the latter's claims (1) that he is able to carry out an autonomous dialectic of concepts on behalf of a self-related Absolute, superseding Kant's constructive "counterproject" to natural or pretheoretical knowledge; (2) that he has shown how philosophy can proceed without presupposition of such pretheoretical knowledge; and (3) that the logical operation of self-relating difference can account for the possibility and fact of consciousness. In Henrich's reinterpretation, the dialectic is *one* possible (not the sole) way of reconstructing the basic world-relation of consciousness, which includes the knowing subject as thinkable only in correlation to the world; and at the same time a constructive method for arriving at and articulating speculative thoughts of closure. In this way Henrich derives a Hegelianism much closer to the intent and procedures of Kant, one that abandons an *explanatory* metaphysical project with respect to the basic "differences" of rational life. See *Fluchtlinien,* pp. 175–179, and "Kant und Hegel: Versuch der Vereinigung ihrer Grundgedanken," in *Selbstverhältnisse,* pp. 173–208.

32. See Chapter 2.

33. See Chapter 4, part I.

34. For the discussion of "reflection" and its role in deduction, see D. Henrich, "Kant's Notion of a Deduction and the Methodological Background of the First Critique," in E. Förster, ed., *Kant's Transcendental Deductions: The Three Critiques and the "Opus Postumum"* (Stanford: Stanford University Press, 1989), pp. 29–64. In this essay Henrich also indicates some changes in his conception of deduction since the early essay "The Proof-Structure of Kant's Transcendental Deduction," in R. C. S. Walker, ed., *Kant on Pure Reason* (Oxford: Oxford University Press, 1982), pp. 66–81.

35. See P. F. Strawson for the most influential statement of this interpretation, in *The Bounds of Sense: An Essay on Kant's "Critique of Pure Reason"* (London: Methuen, 1966); see also P. Guyer's review of the German original of Henrich's essay "Identity and Objectivity," in *Journal of Philosophy*, 76, 3 (March 1979): 151–167, for a critique of Henrich from a related perspective (especially pp. 164–166).

36. See Chapter 4. This argument has been further developed and refined in D. Henrich, "The Identity of the Subject in the Transcendental Deduction," in E. Schaper and W. Vossenkuhl, eds., *Reading Kant: New Perspectives on Transcendental Arguments and Critical Philosophy* (Oxford: Basil Blackwell, 1989), pp. 250–280.

37. See *Critique of Pure Reason*, trans. N. K. Smith (New York: St. Martin's Press, 1965), B 145–146: "The peculiarity of our understanding, that it can produce a priori unity of apperception solely by means of the categories, and only by such and so many, is as little capable of further explanation as why we have just these and no other functions of judgment, or why space and time are the only forms of our possible intuition."

38. In addition to Chapters 2 and 3, see D. Henrich, "Die Deduktion des Sittengesetzes: Über die Gründe der Dunkelheit des letzten Abschnittes von Kants 'Grundlegung zur Metaphysik der Sitten,'" in A. Schwan, ed., *Denken im Schatten des Nihilismus* (Darmstadt: Wissenschaftliche Buchgesellschaft, 1975), pp. 55–112. Henrich's central interest in the practical philosophy is with the account of motivation as indicative of a special problem in the existence of "practical reason" distinguished from "merely" theoretical reason—and not with a "theory of agency," as in some notable current discussions of Kant. Historically, Henrich's emphasis gains support from the consideration that Rousseau's great contribution, according to Kant, was to show not how human reason as free accounts for our actions in the world, but how it can be *self*-determining and thus give itself, and even *be* itself, an end, without dependence on a natural order or a higher being. Hence Kant's turn to freedom is inseparable from the project of justifying *reason as such*, in the light of the collapse of all traditional metaphysics of nature and being (of which collapse Kant was convinced well before 1781). These points generally get missed in presentations which assume that the primary issue surrounding freedom in Kant is whether it commits him to a "two-world" (noumenal-phenomenal) view or a "two-aspect" (imputational-explanatory) view of human action. See H. E. Allison, *Kant's Theory of Freedom* (Cambridge: Cambridge University Press, 1990), and the review of Allison by O. O'Neill in *Mind*, vol. 100 (July 1991): 373–376,

especially the criticism in the final paragraph of the review, wherein O'Neill claims that "the vindication of reason—the grounding of intelligibility—is not a dispensable element of Kant's argumentative strategy." She would seem to agree with Henrich that the moral fact of reason is not a dogmatic "glimpse of some transcendent reality" but instead central to Kant's project of disclosing the freedom-constituted essence of rationality. Again, Henrich intends to show that Kant's practical doctrines entail a new approach to the meaning of metaphysics: they are not "ethics" in a narrow sense but signify a challenge to Western traditions (ancient, medieval, early modern) of thinking about the highest "interest" of human reason. Yet Henrich regards Kant's innovation as a certain rediscovery of a Platonic way of thinking; and one surely sees an intended response to Heidegger in Henrich's revived "ontology of the good."

39. Henrich notes that Leibniz's manner of philosophizing shares with Kant's this character of reflection on diverse forms of knowing, though without Kant's "transcendental" form of systematizing them that accepts the givenness of elements without "sufficient reason." See *Fluchtlinien*, p. 129.

40. Kant has of course made a famous statement about authors not fully understanding themselves. See *Critique of Pure Reason*, A 314/B 370.

41. See the preface to the *Critique of Judgment*: "If only the principle is correctly given, then enough has been done," in *Kants gesammelte Schriften*, vol. 5, p. 170; and Henrich's discussion of this passage in "Kant's Explanation of the Aesthetic Judgment," in D. Henrich, *Aesthetic Judgment and the Moral Image of the World*, pp. 29–56. It should be mentioned that with the account of the deduction of the aesthetic judgment in the essay just cited, Henrich completes a triptych of studies of the Kantian theoretical, moral, and aesthetic deductions.

42. See Chapter 4, part I.

43. D. Henrich, "Zu Kants Begriff der Philosophie," p. 59.

44. A brief guide to selected writings may be helpful. On the possibility of the transcendental "I," in addition to the already-mentioned essays on Fichte, see the following recent books on Hölderlin: *Der Gang des Andenkens: Beobachtungen und Gedanken zu Hölderlins Gedicht* (Stuttgart: Klett-Cotta, 1986), and *Der Grund im Bewusstsein: Untersuchungen zu Hölderlins Denken in Jena (1794/95)* (Stuttgart: Klett-Cotta, 1992); see also "Die Anfänge der Theorie des Subjekts (1789)," in A. Honneth et al., eds., *Zwischenbetrachtungen: J. Habermas zum 60. Geburtstag* (Frankfurt a. M.: Suhrkamp, 1989), pp. 106–170, and D. Henrich, *Konstellationen: Probleme und Debatten am Ursprung der idealistischen Philosophie (1789–1795)* Stuttgart: Klett-Cotta, 1991). Hölderlin's philosophical fragments and programs have been of particular interest to Henrich, in that they point toward a post-Kantian position free of the Fichtean and Hegelian inclination toward demonstrative monism. Henrich's approach to Hölderlin thus suggests an alternative to Heidegger's way of treating this poet-philosopher as authoritative for twentieth-century thinking.

On Hegel's critique of Kant's doctrines of practical reason, in addition to Chapter 3, see Henrich's introduction to *Hegel: Philosophie des Rechts. Vorlesungen 1819/20* (Frankfurt a. M.: Suhrkamp, 1983). Henrich also seeks to disclose, in his studies of the early phases of the emergence of Hegel's philosophy, the grounds for Hegel's departures from Kant and his failures in comprehending the genuine intent of Kantian concepts, especially in the practical philosophy. Henrich has indicated how he would develop an ethical position building critically on a Kantian foundation in *Ethik zum nuklearen Frieden* (Frankfurt a. M.: Suhrkamp, 1990), and "Gedanken zur Dankbarkeit."

For Hegelian reflections on the limitations of Kant's ontology of ordinary things, see "Kant und Hegel," in *Selbstverhältnisse;* "Dunkelheit und Vergewisserung"; "Ding an sich: Ein Prolegomenon zur Metaphysik des Endlichen," in J. Rohls and G. Wenz, eds., *Vernunft des Glaubens: Festschrift zum 60. Geburtstag von W. Pannenberg* (Göttingen: Vandenhoeck und Ruprecht, 1988), pp. 42–92; and "Die Formationsbedingungen der Dialektik: Über die Untrennbarkeit der Methode Hegels von Hegels System," *Revue internationale de philosophie* 139/40 (1982): 139–162.

45. D. Henrich, *Konzepte,* p. 110; and "Karl Jaspers: Thinking with Max Weber in Mind," in W. J. Mommsen and J. Osterhammel, eds., *Max Weber and His Contemporaries* (London: Allen and Unwin, 1987), pp. 528–544. See also Henrich's doctoral dissertation, "Die Einheit der Wissenschaftslehre Max Webers" (Tübingen, 1952).

46. D. Henrich, *Konzepte,* pp. 40–43.

47. See D. Henrich, "Dunkelheit und Vergewisserung." Another example of a direction is Henrich's treatment of "remembrance" in his study of Hölderlin, *Der Gang des Andenkens.* A convergence with the themes and questions of the later Heidegger is unmistakable in these writings.

48. See D. Henrich, "Gedanken zur Dankbarkeit"; and compare with Plato, *Euthyphro,* 14c–15b.

49. See, for example, "Hegels Theorie über den Zufall," in D. Henrich, *Hegel im Kontext* (Frankfurt a. M.: Suhrkamp, 1971), pp. 157–186.

50. See D. Henrich, *Der Grund im Bewusstsein,* chapter 30, "Absolute Erkenntnis und der endliche Gott"; also the essays "The Moral Image of the World" and "The Contexts of Autonomy: Some Presuppositions of the Comprehensibility of Human Rights," in *Aesthetic Judgment and the Moral Image of the World,* pp. 3–28 and 59–84, respectively.

1. On the Unity of Subjectivity

1. Parenthetical page references in the body of the essay refer to M. Heidegger, *Kant and the Problem of Metaphysics,* 4th ed., trans. Richard Taft (Bloomington: Indiana University Press, 1990). Parenthetical page references with preceding 'A' or 'B' refer to the original pagination of the first and second edition, respectively, of the *Critique of Pure Reason.* Quotations from the *Critique* follow the translation by N. K. Smith (New York: St. Martin's Press, 1965). I wish to thank Marlena Corcoran, John Peters, David Stern, and Richard Velkley for their helpful stylistic advice.—*Trans.*

2. This essay presupposes acquaintance with Heidegger's book. It concludes a

series of articles on Kant's philosophy. Although each has a certain independence, they all refer in multiple ways to one another and are intended jointly to guide toward an entire context of problems the discussion of which has also become urgent by the current situation of Kant scholarship. Cf. "Zur theoretischen Philosophie Kants," *Philosophische Rundschau*, 1 (1953/54): 124–149; "Das Prinzip der kantischen Ethik," *Philosophische Rundschau*, 2 (1954/55): 20–38.

3. E. Cassirer, "Kant und das Problem der Metaphysik," *Kantstudien*, 36 (1931): 10–26; H. Levy, "Heidegger's Kant-Interpretation," *Logos*, 21 (1932): 1–43.

4. M. Heidegger, *What Is Called Thinking?* trans. F. Wieck and J. G. Gray (New York: Harper and Row, 1972), p. 128.

5. *Philosophische Enzyklopädie*, in *Kants gesammelte Schriften*, Royal Prussian Academy of Sciences edition (Berlin: W. de Gruyter, 1902–), vol. 29.1,1, p. 29.

6. One may refer here to Vaihinger's commentary *Commentar zu Kants Kritik der reinen Vernunft*, vol. 1 (Stuttgart: W. Spemann, 1881), p. 485ff., which provides a useful survey of the literature without ever reaching the sense of Kant's text. Some, though insufficient, remarks pertaining to what follows can be found in J. Bona-Meyer, *Kants Psychologie* (Berlin: Wilhelm Hertz, 1870), and in A. Apitzsch, *Die psychologischen Voraussetzungen der Erkenntniskritik Kants* (dissertation, Halle, 1897).

7. "Über den Gebrauch teleologischer Principien in der Philosophie," in *Kants gesammelte Schriften*, vol. 8, pp. 180–181, n.

8. Cf. *Kants gesammelte Schriften*, vol. 28.1, p. 261f.; alternatively, *Kants Vorlesungen über Metaphysik*, ed. K. H. L. Pölitz (Erfurt: Keysersche Buchhandlung, 1821; reprint Darmstadt: Wissenschaftliche Buchgesellschaft, 1975), pp. 192–195.

9. "Power representing the universe"; *Kants Vorlesungen über Metaphysik*, pp. 192–195.

10. *Kants gesammelte Schriften*, vol. 28.2,1, p. 674; alternatively, *Die philosophischen Hauptvorlesungen Immanuel Kants*, ed. A. Kowalewski (Hildesheim: Georg Olms, 1965), p. 596f.

11. Kant, "Über den Gebrauch teleologischer Principien," pp. 180–181, n.

12. *Kants gesammelte Schriften*, vol. 28.1, p. 261; alternatively, *Kants Vorlesungen über Metaphysik*, p. 193.

13. Kant, "Über den Gebrauch teleologischer Principien," p. 181, n.

14. In the lectures on metaphysics edited by Pölitz (*Kants Vorlesungen über Metaphysik*) Kant is still defending a different position; he thinks that the identity of the soul and the "I" permits the inference to a basic force which, however, is thought to be unknown. If one wants to trust the lecture notes to this extent, then the essay on teleological principles, as well as the passage concerning the common root, contain a moment of self-criticism. This observation is further confirmation of the need to date the second half of the Pölitz lectures at a considerable interval prior to 1781. On the chronology cf. M. Heinze, *Vorlesungen Kants über Metaphysik aus drei Semestern*. Abhandlungen der philologisch-historischen Classe der Königlich Sächsischen Gesellschaft der Wissenschaften, vols. 14/15 (Leipzig, 1894).

15. Cf. "Monadology," §10ff., in G. W. Leibniz, *Philosophical Essays*, trans. R. Ariew and D. Garber (Indianapolis: Hackett, 1989), p. 214.

16. Cf. "On the Correction of Metaphysics and the Concept of Substance," in G. W. Leibniz, *Philosophical Papers and Letters*, ed. L. E. Loemker (Dordrecht: Reidel, 1969), p. 432f.; "Postscript to a Letter to Basnage de Beauval," in Leibniz, *Philosophical Essays*, pp. 147–149.

17. "Monadology," §§13, 14, in G. W. Leibniz, *Philosophical Essays*, p. 214.

18. Cf. "Principles of Nature and Grace, Based on Reason," §3, in G. W. Leibniz, *Philosophical Essays*, p. 207f.

19. Cf. C. Wolff, *Psychologia Rationalis* (1734), in id., *Gesammelte Schriften*, div. 2, vol. 6, ed. Jean Ecole (Hildesheim: Georg Olms, 1972), p. 40ff. (§62ff.); A. G. Baumgarten, *Metaphysica*, 3rd ed. (1757), in *Kants gesammelte Schriften*, vol. 17, p. 140ff. (§740ff.).

20. "The power that represents the universe according to the location of the body in it."

21. Cf. C. Wolff, *Psychologia Rationalis*, p. 37 (§57); id., *Vernünftige Gedanken von Gott, der Welt und der Seele des Menschen, auch allen Dingen überhaupt* (1720), in id., *Gesammelte Schriften*, div. 1, vol. 2, ed. C. A. Corr (Hildesheim: Georg Olms, 1983), p. 464f. (§745).

22. Cf. C. Wolff, *Psychologia Rationalis*, p. 40 (§61).

23. Cf. C. Wolff, *Philosophia prima sive ontologia* (1736), in id., *Gesammelte Werke*, div. 2, vol. 3, ed. J. Ecole (Hildesheim: Georg Olms, 1962), p. 538ff. (§716ff.).

24. Cf., e.g., A. G. Baumgarten, *Metaphysica*, in *Kants gesammelte Schriften*, vol. 15, p. 46 (§667).

25. I. Kant, *Critique of Judgment*, trans. Werner S. Pluhar (Indianapolis: Hackett, 1987), p. 394f. (translation modified).

26. Cf. I. Kant, *Erste Einleitung in die Kritik der Urteilskraft*, ed. G. Lehmann (Leipzig: Meiner, 1927).

27. On the following one should compare the important work by Heimsoeth on Crusius, which unfortunately has not become sufficiently influential. It is the only work that correctly sees the reference to Crusius in the passage on the common root: "Metaphysik und Kritik bei Ch. A. Crusius," in H. Heimsoeth, *Studien zur Philosophie Immanuel Kants: Metaphysische Ursprünge und ontologische Grundlagen*. Kantstudien Ergänzungshefte, no. 71 (Cologne: Kölner Universitätsverlag, 1956), pp. 125–188. Yet Crusius is by no means Wolff's first opponent in psychology. Rather, Crusius's most essential arguments had already been advanced in 1727, thus even prior to the publication of Wolff's Latin psychology (1734), by Andreas Rüdiger in *Wolff's Opinion on the Essence of the Soul and of a Spirit in General and Andreas Rüdiger's Contrary Opinion*. The immediate connection with Crusius is established through his teacher, Friedrich Hoffmann, who in his refutation of Wolff's logic, published in 1729, calls for a reply to Rüdiger's work. Rüdiger, who agrees with Wolff that the soul is power (§27), holds that it is possible to subsume the functions of the soul under that power, but not to derive the former from the latter. The *vis repraesentativa* is thus said to be a mere *genus remotum*. "An abstractio metaphysica in the sense of a genus, such as the author's power of

the soul, does not remove the real difference of powers but rather confirms it" (r 2, on §754 of Wolff, *Vernünftige Gedanken von Gott*, p. 468f.). The response of a Wolffian, published under the pseudonym Hieronymous Aletophilus (Frankfurt and Leipzig, 1729) correctly points out that the *vis repraesentativa* is supposed to be not "genus remotum, but the ground of everything changeable going on in the soul" (p. 37). *De facto*, though, the task of derivation which follows from such a determination was not solved by Wolff. The contradictions that Rüdiger himself faces, because he retains the Wolffian concept of the soul as power, will be solved only by Crusius.

28. C. A. Crusius, *Entwurf der notwendigen Vernunftwahrheiten: Wiefern sie den zufälligen entgegengesetzt werden*, in id., *Die philosophischen Hauptwerke*, ed. G. Tonelli, vol. 2 (Hildesheim: Georg Olms, 1964), pp. 119–123 (§69f.).

29. Ibid., p. 121 (§70).

30. Notice the analogy with Kant in his essay "On the Use of Teleological Principles in Philosophy."

31. C. A. Crusius, *Entwurf*, p. 128 (§73).

32. Ibid., p. 860 (§444); cf. also C. A. Crusius, *Weg zur Gewißheit und Zuverläßigkeit der menschlichen Erkenntnis* (1747), in id., *Philosophische Hauptschriften*, vol. 3, p. 134 (§75).

33. In Wolff the term "basic power" is absent because he defines power *(vis)* outright as basic power; all derived powers are called faculties *(facultates)*.

34. Cf. C. A. Crusius, *Entwurf*, p. 854f. (§439).

35. "Principiorum primorum cognitionis metaphysicae nova dilicudatio," in *Kants gesammelte Schriften*, vol. 1, p. 411.

36. In *Weg zur Gewißheit und Zuverläßigkeit der menschlichen Erkenntnis* C. A. Crusius shows that he considers it impossible to "discover completely" the "absolutely first basic powers of the human understanding" (p. 111, §63). Here he also attempts to show that certain powers are only "derived powers," which "presuppose the basic ones and follow from them" (pp. 176–179, §101). Yet there is no demonstration of an intelligible system of powers. And this in spite of the definition of the soul given in §75 (p. 134), according to which one has to think of it as a "*systema* of basic powers, connected by certain laws, such that the efficacy of one becomes the condition for the vitality of the other."

37. Charles Bonnet (1720–1793), Swiss naturalist and philosopher, published two psychological treatises: *Essai de psychologie* (1745) and *Essai sur les facultés de l'âme* (1760).

38. *Philosophische Versuche über die menschliche Natur und ihre Entwicklung*, vol. 1, ed. W. Uebele (Berlin: Reuther and Reichard, 1913).

39. Cf. ibid., p. 5.

40. Cf. ibid., p. 4.

41. Ibid., p. 223.

42. *Enquiry concerning the Clarity of the Principles of Natural Theology and Ethics*, in Kant, *Selected Precritical Writings and Correspondence with Beck*, trans. G. B. Kerferd and D. E. Walford (Manchester: Manchester University Press, 1968), p. 33.

43. Ibid., p. 11 (translation modified).

44. *Kants gesammelte Schriften*, vol. 28.2,1, p. 674; alternatively, *Die philosophischen Hauptvorlesungen*, p. 596.

45. *Kants gesammelte Schriften*, vol. 28.1, p. 262; alternatively, *Kants Vorlesungen über Metaphysik*, p. 194.

46. "Imaginary focal point"; cf. A 644/B 672.

47. These Kantian thoughts have to be pieced together through the combination of mostly hidden texts. Many of these thoughts are presented in a systematic manner in the initial sections of C. C. E. Schmid, *Empirical Psychology* (Jena, 1791). This compendium was widely used in its time and is of particular interest because it manages to appreciate, on the basis of Kantian principles, the significance of Crusius's opposition to Wolff.

48. Cf. I. Kant, *On a Discovery according to which Any New Critique of Reason Has Been Made Superfluous by an Earlier One*, in H. Allison, *The Kant-Eberhard Controversy* (Baltimore: The Johns Hopkins University Press, 1973), p. 137, n.

49. Ibid.

50. *Kants gesammelte Schriften*, vol. 28.2,1, p. 563; alternatively, *Kants Vorlesungen über Metaphysik*, p. 55.

51. *Kants gesammelte Schriften*, vol. 18, p. 311 (reflection 5653).

52. Cf. I. Kant, *Dreams of a Spirit-Seer and Other Related Writings*, trans. J. Manolesco (New York: Vintage Press, 1969), p. 43.

53. *Kants gesammelte Schriften*, vol. 18, p. 414 (reflection 5979).

54. I. Kant, *Critique of Practical Reason*, in *Critique of Practical Reason and Other Writings in Moral Philosophy*, trans. L. W. Beck (Chicago: University of Chicago Press, 1949), p. 142.

55. Thus in the categorical imperative self-consciousness is, as it were, confirmed in its status as substance. Without the consciousness of obligation, self-consciousness cannot be certain of its "mode of being," since it could as well be the accident or state of some nonrational transcendent matter. Initially it might seem that from here one could gain a modern understanding of the "elevation of the mind" and the "sublime character of the law," arguing that self-consciousness is concerned with its *Geborgenheit* (securedness) in Being, of which it becomes certain in the categorical imperative. That would also explain its binding force. But all such attempts fail to realize that according to Kant, and maybe also according to the way things are, a concern of the soul for itself already presupposes the consciousness of obligation. If there were rational beings that did not stand under moral obligation (for Kant that is not a contradiction), they could seek their "happiness" without being in the least interested in their origin, which they might at most turn into one of the objects of their purely theoretical cognition. Only the fact of obligation brings with it necessarily the problem of freedom as such. It should be remembered that Kant interprets the entire system of metaphysics as an attempt to solve the problem of freedom. Metaphysics itself would, according to him, hardly have come into existence were it not for the fact that the moral vocation of human beings had to fight off the subtleties advanced by the understanding in the interest of sensibility against the validity of the law.

Furthermore, the satisfied concern over whether self-consciousness is a subject with a being of its own is in itself an instance of vanity and cannot possibly explain the consciousness of being able to overcome all obstacles, which lies in the "you ought" of the categorical imperative.

56. J. Locke, *An Essay concerning Human Understanding,* book 2, chapter 27.

57. Kant, *Über den Gebrauch teleologischer Principien,* pp. 180–181, n.

58. *Prolegomena to Any Future Metaphysics,* ed. L. W. Beck (Indianapolis: Bobbs-Merrill, 1950), p. 65 (§36).

59. I. Kant, *Anthropology from a Pragmatic Point of View,* ed. H. H. Rudnick (Carbondale and Edwardsville: Southern Illinois University Press, 1978), p. 68 (§31).

60. Kant, *Critique of Practical Reason,* p. 197.

61. Letter to Marcus Herz, May 26, 1789 (Kant, *Philosophical Correspondence,* trans. A. Zweig [Chicago: University of Chicago Press, 1967], p. 153f., translation modified). It must be kept in mind that the teleology involved here, like all teleology in Kant, is not sufficient for objective knowledge. To derive the joining of the faculties from a divine originator is a subjective need, not an absolute necessity. The same holds even for the God of the postulates and the originator of a nature that seems made purposively for us. One has to remember that it is a possible thought that the subject is a function of matter. Given such a possibility, one could easily think of the togetherness of the faculties as having arisen from the laws governing that matter. To be sure, that is not an explanation, since we have no conception of a matter that is capable of bringing about an intellect. Viewed that way, a rational God or at least a demiurge, using the analogy of our own faculty to arrange parts in a purposive order, is a better hypothesis, but nothing more.

62. Kant, *Anthropology,* p. 68 (§31).

63. Kant, *Critique of Judgment,* p. 214.

64. The degree of significance which Kant might accord to all thoughts about the common root can also be detected from the lack of precision in the use of the concepts of power, faculty, activity, and capacity. Those concepts are not strictly distinguished, and the attention given to them does not even come close to the attention they received from Wolff and his successors. All energy is devoted to the analysis of the objective principles.

65. Kant, *Anthropology,* p. 263 (translation modified).

66. *Kants gesammelte Schriften,* vol. 18, p. 319 (reflection 5661).

67. It seems to me a striking deficiency of Heidegger's interpretation that he does not face Kant's thesis about the contingency of space and time. This thought obviously became impossible to entertain once Heidegger established that the categories themselves stem from time *qua* imagination. Yet even in the case of the problem of space and time, Heidegger's assertion of the derived status of everything abstract is not, as far as I can see, supported through a truly conclusive proof of derivation. The peculiar philosophical problem that is posed, e.g., by the contingent fact that the space of experience has three dimensions, is not settled by indicating that there are spatial structures that are more concrete and richer in content. The observation that the space pertaining to extension is only represented by way

of abstraction from a more original experience of space, as in the example of the "space allowed by the bridge," leaves the problem of extension untouched and unresolved, just as it stood in the tradition. Furthermore, it seems to me that the space of extension compared to that of the bridge, which one can *only* get on, step on and cross, is not as external as suggested by the argument from the superordination of more abstract concepts (cf. "Building, Dwelling, Thinking," in M. Heidegger, *Basic Writings from "Being and Time" (1927) to "The Task of Thinking" (1964)*, ed. D. F. Krell [New York: Harper and Row, 1977], p. 333). The impossibility of asserting a unity of sensibility and understanding follows immediately from the contingency of the forms of intuitions, just as the latter's discovery was for Kant a decisive motive for the thesis that the root is unknown to us. Every theory that claims to know that root has to perform a "deduction" of space and time, as it has been attempted from Wolff to Hegel—with obvious failure. The development of geometry during the nineteenth century has made that even clearer. Yet whereas one might at most admit the contingency of space, any such contingency seems unacceptable for time. The two arguments often mounted against the contingency of time are the one from the successive nature of thinking and that from the structural identity of "I" and time. The first argument does not suffice, since the thinking that always occurs in temporal succession must be able to and needs to think that those same thoughts could be expressed in a different medium. Heidegger clearly saw that his enterprise, which concerns not existence in time but the temporality of thinking, is not helped by this argument and employs it nowhere. The second argument is insufficient in that the structural identity in question is indeed asserted by Kant, but only in such a way that "I" and time correspond to each other, not that they coincide. The necessity of this analogical sameness is already given with the discursive nature of thinking according to which several subordinated particulars have to be thought through universal concepts. Transposed to intuition, the latter must be a medium in which the homogeneous can be intuitively presented as different. Nothing more can be said, and the successiveness of intuitions remains a contingent matter. The only way to avoid the consequence of an intrasubjective teleology is to bracket out of ontology the very question concerning the mode of jointness as an ontic and moreover derivative question. I may be permitted to note that it has always puzzled me why Gerhard Krüger, in his teleological counterinterpretation to Heidegger's Kant book, "Über Kants Lehre von der Zeit," in *Anteile: Martin Heidegger zum 60. Geburtstag* (Frankfurt a. M.: Vittorio Klostermann, 1950), pp. 178–211, did not resort to this most basic thought of Kant's. I can only explain it to myself as a result of the force of the Hegelian tradition which no longer permits realizing the thought of an *intrasubjective* teleology.

There is yet another place where Heidegger brackets out the thought of contingency in the subject, viz., in the question of the "fact" of moral obligation. But it is not possible to deal here with this problem, which would show the question about the unity of subjectivity in even greater principal significance.

68. Here I should mention the work by H. Mörchen (*Die Einbildungskraft bei Kant*, first published in *Jahrbuch für Philosophie und phänomenologische Forschung*,

11 (1930); references are to the second edition [Tübingen: Max Niemeyer, 1970]), which can be used with much gain to supplement the reading of Heidegger's Kant book. In its disposition, Mörchen's study is more historically oriented than Heidegger's, but with the same intent of rendering Kant's concepts problematic (p. 12). Over long stretches Mörchen engages in a careful and methodologically correct reading of Kant. But this makes all the more clear that his arguments lack conclusiveness at the crucial points (e.g., pp. 51, 94). Moreover, Mörchen's study lacks the entire horizon of the contrast to Hegel and the question of the meaning of Being that secretly determine Heidegger's book and constitute its true significance. Mörchen employs the philological exegesis of Kant's theory in an effort to identify those points at which the nature of the subject matter requires leaving Kant behind, without, however, raising this philosophical necessity to the status of the secret center of Kant's philosophy (e.g., p. 83). This manner of proceeding allows a philosophically beneficial separation of the interpretation from the question whether the interpreted text is true or provisional and caught up in forgetfulness.

69. Heidegger confirms this in *Being and Time*, trans. J. Macquarrie and E. Robinson (New York: Harper and Row, 1962), p. 45, by saying that Kant shrinks back, "as it were."

70. J. G. Fichte, *Science of Knowledge, with the First and Second Introductions*, trans. P. Heath and J. Lachs (Cambridge: Cambridge University Press, 1992).

71. Ibid., p. 193.

72. Ibid., p. 202.

73. F. W. J. Schelling, *System of Transcendental Idealism (1800)*, trans. P. Heath (Charlottesville: University of Virginia Press, 1978), p. 44.

74. Cf. "Of the 'I' as Principle of Philosophy, or On the Unconditional in Human Knowledge," in F. W. J. Schelling, *The Unconditional in Human Knowledge: Four Early Essays (1794–1796)*, trans. F. Marti (Lewisburg: Bucknell University Press, 1980), pp. 63–128.

75. F. W. J. Schelling, "Of the 'I' as Principle of Philosophy," p. 125, n.

76. Cf. G. W. F. Hegel, *Faith and Knowledge*, trans. W. Cerf and H. S. Harris (Albany: State University of New York Press, 1977), p. 160.

77. Cf. ibid., p. 70.

78. Cf. ibid.

79. Ibid., p. 72f. (translation modified).

80. F. A. Lange, *History of Materialism and Criticism of Its Present Importance*, trans. E. C. Thomas, 3rd ed. (3 vols. in 1), with an introduction by B. Russell (New York: Harcourt, Brace and Co., 1925), vol. 2, p. 196.

81. Cf. H. Cohen, *Kants Theorie der Erfahrung* (1871), in id., *Werke*, eds. Helmut Holzhey et al., vol. 1, part 1.3 (Hildesheim: Georg Olms, 1987), pp. 83, 164; id., *Kommentar zu Immanuel Kants Kritik der reinen Vernunft*, 5th ed., in id., *Werke*, vol. 4, pp. 20, 59.

82. M. Heidegger, *Being and Time*, p. 241; cf. also pp. 65, 169ff., 225f., 235f., 276f., 285ff., and elsewhere.

83. Ibid., p. 383 (translation modified).

84. Cf. ibid., pp. 65, 78.

85. Ibid., p. 170.

86. Ibid., p. 170.

87. Cf. ibid., p. 402.

88. To be sure, we learn a lot in *Being and Time* on the point that the concept of a basic power of the soul has to be understood as a product of a form of falling on the part of *Dasein*, in which the latter interprets itself from the kind of being characteristic of the present-at-hand. (M. Heidegger, *Being and Time*, pp. 225, 287, 350). This destruction, though, already presupposes the view toward a totality of equiprimordial moments. It can at most provide a subsidiary justification.

89. M. Heidegger, *Being and Time*, p. 240f. In his essay on Heidegger's place in the history of philosophy, Walter Schulz, "Über den philosophiegeschichtlichen Ort Martin Heideggers," in O. Pöggeler, ed., *Heidegger: Perspektiven zur Deutung seines Werks* (Cologne: Kiepenheuer and Witsch, 1970), pp. 95–139, has undertaken, in a most impressive manner, to elucidate the unity of Heidegger's thinking. Schulz sees *Being and Time* as the attempt to bring the philosophy of subjectivity to a radical conclusion by having subjectivity entirely closed up in itself as *Dasein* exclusively engaged in interpreting itself in a self-sufficient manner, so that subjectivity even includes the fact of its own existence. The view toward totality supposedly can be understood from this attempt. Schulz's attention is so focused on Heidegger's position in history that the philosophical motives and necessities underlying the explication of the totality of *Dasein* do not quite become visible.

One could consider it a difficulty for the interpretation I have given that, at the culmination of the question concerning the totality of *Dasein*, Heidegger takes back the assertion that this is a methodological question pertaining to the analytic of *Dasein*, instead characterizing it as a factual-existential question to be answered by *Dasein* in its resoluteness (cf. *Being and Time*, p. 357). One might think that as a result *Being and Time* would become nothing but the explication of an existential ideal. Yet this would be entirely at odds with the problem posed in *Being and Time*. One has to realize that the turning of the question concerning the totality into an existential question follows from the methodological guiding thread of the book. *Dasein* was defined as relation to Being, and nothing else. That means that everything *Dasein* is must be in the manner of self-understanding. If *Dasein* is therefore to be interpreted in its totality (for which the reasons will be stated), then this totality must be one that is attested to by *Dasein* itself. Otherwise *Dasein* would be thematized and analyzed like something present-at-hand (as "givenness"). Even in passages that do not yet presuppose the statements expressed on p. 357, Heidegger states that the explication toward totality has to look for an originary possibility of disclosure, "one that lies in *Dasein* itself" (ibid., p. 226). On p. 365 the question how to understand the unity of *Dasein* is outright called identical to the one asking how *Dasein* can exist in a unitary manner in the specified modes and possibilities of its being.

90. "[Being] is predicated in manifold ways."

91. Cf. M. Heidegger, "Letter on Humanism," in id., *Basic Writings*, p. 207f.

92. Cf. "The Age of the World Picture," in *The Question concerning Technology and Other Essays*, trans. W. Lovitt (New York: Harper and Row, 1977), p. 141.

93. Ibid., p. 147.
94. Cf. M. Heidegger, "Building, Dwelling, Thinking," p. 327 (translation modified).
95. Cf. M. Heidegger, *What Is Called Thinking?* p. 79.
96. M. Heidegger, *Being and Time,* p. 383.

2. The Concept of Moral Insight and Kant's Doctrine of the Fact of Reason

1. The classical works of Plato, Aristotle, and Kant are still the most fruitful for an analysis of moral insight. In more recent times we find such investigations in Dilthey, *Versuch einer Analyse des moralischen Bewusstseins* (1864), in *Gesammelte Schriften* (Leipzig and Berlin: Teubner, 1914–1936), vol. 6, pp. 1–56, and in the phenomenological school in Brentano, Scheler, Hartmann, and von Hildebrandt. Von Hildebrandt's work "Sittlichkeit und ethische Werterkenntnis" is seldom consulted. See *Jahrbuch für Philosophie und phänomenologische Forschung,* 5 (1922): 462ff.

2. Compare D. von Hildebrandt, "Die Idee der sittlichen Handlung," *Jahrbuch für Philosophie und phänomenologische Forschung,* 3 (1916): 126ff.

3. Although the question is also raised by moral consciousness itself, it is not a condition of its *complacentia.*

4. See Aristotle, *Nicomachean Ethics,* book 2, chapter 3, in J. Barnes, ed., *The Complete Works of Aristotle* (Princeton: Princeton University Press, 1984), vol. 2.

5. This is Kierkegaard's view. The aesthetic stage of existence is overcome and taken up in the ethical by the event in which an existence chooses itself. Through this choice it becomes first spiritual (or enters into an infinite relation to itself). The self of concrete existence can become itself not by abstractly knowing of something ideal (the good), but by making a factual *choice.* For Kierkegaard, this choice precedes the constitution of the opposition between good and evil. However, Kierkegaard does not contest the truth that the decision to become a moral self already presupposes the *demand* of the good. Kierkegaard never reflected on how this demand confronts us, and how the opposition of good and evil originates in its substance. This problem is the modern version of the Platonic paradox that the person who wants truly to know the good must already have decided in favor of it. Plato's myth of *Eros* hides an attempt at solving this paradox. Kierkegaard cannot get beyond the succession of stages: despair, choice of self, recognition of good and evil, moral existence. If (contrary to Kierkegaard's aim) we obstinately cling to this succession, then the way to Sartre's "Goetz" in *Le diable et le bon dieu* is not far.

6. Plato, *Laws,* 653ff.

7. Aristotle, *Nicomachean Ethics,* book 6, chapter 5, 1140b13–20, pp. 1800–1801.

8. I. Kant, *Foundations of the Metaphysics of Morals,* in I. Kant, *Critique of Practical Reason and Other Writings in Moral Philosophy,* trans. and ed. L. W. Beck (Chicago: University of Chicago Press, 1949), p. 65.

9. See I. Kant, *Lectures on Ethics,* trans. L. Infield, ed. L. W. Beck (Indianapolis: Hackett, 1980), p. 137.

10. S. Clarke, *A Discourse concerning the Unchangeable Obligations of Natural Religion* (London, 1706); W. Wollaston, *The Religion of Nature Delineated* (London, 1722); C. Wolff, *Philosophia Practica Universalis,* 2 vols. (Frankfurt, 1736–1739); Lord Shaftesbury, *An Inquiry concerning Virtue* (London, 1699); F. Hutcheson, (especially) *Essay on the Nature and Conduct of the Passions and Affections* (London, 1728). Compare D. Henrich, "Hutcheson and Kant," *Kantstudien* 49 (1957/58): 49–69. J. Butler, *Fifteen Sermons upon Human Nature, or Man Considered as a Moral Agent* (London, 1726).

11. G. Hegel, *Lectures on the History of Philosophy,* trans. E. S. Haldane and F. H. Simson, vol. 3 (Atlantic Highlands, New Jersey: Humanities Press, 1974), p. 461.

12. A. Schopenhauer, *The Basis of Morality,* trans. A. B. Bullock (London: S. Sonnenschein, 1903), pp. 68–69.

13. The deeper reason for this piece of sophistry is the fact that even the concept of a *vis repraesentativa universi* is already ambiguous. As *vis repraesentativa* it signifies the aggregate of all thoughts. It already contains the entire content of all possible beings by way of obscure representations. However, *vis* means the constant striving to change whatever is represented at a particular moment. It is a *nisus* for the change of representations. It thus refers to both *repraesentatio* and *appetitus.*

14. C. A. Crusius, *Entwurf der notwendigen Vernunftwahrheiten* (Leipzig, 1745); see especially §§70ff. and 449ff.

15. *Die philosophischen Hauptvorlesungen I. Kants,* ed. A. Kowalewski (Hildesheim: G. Olms, 1965), p. 144. Subsequent reflections of the literary remains are quoted with their numbers in parentheses. They are to be found in *Kants gesammelte Schriften,* Royal Prussian Academy of Sciences edition (Berlin: W. de Gruyter 1902–).

16. F. Hutcheson, in making this distinction, appeals explicitly to the "ancients" who in the *logikon meros* of the soul differentiated two different faculties. "However, the will has been forgotten in more recent times." *Abhandlung über die Leidenschaften* (Leipzig, 1760), p. 230; German translation of *An Essay on the Nature and Conduct of the Passions* (London, 1728).

17. Quoted from the German translation of *An Essay on the Nature and Conduct of the Passions,* p. 261.

18. The most important sources that support this unexpected fact are the Latin reflections in Kant's interleaved copy of *Observations on the Feeling of the Beautiful and Sublime,* printed in vol. 20 of the Academy edition. (See D. Henrich's "Selbstbewusstsein und Moralität," habilitation dissertation, Heidelberg, 1956, pp. 130–172).

19. H. J. Paton first showed in his commentary on the *Foundations of the Metaphysics of Morals* that this work, published in 1785, still shows traces of a deductive moral philosophy. See Paton, *The Categorical Imperative: A Study in Kant's Moral Philosophy* (Chicago: University of Chicago Press, 1948), pp. 226, 242ff. Although the doctrine of the fact of reason is already present in substance even here, it has not been formulated in all clarity. See D. Henrich, "Das Prinzip der kantischen Ethik," *Philosophische Rundschau,* 2 (1954/55), p. 36.

20. Kant, *Lectures on Ethics*, pp. 44–45 (emphasis added).

21. I. Kant, *Philosophical Correspondence, 1759–1799*, trans. and ed. A. Zweig (Chicago: University of Chicago Press, 1967), p. 78.

22. The first examination of these attempts can be found in F. W. Foerster's dissertation "Der Entwicklung der kantischen Ethik bis zur Kritik der reinen Vernunft" (Berlin, 1893). Foerster was a student of Riehl. He had access only to the incomplete edition by Erdmann; nevertheless, some of his conclusions are still useful.

23. Kant, *Lectures on Ethics*, p. 45.

24. In the *Critique of Practical Reason*, Kant also places the pleasure we take in the happiness of ourselves and others under the condition of the good will. However, in this work it is no longer part of the nature of the good itself. Someone who possesses a good will is worthy of happiness, but he is no longer good because he is worthy of happiness.

25. During the deductive phase of his moral philosophy, Kant considers moral theology one of the constitutive elements of moral consciousness. In his doctrine of the fact of reason it is only a complement of the good will that prevents us from despairing in the face of its nothingness. For this reason the importance of moral theology has already decreased in the *Critique of Practical Reason*. It is still less important in *Religion within the Limits of Mere Reason Alone*; see I. Kant, *Religion within the Limits of Mere Reason Alone*, trans. T. M. Greene and H. H. Hudson (New York: Harper Torchbooks, 1960), p. 1ff. Kant still held to the doctrine of the worthiness of happiness in the *Critique of Pure Reason* (B 837ff). However, in his moral writings (beginning with the *Foundations*) he always rejected faith in God as a *motive* for the good will. The accusations that Kant again introduced heteronomy with his moral theology are unfounded, though they are still made. In Kant's mature works the moral faith is a *consequence*, not a condition, of the good will.

26. I. Kant, *Vorlesungen über Metaphysik*, ed. K. H. L. Pölitz (Erfurt, 1821; reprinted Darmstadt: Wissenschaftliche Buchgesellschaft, 1975), pp. 205–207.

27. Compare H. J. Paton, *The Categorical Imperative*. In the last paragraph of his review of Schulz, Kant wants to force the author to admit freedom of the will by referring to the reflective freedom of thinking.

28. Kant intentionally chose the title "Critique of Practical Reason." He did not call it "Critique of Pure Practical Reason," for pure practical reason (i.e., moral insight and its power to act) "does not require any critique." It does not get embroiled in an antinomy of contradictions; see Kant, *Critique of Practical Reason*, p. 129. The *Critique of Practical Reason* criticizes the kind of reason that serves pleasure and has become the sophistical defender of pleasure. This practical reason is "empirically determined." Its claims must be rejected in the interest of morality and the unclouded clarity of moral insight.

29. Kant, *Religion within the Limits of Reason Alone*, p. 21, n. (emphasis added).

30. *Kants gesammelte Schriften*, vol. 20, p. 44.

31. Compare E. Kapp, *The Greek Foundations of Traditional Logic* (New York: Columbia University Press, 1942). See also the article "Syllogistik" in A. F. Pauly and G. Wissowa, *Realenzyklopädie der klassischen Altertumswissenschaft*.

32. Compare R. P. Sertillanges, "La morale ancienne et la morale moderne," *Re-

vue philosophique, 51 (1901): 280ff.; E. Gilson, *The Spirit of Medieval Philosophy,* trans. A. H. C. Downes (London: Sheed and Ward, 1936).

3. Ethics of Autonomy

1. See *Critique of Practical Reason,* in I. Kant, *Critique of Practical Reason and Other Writings in Moral Philosophy,* trans. L. W. Beck (Chicago: University of Chicago Press, 1949), p. 130.
2. See ibid., p. 129.
3. See Kant, *Foundations of the Metaphysics of Morals,* in *Critique of Practical Reason and Other Writings in Moral Philosophy,* p. 55.
4. The proof of this is based on the Latin reflections in Kant's own manuscript of the *Observations on the Feeling of the Beautiful and Sublime;* see *Kants gesammelte Schriften,* Royal Prussian Academy of Sciences edition (Berlin: W. de Gruyter, 1902–), vol. 20, pp. 1–192.
5. I. Kant, *Critique of Pure Reason,* trans. N. K. Smith (New York: St. Martin's Press, 1965), B xvi.
6. Ovid, *Ex Ponto* III 4, 79.
7. Propertius, *Elegies* II 10, 6.
8. See *Remarks to Observations,* in *Kants gesammelte Schriften,* vol. 20, p. 148, 13 ff. Quotation translated from the Latin.
9. Ibid., vol. 20, p. 156, 2.
10. Kant, *Foundations of the Metaphysics of Morals,* p. 80ff.; compare id., *Critique of Practical Reason,* p. 142ff.
11. See Kant, *Metaphysics of Morals* (1797) and *Opus Postumum.*
12. The *Remarks,* in *Kants gesammelte Schriften,* vol. 20, p. 161, 5ff. The subsequent translation is from the Latin.
13. Ibid, p. 148, 13.
14. See Kant, *Foundations of the Metaphysics of Morals,* p. 81.
15. D. Henrich, "Das Prinzip der kantischen Ethik," *Philosophische Rundschau,* 2 (1954/55): 28ff.
16. One can find the best analyses of these procedures of deduction in H. J. Paton, *The Categorical Imperative: A Study in Kant's Moral Philosophy* (Chicago: University of Chicago Press, 1948), and J. Ebbinghaus, "Die Formeln des Kategorischen Imperativs und die Ableitung inhaltlich bestimmter Pflichten," *Studie e ricerche di storia della filosofia,* 10 (1959): 733ff.
17. In contrast to J. Ebbinghaus, "Die Formeln," 749ff.
18. G. W. F. Hegel, *Lectures on the History of Philosophy,* vol. 3, trans. E. S. Haldane and F. H. Simson (Atlantic Highlands, New Jersey: Humanities Press), p. 461.
19. See Kant, *Foundations of the Metaphysics of Morals,* p. 59ff.
20. I. Kant, *Metaphysics of Morals,* trans. with an introduction by M. Gregor (Cambridge: Cambridge University Press, 1991), part two, "The Doctrine of Virtue," p. 270.
21. See D. Henrich, "Hutcheson und Kant," in *Kantstudien: Festschrift für H. J. Paton,* 49 (1957/58): 46–69.

22. I. Kant, *Lectures on Ethics*, trans. L. Infield, ed. L. W. Beck (Indianapolis: Hackett, 1980), pp. 44–45.

23. See Chapter 2.

24. This is the logical connection between these two theories. The developmental history of Kantian ethics led first to the theory of respect for the law (after 1781) and then to the theory of the fact of reason (after 1785).

25. See Kant, *Critique of Practical Reason*, pp. 181, 186–187.

26. See Kant, *Metaphysics of Morals*, p. 204.

27. We are still waiting for an investigation into the history of the word *Achtung*. An initial survey can be found in the dictionaries of Walch, Adelung, and Grimm.

28. Kant, *Critique of Practical Reason*, pp. 186–187.

29. Ibid., p. 183.

30. C. Thomasius (1655–1728); see G. Tonelli, *Elementi metodologici e metafisici in Kant dal 1745 al 1768* (Turin: Edizioni di filosofia, 1959).

31. *Briefe über kantische Philosophie* (Jena, 1792), vol. 2.

32. See above all G. C. Storr, *Bemerkungen über Kants philosophische Religionslehre* (Tübingen, 1794).

33. D. Henrich, "Beauty and Freedom: Schiller's Struggle with Kant's Aesthetics," in T. Cohen and P. Guyer, eds., *Essays in Kant's Aesthetics* (Chicago: University of Chicago Press, 1982), pp. 237–257.

34. Letter to F. Huber, Feb. 19, 1795, in *Schillers Briefe*, ed. F. Jonas, vol. 4 (Stuttgart: Deutsche Verlags-Anstalt, 1892), pp. 125–128.

35. Kant, *Critique of Practical Reason*, 2nd ed. (Riga, 1792), B 11, note.

36. *Über Anmut und Würde* (1793), in *Schillers philosophische Schriften und Gedichte*, ed. E. Kühnemann (Leipzig: Dürr, 1922) p. 151, note.

37. G. W. F. Hegel, *Theologische Jugendschriften*, ed. H. Nohl (Tübingen: J. C. B. Mohr (Paul Siebeck), 1907), p. 390.

38. F. Schiller, *Kallias-Briefe*, Feb. 18 and 19, 1793.

39. See especially J. G. Fichte, *System der Sittenlehre* (1798), in id., *Sämtliche Werke*, ed. I. H. Fichte, vol. 4 (Berlin: Veit, 1845/46; reprint W. de Gruyter, 1965), pp. 13–62. In this connection the thought in §2 of the first division of *System der Sittenlehre* could be ignored.

40. See above all G. W. F. Hegel, *Elements of the Philosophy of Right*, trans. H. B. Nisbet, ed. A. Wood (Cambridge: Cambridge University Press, 1991), §5.

4. Identity and Objectivity: An Inquiry into Kant's Transcendental Deduction

1. Despite many new and important titles, the two publications carrying the greatest philosophical weight are still Jonathan Bennett, *Kant's Analytic* (Cambridge: Cambridge University Press, 1966), and Peter Strawson, *The Bounds of Sense* (London: Methuen, 1966).

2. The form of the presentation of the present essay as given in the meeting of the Philosophic-Historical Class of the Heidelberg Academy of Sciences has been retained only in the Introduction and Conclusion. The two main sections have

been written entirely anew. I have been aided in this rewriting by the arguments formulated by a number of colleagues and by discussions after talks given at Frankfurt University, Harvard University, and the University of Pittsburgh. The sequence of theses and arguments, however, remains nearly the same as in the presentation at the Academy. (A summary of this can be found in *Jahrbuch der Heidelberger Akademie der Wissenschaften für das Jahr 1974,* Heidelberg, 1974, pp. 129–131.) The investigation that originated in this manner is in no way intended to be a commentary upon the entire transcendental deduction; it does not even investigate all the principal arguments of the deduction. It develops only a theoretical complex that is indispensable for, and central to, understanding this aspect of Kant's thought. Of the philosophical problems that must be treated by a complete and comprehensive interpretation of the deduction, not more than roughly 10 percent (and far fewer of the exegetical problems) are covered here. Citations are made in parentheses, and the first (A) and second (B) editions of the *Critique of Pure Reason* are referred to in the way customary in the literature on Kant. Quotations, with slight modifications, are from N. K. Smith, trans., *Critique of Pure Reason* (New York: St. Martin's Press, 1965).

3. A textually faithful investigation into the organization of the deduction's proof-procedure is to be found in D. Henrich, "The Proof-Structure of Kant's Transcendental Deduction," in R. C. S. Walker, ed., *Kant on Pure Reason* (Oxford: Oxford University Press, 1982), pp. 66–81.

4. An attempt to achieve clarity about the possible meanings of "objective" is made by R. Ingarden in his article "Betrachtungen zum Problem der Objektivität," *Zeitschrift für philosophische Forschung,* 21 (1967): 31ff., 242ff.

5. Kant never did, and never could, claim anywhere that the basic structure of judgment could be obtained deductively by an analysis of self-consciousness.

6. *Kants gesammelte Schriften,* Royal Prussian Academy of Sciences edition (Berlin: W. de Gruyter, 1902–), vol. 4, p. 475, remark.

7. In what follows, the German *Satz* will generally be translated as "proposition" in order to distinguish it from *Aussage,* which will be translated as "statement." When Henrich's primary focus is upon *Satz* as a linguistic or grammatical unit, it will be rendered as "sentence." In view of the great number of philosophical issues connected with the use of these terms, the translations will on occasion appear rather arbitrary. But there is no good reason to contribute further to the general confusion historically associated with the translation of *Satz.* Cf. Kneale and Kneale, *The Development of Logic* (Oxford, 1962), pp. 361–362, 592–593.—*Trans.*

8. P. F. Strawson, *Subject and Predicate in Logic and Grammar* (London, 1974). See also W. v. O. Quine, *Word and Object* (Cambridge, Mass.: MIT Press, 1960), p. 96. It may be said in anticipation that Strawson's contributions to the understanding of the relationship between the form of the subject-predicate proposition and the concept of an object will not be entered into in what follows, even though they are of the highest importance in the contemporary theoretical context and can be developed in connection with a focus upon Kant. For reasons which will not be discussed here, they distance themselves from the outset from drawing any conclusions whatever concerning the concept of an object from the form of the

subject-predicate statement. But as will be seen, just such a conclusion was what Kant had in mind in the clearest, and philosophically most interesting, passage in his work on this topic.

9. I adopt this term from W. Sellars, who introduced it in his article "Particulars," *Philosophy and Phenomenological Research*, 13 (1952), p. 187. However, it may be noted that my use of the term diverges from that of Sellars. (For Sellars, a quale is something general which completely characterizes simple occurrences. But in the present context it is advisable to apply the term to particular occurrences that can be completely characterized by a predicate of quality.) Sellars's article is reprinted in W. Sellars, *Science, Perception, and Reality* (London: Routledge and Kegan Paul, 1963). The following articles by Sellars also belong to the same complex: "On the Logic of Complex Particulars," *Mind*, 58 (1948); "Logical Subjects and Physical Objects," *Philosophy and Phenomenological Research*, 17 (1957); "Aristotle's Metaphysics: An Interpretation," in id., *Philosophical Perspectives* (Springfield, Ill: C. C. Thomas, 1967), p. 73ff. (especially p. 74), and "Substance and Form in Aristotle" (ibid., p. 125ff.). The note on pages 130–131 of the last cited article shows the sense in which one of the fundamental perspectives of Sellars's later work was disclosed in these articles. W. Alston's criticism, "Particular—Bare and Qualified," *Philosophy and Phenomenological Research*, 15 (1955), strikes at the weak points in the argument for the thesis that the supposition of qualia as basic particulars is unavoidable. However, it leaves untouched Sellars's theses about the connection between judgment and object. The arguments of my essay have a good deal in common with those theses.

10. According to W. v. O. Quine, this connection defines the very meaning of predication. See, for example, "Speaking of Objects," in *Ontological Relativity and Other Essays* (New York: Columbia University Press, 1969), pp. 1–25; and id., *The Roots of Reference* (La Salle, Ill.: Open Court, 1973).

11. It is well known that Kant counted solely forms of the "universal" and the "particular" judgments as part of formal logic. The special form of the "singular" judgment was first introduced in the transition to transcendental philosophy (*Critique of Pure Reason*, B 96). Kant's thoughts about this matter remain unelucidated. They are, of course, also a consequence of the formal difficulties which traditional logic had in treating propositions with singular terms or names in the subject position.

12. A variation (likely problematic) on *Critique of Pure Reason*, A 126.

13. *Kants gesammelte Schriften*, vol. XVII.

14. Kant no doubt has in mind here the physical concept of heat (or caloric). Compare, for example, the use of the concepts *Wärme* and *Wärmestoff* in Kant's fragments on physics of the 1770s (*Kants gesammelte Schriften*, vol. XIV) and in the *Opus postumum*. As employed in the quoted passage, *Wärme* should technically be translated accordingly; but in the present context it is important to bring out clearly in English the connection between this term and the corresponding adjective (i.e., "warm").—*Trans.*

15. Kant's letter to Tieftrunk, Oct. 13, 1797. After the extensive correspondence Kant had received concerning the philosophical development of Reinhold and

Fichte, this attempt was evoked by the appearance of the third volume of J. S. Beck's *Erläuternder Auszug aus den critischen Schriften des Herrn Prof. Kant* [Explanatory Excerpt from the Critical Writings of Professor Kant], which had been published in 1796 by Hartknoch (Riga), publisher of the *Critique of Pure Reason*. Beck's third volume bears its own title: *Einzig möglicher Standpunkt: Aus welchem die critische Philosophie beurteilt werden muß* [The Sole Possible Standpoint from Which the Critical Philosophy Must Be Judged]. In its first part it primarily constitutes an independent investigation by Beck and a defense of the *Critique* by means of its own resources. The title *Erläuternder Auszug . . .*, which applies to all three volumes and which also appears in the third volume, contains, with reference to Kant, the additional remark, *auf Anrathen desselben* [on the advice of the same]. In point of fact, Beck had been encouraged by Kant to publish an excerpt from his work. However, it could now appear that also Beck's independent explications had been authorized by Kant. Pastor Schulz, whom Kant had declared to be the best exegete of his doctrine (see statement against Schlettwein, May 29, 1797), had taken exception to Beck's argumentation. As a result, Kant must have called upon Beck, in a letter now lost, to alter and retract his interpretation (letter to Tieftrunk, Oct. 13, 1797). In response, Beck sent Kant lengthy philosophical explanations of his standpoint. In addition, a correspondence was engendered with Beck's colleagues Tieftrunk and Jacob, both of whom were Kantians truer to the letter of Kant's writings. Since by this time Tieftrunk, too, was planning an explanatory excerpt from Kant's work, it was he, and not Beck, who received from Kant an extended reply to his communications and inquiries.

That there is a relationship between reflection 6350 and Kant's philosophical efforts in this context is made probable by the mention of Reinhold's name in the reflection. At such a late date Reinhold's name is to be found only once outside Kant's correspondence, namely, in the *Opus postumum,* and there manifestly in connection with Beck's letter of June 20, 1797. In this letter Beck announces the "retractions" of his doctrine of the standpoint [*Standpunktlehre*] written in the spirit of "Saint Augustine." Kant notes in volume 2, page 54, of the *Opus postumum:* ". . . Augustini retractatio. Reinhold" (see also G. Lehmann's editorial comments upon the passage in the same volume, p. 817). In Beck's third volume, 1797, Reinhold's theory is subjected to extensive criticism. But the reasons for which Kant associates Beck's possible self-revision with Reinhold's name cannot be clarified here.

16. Kant's considerations on the method of presentation of the transcendental deduction have been elucidated in D. Henrich, "The Proof-Structure of Kant's Transcendental Deduction."

17. See J. S. Beck, *Einzig möglicher Standpunkt,* p. 134.

18. With the definition of the category of substance as that of a particular, Kant shows himself to be operating within an Aristotelian tradition. But here it becomes apparent once and for all that for Kant no consequences are yielded by this definition which would require an Aristotelian formulation of the concept of nature. Kant puts to question the conditions of the application of the category of substance, determines these as permanence, and then investigates the conditions of

the cognizability of enduring objects. In this way he is able to reinterpret substance as matter. The problematic of this transition from the normal to the scientific concepts of substance and nature is, to be sure, taken up only in small part in the *Critique*.

19. An exposition of Kant's definition of "category" (*Critique of Pure Reason*, B 128) would be indispensable in this context. According to that definition, categories are interpreted as concepts of an object "whose intuition is regarded as determined in respect of one of the logical functions of judgment." In fact, this definition could, and should, be investigated even in the present chapter. But this task has been forgone because of the difficulties it raises. Let it merely be noted first that Kant himself gave at least two mutually irreconcilable readings of this definition (*Prolegomena*, §20, does not accord with *Critique of Pure Reason*, B 128, and reflection 5555); and second, that the relationship between the subject of judgment and object is not, according to the interpretation provided here, in agreement with either of these two interpretations. The treatment of this and many other problems must be the job of a philosophical commentary upon the entire transcendental deduction.

20. The problems that arise when one attempts to understand how it is that the knowledge of a subject of consciousness can come about within consciousness will not at all be subjected to scrutiny in what follows. Kant entertained two divergent solutions to this problem, both of which are equally unsatisfactory. I have treated this problematic in "Self-Consciousness: A Critical Introduction to a Theory," *Man and World*, 4 (1971): 3–28.

21. D. Hume, *A Treatise of Human Nature*, book 1, part 4, §§4, 6.

22. A complication arises here in view of the distinction that Kant makes (and must make) between two ways of comprehending the given qua sensation, i.e., "perception" and "concept." In order to provisionally circumvent this difficulty, I shall write first merely of the relationship between the "given" and the "thought."

23. As we know, Kant teaches that it is impossible as a matter of principle to have theoretical knowledge of the real conditons of the possibility of self-consciousness.

24. The investigation concerning the concepts of object and judgment in the first part of this essay proceeded on the basis of a rule and derived from it the necessity of there being a certain type of complex thought, viz., the thought of objects. From a certain type of complex thought (namely, of subject-predicate propositions), the investigation actually obtained an a priori rule for another type of complex thought. However, this argument does not thereby have the generality of a deduction of necessary conditions to which complex thoughts are subject.

25. It is appropriate at this point to go into two of the more voluminous publications on the transcendental deduction. The criticism of the argument for Kant's transcendental logic which M. Aebi published under the title *Kants Begründung der "deutschen Philosophie": Kants transzendentale Logik, Kritik ihrer Begründung* (Basel: Verlag für Recht und Gesellschaft, 1947), claims to show that Kant surreptitiously accomplished the transition from the necessary unity of all thoughts in self-consciousness to the necessity of the relation of all representations, and then to concepts of unity on the basis of a *homonymia in termino* pertaining to the concept

of the "unity of apperception." In Aebi's book, the text of all versions of the transcendental deduction is worked through and declared to be the product of this fallacy, which repeats itself in changing circumstances and disguises. J. Ebbinghaus (see *Archiv für Philosophie*, 5/1 (1954), p. 37ff.) rightly reproaches this author for failing to recognize the actual standing of Kant's problem in her articulation of the proof program of the *Critique*. However, he, too, leaves a fully justified question without any prospect of receiving an answer, a question into which Aebi's badly formulated criticism of the proof procedure of the transcendental deduction can easily be transformed. That is, what reason and context are there which compellingly ground the thesis that the unity of self-consciousness is only possible through synthesis in conformity with a priori principles? Kant, too, does not give an adequately formulated solution to this problem, which is what makes possible a criticism such as that of Aebi. But in this criticism the potential of Kant's theoretical blueprint is nowhere explored. And the complicated argumentative associations and superimpositions within the text of the *Critique*—factors which yield not only many faulty inferences but also the outlines of many important conclusions—are reduced to a single fallacy.

Although rich in insights and arguments, R. P. Wolff's work *Kant's Theory of Mental Activity: A Commentary on the Transcendental Analytic of the Critique of Pure Reason* (Cambridge, Mass.: Harvard University Press, 1963), unfortunately neglects almost entirely the problem of substantiating the first series of moves in the transcendental deduction. Wolff does comment upon why it is that the unity of consciousness is a different type of unity than that of a sequence of objective happenings (p. 106). He also makes evident the special features of synthesis according to a rule (p. 120ff.). Still, he does not show that the unity of consciousness is possible only as the consciousness of synthesis according to a rule, or that the unity of self-consciousness requires such a regulated synthesis. Where this problem ought to be discussed Wolff gives merely a variant of Kant's analysis of recognition (p. 129), an analysis which (as will be shown later) cannot bear the burden of proof. Wolff's book thereby overlooks Kant's most crucial problem—just as Kant himself overlooked it. Wolff finds Kant's thesis to be a sensible one, but he does not attribute any force to the latter's validative labors at the most elementary stage of the deduction, which is to say, at the stage where its premises must be secured. For an understanding of the proof derived from these premises, however, Wolff's book represents a considerable achievement.

26. C. Wolff, *Philosophia prima sive ontologia* (1736), in C. Wolff, *Gesammelte Werke*, div. II, vol. 3, ed. J. Ecole (Hildesheim and New York: G. Olms, 1962), §182.

27. For one to be in a position to speak at all about states of the subject in a sufficiently specific sense, representations cannot be comprehended merely as elements of a relation whose further element is identical self-consciousness. But that is already avoided if this self-consciousness is assumed to structure the mode of givenness of representations by rules of synthesis. It can then be the same self-consciousness in the sequence of representations in just as strict a sense as a type case remains the same for changing sets of type settings (or better yet, a movie screen for sequences of pictures).

28. One can find in this relation of conditionality an analogy with the normative component attributable to the meaning of the concept of rule in its normal employment: what is manifold must be submitted to the constant form of the subject-combination; otherwise consciousness is not engendered in relation to that manifold. Since consciousness is an active principle of combination, it can be said that in the latter case consciousness has *miscarried,* although it makes no sense to say that the rules are *incorrectly* applied. A clarification of the concept of rule which permits such an extension of its meaning is provided by S. Cavell in *Must We Mean What We Say?* (New York: Scribners, 1969), p. 46ff.

29. See D. Henrich, "Selbsterhaltung und Geschichtlichkeit," in H. Ebeling, ed., *Subjektivität und Selbsterhaltung* (Frankfurt a. M.: Suhrkamp, 1976), pp. 303–313.

30. The subsequent considerations represent a first attempt at working out a line of argument on this matter. They have been expanded in my paper, "The Identity of the Subject in the Transcendental Deduction," in E. Schaper and W. Vossenkuhl, eds., *Reading Kant: New Perspectives on Transcendental Arguments and Critical Philosophy* (Oxford: Basil Blackwell, 1989), but are in need of further amplification.

31. The knowledge of transition implicit in the concept of subject identity differs in this respect from the aprioricity which, according to E. Husserl, accrues to consciousness in the actual course of transitions.

32. *Metaphysica* §83. A. G. Baumgarten, *Metaphysica,* 3d ed. (1757), in *Kants gesammelte Schriften,* vol. XVII, §83.

33. What "transition" is for states of consciousness is called "synthesis" of representational states.

34. The first of these arguments already leads to a form of argumentation which refers in equal measure to the identity *and* the simplicity of the subject.

35. To elaborate upon this argument, which is given here in rudimentary form, one would have to show (a) that a manifold must in every instance be combined with a determinate manifold in the unity of an object; (b) that such elementary combinations have regulated relations to other elementary objects; (c) that these relations in turn yield a universal nexus of determinateness; and (d) that even arbitrary transitions between representations can be *definite* transitions only on the presuppositions of, and in relation to, this nexus.

36. An as yet unpublished lecture on the transcendental deduction, which I gave at Columbia University, is constructed entirely upon the investigation of this problematic.

37. See J. Piaget, *The Mechanisms of Perception* (London: Routledge and Kegan Paul, 1969).

38. The argument differs from the one used in the analysis of recognition in that it has in view not the consciousness of transitions, but rather the consciousness of the past. Of course, both modes of consciousness can only be realized together. But that does not hinder them from being distinct in themselves.

39. The Kantian concept of a "transcendental deduction" admits arguments which are not deductive in the formal sense. I have shown this in my article "Die Deduktion des Sittengesetzes: Über die Gründe der Dunkelheit des letzten Ab-

schnittes von Kants 'Grundlegung zur Metaphysik der Sitten,'" in A. Schwan, ed., *Denken im Schatten des Nihilismus* (Darmstadt: Wissenschaftliche Buchgesellschaft, 1975), pp. 55–112, §VI.

40. In following (and correcting) Wittgenstein, S. Shoemaker has occasionally come close to the thesis that this is, in fact, the case. See Shoemaker, "Self-Reference and Self-Awareness," *The Journal of Philosophy,* 65 (1968), p. 568. All the studies on the identity of the person by R. Chisholm are guided by the intention to refute the currently dominant thesis that the subject is reducible to the process of communication. However, the discussion of this problem has generally not gone beyond its beginnings.

Sources

Essays in This Volume

1. "On the Unity of Subjectivity," originally published in *Philosophische Rundschau*, 3 (1955): 28–69, as a review essay of M. Heidegger, *Kant und das Problem der Metaphysik*, on the occasion of the second edition of this work (Frankfurt a. M.: V. Klostermann, 1951).
2. "The Concept of Moral Insight and Kant's Doctrine of the Fact of Reason," originally published in *Die Gegenwart der Griechen im neueren Denken: Festschrift für Hans-Georg Gadamer zum 60. Geburtstag*, eds. D. Henrich, W. Schulz, K. H. Volkmann-Schluck (Tübingen: J. C. B. Mohr, 1960), pp. 77–115.
3. "Ethics of Autonomy," originally published as "Das Problem der Grundlegung der Ethik bei Kant und im spekulativen Idealismus," in *Sein und Ethos: Walberberger Studien*, vol. 1 (Mainz, 1963): 350–386; reprinted in D. Henrich, *Selbstverhältnisse: Gedanken und Auslegungen zu den Grundlagen der klassischen deutschen Philosophie* (Stuttgart: Philipp Reclam, 1982), pp. 6–56.
4. "Identity and Objectivity: An Inquiry into Kant's Transcendental Deduction," originally published in *Sitzungsberichte der Heidelberger Akademie der Wissenschaften: Philosophisch-historische Klasse*, essay 1 (Heidelberg: Carl Winter Universitätsverlag, 1976).

Other Works by Dieter Henrich

Aesthetic Judgment and the Moral Image of the World: Studies in Kant (Stanford: Stanford University Press, 1992).

"Die Anfänge der Theories des Subjekts (1789)," in A. Honneth et al., eds., *Zwischenbetrachtungen: Im Prozess der Aufklärung. Jürgen Habermas zum 60. Geburtstag* (Frankfurt a. M.: Suhrkamp, 1989), pp. 106–170.

"Art and Philosophy of Art Today: Reflections with Reference to Hegel," in R. E.

Amacher and V. Lange, eds., *New Perspectives in German Literary Criticism: A Collection of Essays* (Princeton: Princeton University Press, 1979), pp. 107–133.

"The Basic Structure of Modern Philosophy," *Cultural Hermeneutics,* 2/1 (1974): 1–18.

"Beauty and Freedom: Schiller's Struggle with Kant's Aesthetics," in T. Cohen and P. Guyer, eds., *Essays in Kant's Aesthetics* (Chicago: University of Chicago Press, 1982), pp. 237–257.

"The Contexts of Autonomy: Some Presuppositions of the Comprehensibility of Human Rights," in D. Henrich, *Aesthetic Judgment and the Moral Image of the World,* pp. 59–84.

"Die Deduktion des Sittengesetzes: Über die Gründe der Dunkelheit des letzten Abschnittes von Kants 'Grundlegung zur Metaphysik der Sitten,'" in A. Schwan, ed., *Denken im Schatten des Nihilismus* (Darmstadt: Wissenschaftliche Buchgesellschaft, 1975), pp. 55–112.

"Die deutsche Philosophie nach zwei Weltkriegen," in D. Henrich, *Konzepte: Essays zur Philosophie in der Zeit* (Frankfurt a. M.: Suhrkamp, 1987), pp. 44–65.

"Dimensionen und Defizite einer Theorie der Subjektivität," *Philosophische Rundschau* (1989): 1–24.

"Ding an sich: Ein Prolegomenon zur Metaphysik des Endlichen," in J. Rohls and G. Wenz, eds., *Vernunft des Glaubens: Festschrift zum 60. Geburtstag von W. Pannenberg* (Göttingen: Vandenhoeck and Ruprecht, 1988), pp. 42–92.

"Dunkelheit und Vergewisserung," in D. Henrich, ed., *All-Einheit: Wege eines Gedankens in Ost und West* (Stuttgart: Klett-Cotta, 1985), pp. 33–52.

"Die Einheit der Wissenschaftslehres Max Webers" (doctoral dissertation, Tübingen, 1952).

Ethik zum nuklearen Frieden (Frankfurt a. M.: Suhrkamp, 1990).

"Fichtes 'Ich,'" in D. Henrich, *Selbstverhältnisse* (Stuttgart: Philipp Reclam, 1982), pp. 57–82.

"Fichte's Original Insight," in *Contemporary German Philosophy,* 1 (University Park: The Pennsylvania State University Press, 1982): 15–53.

Fluchtlinien: Philosophische Essays (Frankfurt a. M.: Suhrkamp, 1982).

"Die Formationsbedingungen der Dialektik: Über die Untrennbarkeit der Methode Hegels von Hegels System," *Revue internationale der philosophie,* 139/40 (1982): 139–162.

"The French Revolution and Classical German Philosophy: Toward a Determination of Their Relation," in D. Henrich, *Aesthetic Judgment and the Moral Image of the World,* pp. 85–99.

Der Gang des Andenkens: Beobachtungen und Gedanken zu Hölderlins Gedicht (Stuttgart: Klett-Cotta, 1986).

"Gedanken zur Dankbarkeit," in R. Löw, ed., *Oikeiosis: Festschrift für R. Spaemann* (Weinheim: Acta Humaniora, 1987), pp. 69–86.

Der Grund im Bewusstsein: Untersuchungen zu Hölderlins Denken in Jena (1794/95) (Stuttgart: Klett-Cotta, 1992).

"Grund und Gang spekulativen Denkens," in D. Henrich and R. P. Horstmann, eds., *Metaphysik nach Kant? Stuttgarter Hegel-Kongress* (Stuttgart: Klett-Cotta, 1988), pp. 83–120.

Hegel im Kontext (Frankfurt a. M.: Suhrkamp, 1971).

Hegel: Philosophie des Rechts. Vorlesungen (1819/20), introduction by D. Henrich (Frankfurt a. M.: Suhrkamp, 1983).

"Hegels Grundoperation: Eine Einleitung in die 'Wissenschaft der Logik,'" in U. Guzzoni et al., eds., *Der Idealismus und seine Gegenwart: Festschrift für W. Marx* (Hamburg: Meiner, 1976), pp. 208–230.

"Hegels Theorie über den Zufall," in D. Henrich, *Hegel im Kontext*, pp. 157–186.

"Hutcheson und Kant," *Kantstudien: Festschrift für H. J. Paton*, 49 (1957/58): 49–69.

"Identität—Begriffe, Probleme, Grenzen," in O. Marquard and K. H. Stierle, eds., *Poetik und Hermeneutik*, 8 (Munich: Wilhelm Fink, 1979), pp. 133–186.

"The Identity of the Subject in the Transcendental Deduction," in E. Schaper and W. Vossenkuhl, eds., *Reading Kant: New Perspectives on Transcendental Arguments and Critical Philosophy* (Oxford: Basil Blackwell, 1989), pp. 250–280.

"Kant und Hegel: Versuch der Vereinigung ihrer Grundgedanken," in D. Henrich, *Selbstverhältnisse*, pp. 173–208.

"Kants Denken, 1762/63: Über den Ursprung der Unterscheidung analytischer und synthetischer Urteile," in H. Heimsoeth, D. Henrich, and G. Tonelli, eds., *Studien zu Kants philosophischer Entwicklung* (Hildesheim: G. Olms, 1967), pp. 7–36.

"Kant's Explanation of the Aesthetic Judgment," in D. Henrich, *Aesthetic Judgment and the Moral Image of the World*, pp. 29–56.

"Kant's Notion of a Deduction and the Methodological Background of the First Critique," in E. Förster, ed., *Kant's Transcendental Deductions: The Three Critiques and the "Opus Postumum"* (Stanford: Stanford University Press, 1989), pp. 29–46.

"Karl Jaspers: Thinking with Max Weber in Mind," in W. J. Mommsen and J. Osterhammel, eds., *Max Weber and His Contemporaries* (London: Allen and Unwin, 1987), pp. 528–544.

Konstellationen: Probleme und Debatten am Ursprung der idealistischen Philosophie (1789–1795) (Stuttgart: Klett-Cotta, 1991).

Konzepte: Essays zur Philosophie in der Zeit (Frankfurt a. M.: Suhrkamp, 1987).

"The Moral Image of the World," in D. Henrich, *Aesthetic Judgment and the Moral Image of the World*, pp. 3–28.

"Noch einmal in Zirkeln: Eine Kritik von Ernst Tugendhats semantischer Erklärung von Selbstbewusstsein," in C. Bellut and U. Müller-Scholl, eds., *Mensch und Moderne: Festschrift für H. Fahrenbach* (Würzburg: Königshausen und Neumann, 1989), pp. 89–128.

"Nuklearer Frieden," in D. Henrich, *Konzepte*, pp. 103–113.

"Das Prinzip der kantischen Ethik," *Philosophische Rundschau*, 2 (1954/55): 20–38.

"The Proof-Structure of Kant's Transcendental Deduction," in R. C. S. Walker, ed., *Kant on Pure Reason* (Oxford: Oxford University Press, 1982), pp. 66–81.

"Selbstbewusstsein und Moralität" (habilitation dissertation, Heidelberg, 1956).

"Selbstbewusstsein und spekulatives Denken," in D. Henrich, *Fluchtlinien*, pp. 125–181.

"Selbsterhaltung und Geschichtlichkeit," in H. Ebeling, ed., *Subjektivität und Selbsterhaltung* (Frankfurt a. M.: Suhrkamp, 1976), pp. 303–313.

Selbstverhältnisse: Gedanken und Auslegungen zu den Grundlagen der klassischen deutschen Philosophie (Stuttgart: Philipp Reclam, 1982).

"Self-Consciousness: A Critical Introduction to a Theory," *Man and World*, 4 (1971): 3–28.

"Über Kants Entwicklungsgeschichte," *Philosophische Rundschau*, 13 (1966): 252–263.

"Über Kants früheste Ethik," *Kantstudien*, 54 (1963): 404–431.

"Über Selbstbewusstsein und Selbsterhaltung," in D. Henrich, *Selbstverhältnisse*, pp. 109–130.

"Was ist Metaphysik—Was Moderne? Zwölf Thesen gegen Jürgen Habermas," in D. Henrich, *Konzepte*, pp. 11–43.

"Wohin die deutsche Philosophie?" in D. Henrich, *Konzepte*, pp. 66–75.

"Zu Kants Begriff der Philosophie: Eine Edition und eine Fragestellung," in F. Kaulbach and J. Ritter, eds., *Kritik und Metaphysik: Heinz Heimsoeth zum 80. Geburtstag* (Berlin: W. de Gruyter, 1966), pp. 40–59.

"Zur theoretischen Philosophie Kants," *Philosophische Rundschau*, 1 (1953/54): 124–149.

"Zwei Theorien zur Verteidigung des Selbstbewusstseins," *Grazer philosophische Studien*, 7/8 (1979): 77–99.

Acknowledgments

Many thanks are owed to the following individuals: Paul Guyer and Eckart Förster for crucial assistance in the early phases of preparing this volume; Lindsay Waters, Christine Thorsteinsson, and Alison Kent at Harvard University Press for their patient and kind attention to countless details; Karl Ameriks, Manfred Frank, Lindsay Waters, and Guenter Zoeller for their helpful remarks on the Introduction; Jim McKinsey, Kathy MacKenzie, and Jim Burns at the Stonehill College computer center for technical support; Dean Jo-Ann Flora, S.N.D., and Elaine Melisi at Stonehill for procuring financial and institutional backing; the four translators for giving their time and talent to a very demanding task; and above all Dieter Henrich for generously contributing so much interest, insight, and careful reflection to all aspects of this project.

—Editor

Index

Absolute: activity of "I," 41–43; subject, 44, 47
Achtung. See Respect
Activity of subject, 80, 133–134, 165–166, 169, 181, 184–186, 191, 199–202, 208
Aesthetics, 107, 115
Anthropology. *See* Human nature
Aporia in ethics, 98, 106–107
Apperception, 30–31, 35–37, 44, 50, 74, 82, 100, 129, 135–136, 164, 183–184, 186–187, 197, 200
Approval of the good, 61–66, 71, 73, 77, 81, 106
Aprioricity of self-consciousness, 168–169, 184–185, 187–189
Aristotle, 52, 55, 67, 126, 144; ethics, 57–60, 62, 65, 66, 70, 85, 86, 90, 113, 121
Austin, J., 127
Autonomy, 85, 101, 105, 111–114, 119–121; in Idealism, 90–92

Basic power, 20–29, 31–32, 34–36, 40, 42, 49–50, 70, 71
Baumgarten, A., 22, 179, 189
Beck, J. S., 126
Being, 55–56, 64, 66–67, 87, 94; knowability of, 35–38
Bonnet, C., 25
Butler, J., 68

Cartesian certainty, 164, 169, 173, 186–187
Cartesianism, 113, 164, 184
Cassirer, E., 17
Categorical judgments, 146, 149, 150, 151, 154–156, 205–206

Categories, 31, 35–37, 46, 74, 134, 136, 159–160, 165–168, 171, 174, 176–178, 182, 184, 191–192, 197, 200
Causality, 27–28, 66, 80
Christian philosophy, 87, 104, 105, 121
Cicero, 90, 105
Clarke, S., 67, 72
Cognition of objects, 133–138, 142, 151–152, 155, 159–160, 188
Cohen, H., 19, 45–47
Combination, 132–134, 137–139, 141–142, 152–153, 159–174, 181–184, 192–197, 205
Commentary on philosophical texts, 124–129
Common root of faculties, 19–21, 26–27, 29–30, 32–34, 36, 38, 40, 43–49, 54. *See also* Basic power
Complex thoughts, 132–133, 137–141, 143, 150–151, 156–158, 167, 171–173, 193, 195–196
Concepts: as predicates, 27, 38–39, 74; in Hegel, 45; role in morality, 105, 107; of synthesis, 139, 142, 144, 150, 153, 156–157, 200–201. *See also* Synthesis
Conditions of experience, 129, 134–135, 158, 174, 208
Conditions of thought, 36, 39, 42, 167–168, 170–171
Constitution, 152, 157, 169, 171, 177, 194–195, 201–202, 207
Contemporary philosophy, 127–129, 206–207. *See also* Semantic theory
Contradiction of the will, 75, 77–78, 82, 99, 102

Copernican turn, 96, 98
Critical philosophy, 32, 84–86, 91, 107, 114, 126, 144
Critique of Judgment (Kant), 23, 77, 85
Critique of Practical Reason (Kant), 68, 73, 80, 81, 84, 85, 92–95, 102, 113, 114, 118
Critique of Pure Reason (Kant), 19–20, 21, 26–27, 32–33, 38, 42, 54, 60, 68, 73, 93, 98, 108, 126, 128, 136, 138, 155, 161, 164, 166, 169, 175, 201, 202–204; paralogisms, 28–29, 36, 82, 161, 183; aesthetic, 29, 47; analytic, 47, 50, 139, 160; metaphysical deduction, 141. *See also* Transcendental deduction
Crusius, C. A., 23–25, 27, 71–72, 105, 180

Data-sensualism, 133–135, 140, 141, 149, 151, 155–158, 206
Demonstratives, 137, 140, 146, 147
Desire, 21, 24, 66, 67, 71, 72, 74, 77, 78, 100, 113, 117
Dialectic in morality, 66–67
Drives, 74, 94, 106, 117
Dualism in ethics, 115, 120
Duty, 66, 69, 72, 76, 81–82, 101, 103–105, 115–117; to self, 102, 104; to others, 102, 104, 109, 111, 115, 121

Eberhard, J. A., 27
Emotion, 63, 73, 76–78, 81, 84, 106
Empirically conditioned practical reason, 93–94, 100–101, 109
Empirical psychology, 20–23, 25, 33, 36–37, 44, 46, 49, 56, 64
Empiricist philosophy, 59, 107, 130
Entelechy, 22, 24, 55, 112
Epistemology. *See* Theory of knowledge
Equiprimordiality, 49–53
Ethics: relation to ontology, 55–61, 64, 66–67, 85–87, 91, 113; history of, 58–59, 61–62, 67, 90, 98, 104–105, 110
Execution in ethics, 79, 111, 114; principle of, 95–96, 105, 112

Facticity, 83, 85, 108, 111, 115, 203, 208
Feeling, 25, 57, 63, 64, 73, 97, 103, 109–111, 116, 117
Fichte, J. G., 19, 38, 40, 44, 47, 53, 62, 90, 127; on imagination, 41–43; on morality, 41, 58–59, 86, 112, 113–114, 119–121; critique of Kant, 60, 120
Finite mind, 31, 35–36, 50
First philosophy, 56, 57, 61, 67, 86, 207
Forms of intuition. *See* Sensible intuition
Forms of judgment, 203–206

Foundations of the Metaphysics of Morals (Kant), 81, 95
Freedom, 28–29, 35, 67, 74–76, 80–85, 94, 105, 107, 108, 110, 113, 120, 127
Frege, G., 138
Functions of understanding, 32, 36, 37, 74, 134, 135, 165–168, 173, 174, 188, 200, 201

German Idealism. *See* Speculative Idealism
God, 42, 78–80, 87
Good, 55–58, 60–68, 70, 71, 73, 76, 78–87, 95–97, 100, 101, 105–108, 111, 112, 116–118, 121
Greek philosophy, 61, 86, 105, 121

Happiness, 76–79, 99–101, 103
Harmony of human faculties, 26–27, 32–33, 78, 99
Hegel, G. W. F., 18, 19, 38, 62, 89; on speculative concept and logic, 28, 38, 44–45, 50; on unity of subjectivity, 43–48; on imagination, 44, 50; on basis of morality, 58, 59, 61, 70, 90, 114, 117–119, 121; critique of Kant's ethics, 69, 98, 103, 114, 118, 121
Heidegger, M.: interpretive method, 17–18, 33–35, 44, 49, 53–54; Kant-interpretation, 17–20, 33–54; relation to speculative Idealism, 18, 41, 48, 50, 52–53; *Being and Time*, 34, 48–54
Herbart, J. F., 46
Hobbes, T., 67, 68, 104
Hönigswald, R., 46
Human nature, 94, 97, 116, 186
Hume, D., 105, 135, 142, 157, 162
Husserl, E., 38
Hutcheson, F., 25, 70–74, 83, 104, 105

"I": in Kant, 29, 30, 37–38, 40, 80; in Hegel, 38, 44–45, 121; in Fichte, 41–42, 119–121; in Schelling, 42–43. *See also* Apperception; Identity of subject; Self-consciousness
Idealistic ethics, 89–92, 94–95, 102, 112–114, 121
Ideal of happiness, 77–78
Identity criteria, 138–140, 144, 188
Identity of subject, 28, 129, 130, 164, 188–191, 195–199, 201, 203–205, 208; numerical, 163, 175–176, 178–181, 187; strict, 180, 181–185, 202; moderate, 180, 183, 185, 186, 192, 193, 202; relation to objectivity, 204
Identity principle (Leibniz), 179–180
Imagination, 19, 29, 31, 33–36, 38–44, 47, 50, 52, 53, 71, 77–79

Index

Imperative. *See* Kant's moral philosophy
"Inaugural Dissertation" (Kant), 60
Incentives. *See* Motives
Inclinations, 66, 72, 84, 100, 103, 105, 107, 109, 111, 115–118
Intellectual intuition, 30, 35, 38, 44
Intelligible ground, 28, 40, 82–83
Intention in ethics, 95, 99, 100–104, 109, 111, 113, 115, 116, 121
Interest, 78, 95, 99, 100, 103, 107, 127
Interpretation of philosophic texts, 123–129
Intrasubjective teleology, 31–33, 40, 45
Intuition. *See* Intellectual intuition; Sensible intuition
"I think." *See* Apperception; "I"; Identity of subject; Self-consciousness

Jacobi, F. H., 69
Judgment, 37, 74; relation to object, 136–141, 144–155, 159–160, 204; structure of, 136–144, 152–155, 159–160, 203–205. *See also* Forms of judgment; Subject-predicate form
Judgment in ethics, 57, 68, 73–79, 110–111; principle of, 96–98, 104, 112, 114

Kant, I.: systematic intentions, 56, 84, 85, 91–92, 105, 121, 127; methodology, 85, 112; unity of system, 107, 112, 121; view of own work, 126–128, 154, 160, 198. *See also* Kant's moral philosophy; *individual works*
Kant-scholarship, 17–18, 127, 138. *See also* Heidegger, M.
Kant's moral philosophy, 65; theoretical foundations of morality, 25, 56, 60, 69, 71–74, 77, 79, 80, 83–87, 90, 92, 94, 105–108, 113–114, 119, 126, 198; moral law as fact of reason, 28, 60, 69, 72, 83–85, 108, 111–112, 120; practical reason, 31, 80, 93, 97, 110, 111, 113; relation of speculative to practical reason, 31–32, 59–60, 69–74, 81, 85, 91–92, 105, 107, 186; deduction of moral law, 32, 70, 84, 93, 106–108; categorical imperative, 63, 66, 68–69, 72, 74, 75, 83, 98–102, 108, 111; good will, 67, 85, 96–98, 100, 103, 104, 106, 107, 112, 113, 116, 117; grounding of moral insight, 72–87; hypothetical imperative, 76, 78, 83. *See also* Autonomy; Execution in ethics; Freedom; Judgment in ethics; Law; Moral insight; Respect

Lange, F. A., 46
Law: of reason in general, 76, 78, 79, 82, 104, 120, 121, 182, 189; moral, 79–80, 83–84, 102–103, 109, 110–111, 115, 118; as rule of cognition, 159–160, 177, 187, 195, 202. *See also* Kant's moral philosophy
Lehmann, G., 23
Leibniz, G. W., 22, 24–25, 28, 32, 42, 178–182
Levy, H., 17
Limits of reason, 32, 91–93
Locke, J., 24, 29
Logic, 26, 32, 35–37, 55, 61, 68, 72–75, 86, 106, 126, 137, 148, 184, 189–190, 201, 206–208. *See also* Hegel, G. W. F.; Judgment; Subject-predicate form

Materialism, 24, 27
Matter, 28, 29, 83, 85
Maxim, 99–101
Metaphysical Principles of Natural Science (Kant), 136
Metaphysics, 35, 38, 55–57, 59, 61, 126, 198
Monism, 23, 26, 34, 71
Moral evil, 64–66, 74–76, 79, 98
Moral insight, 56–87, 111, 121; distinguished from theoretical insight, 68, 72–73, 111
Moral sense, 68, 72, 73, 83, 106
Moral sense philosophy, 68, 69, 105, 106, 113
Moral subjectivity, 57, 79, 83, 112, 114
Motives, 63–67, 71–79, 84, 93, 94, 105–107, 111, 116

Natorp, P., 46
Nature, 77, 78, 159, 192, 197, 205, 206
Negation, 145, 149
Neo-Kantianism, 46
Newton, I., 67

Object-concept, 130–137, 144, 153–156, 160, 204
Objectivity, 74, 129–139, 142, 155–161, 204–206
"On the Use of Teleological Principles in Philosophy" (Kant), 20–21, 27
Ontology, 55–61, 64–67, 70, 74, 80, 82, 83, 85, 106, 113, 180
Opus postumum (Kant), 154

Particulars, 93, 130–134, 138–144, 150–159, 163, 166, 171, 180, 184, 185, 200, 205, 207
Perception, 162, 194–196
Perfection in ethics, 70–71, 96
Person, 162–163, 190, 200
Phronesis, 60, 86
Physics, 55, 67, 147, 154, 158, 198
Plato, 55–56, 59–67, 85, 113, 139, 142, 144, 150; doctrine of ideas, 66, 86, 123
Pleasure, 21, 24, 65, 66, 70–78, 84, 107, 116

Pluralism of faculties, 21–26, 30–34, 36, 43–45, 47, 64
"Pölitz Metaphysics" (Kant), 27
Power (metaphysical), 21–24, 27, 35
Predicate-concept, 139–157, 163
Preestablished harmony, 22, 32
Presocratics, 55, 58
Properties, 132, 139–143, 151, 152, 156–158, 179
Proposition. *See* Categorical judgments; Subject-predicate form
Protagoras, 57
Purposiveness, 31, 93

Qualia, 130–133, 137–152, 155–157

Rational psychology, 70, 106, 163, 183
Reflection, 41, 62, 63, 165, 166, 169, 174, 183, 184, 191, 208
Reinhold, K. L., 19, 60, 113, 127
Relational concepts, 35, 134, 179
Representational power. *See* Vis repraesentativa
Resistance to moral law, 76, 77, 85, 109–110, 115, 116
Respect, 82, 84, 85, 95, 107–112, 115, 117, 118, 120
Rousseau, J. J., 83, 97, 98, 127
Rüdiger, A., 24
Rules: of synthesis, 74, 75, 133–135, 139, 142, 157–160, 164, 168, 171, 177, 178, 182, 185, 187, 192–205, 208; of transition between subject-states, 189–195

Schelling, F. W. J., 42–44, 50, 90, 114
Schiller, F., 112–119
Scholasticism, 57, 67
Schopenhauer, A., 69, 70, 98, 198
Schultz, J., 81
Self, 42, 66, 76, 80, 84, 120–121; theoretical, 63–64, 78, 81–83, 168, 169, 183, 185; moral, 64, 81–83, 119
Self-consciousness, 28, 31, 35–37, 41–42, 47, 91, 129, 130, 136, 142, 160–161; unity of, 29–30, 43–44, 46, 162–174, 178, 185, 192, 196, 200–201; simplicity of, 162–164, 170–171, 178, 186, 192–193, 195–198, 203–204; particularity of, 172–175. *See also* Unity of subject
Self-love, 68, 101
Self-relation of will, 42, 96, 98, 112, 119, 120
Semantic theory, 138, 144, 207–208. *See also* Contemporary philosophy
Sensation, 74, 130–133, 138, 144, 150, 156, 158, 159

Sensibility. *See* Sensible intuition
Sensible intuition, 19, 21, 25, 29–33, 36, 38, 40, 46, 54, 92, 110, 111, 115, 117, 133, 134, 137, 151, 155, 157, 158, 167, 181, 183
Shaftesbury, Earl of, 68
Simple qualities. *See* Qualia
Socrates, 55, 60, 84, 86
Sophists, 86
Soul, 20–24, 26–27, 34–35, 64, 65, 70, 71, 76, 80, 99
Space, 31, 47, 74, 130, 133, 140, 156, 157, 163, 180
Speculative Idealism, 18, 25, 33, 40, 44–46, 52, 53, 56, 62, 87, 113, 114, 121, 207; critique of Kant in, 60, 85, 92, 104; demand for unity of principles, 85, 86, 91, 108. *See also* Idealistic ethics
Spinoza, 27, 42
Spontaneity of subject, 28, 31, 35, 37, 47, 63, 82, 106, 107, 165, 179, 207, 208; distinguished from moral freedom, 29, 80–81, 84–85
Stoics, 63, 96, 105
Subject-concept, 139–149, 152–155, 158; as plurality in unity, 150, 154, 156, 157
Subject-predicate form, 139–151, 153, 157, 160
Substance, 22, 26, 27–29, 32, 35, 132, 155, 158, 163, 164, 179, 180, 181–183, 185
Synthesis, 50, 86, 106, 191–204; of objects, 133–135, 139, 140, 156; of thoughts, 168; of representations, 176–177; of recognition, 177–178; of apprehension, 187, 200, 203. *See also* Complex thoughts
Synthetic unity of apperception. *See* Apperception

Teleology, 57, 67, 68, 87, 112
Tetens, J. N., 25–27, 35
Theory of knowledge, 56, 57, 60, 61, 68, 69, 81, 100, 107, 130, 133, 135, 139, 151, 157, 159, 160, 186, 197, 207–208
Thing in itself, 40, 46
Thomas Aquinas, 121
Thomasius, C., 113
Thoroughgoing interconnection, 159–160, 166, 196–197, 203, 205
Time, 31, 39, 47, 49, 52, 53, 74, 140, 157, 163, 180, 183, 189, 200, 203
Transcendental argument, 127, 129
Transcendental deduction, 19, 32, 33, 37, 39, 44, 46, 50, 126, 128–130, 158–208; first edition version, 36, 47, 177, 198; second edi-

Index

tion version, 36, 47, 198–199; underdevelopment of argument in, 160–161, 164, 197–199, 204, 207–208; criticism of, 199, 207–208
Transcendental subject, 181, 183, 184, 202
Transcendental unity of apperception. *See* Apperception
Transition between states of subject, 175–178, 181, 186; a priori knowledge of, 187–190, 201–205
Tübingen theology, 113–114

Unconditioned worth, 84, 96, 107, 108, 112
Understanding, 19–32, 38–46, 54, 71–81, 100, 106, 151, 203
Unity as regulative demand of reason, 26–27, 32–33, 40, 74–75
Unity of reason, 76, 78, 92, 94

Unity of subject, 162–175, 181, 184–186, 192, 206. *See also* Self-consciousness
Universality in ethics, 74, 75, 77–78, 83, 96–102

Virtue, 56, 63, 65, 67, 102
Vis repraesentativa, 20–28, 70, 71, 80

Will, 70–81, 93–119. *See also* Kant's moral philosophy
Wittgenstein, L., 127
Wolff, C., 20–27, 33, 36, 47, 48, 68, 70–72, 97–99, 104, 105, 107
Wollaston, W., 67–68, 72, 97–99
Worthiness to be happy, 77, 79, 84, 86
Worth of persons, 100, 102, 104, 108, 110

Xenocrates, 55